Reckoning

JOURNALISM AND POLITICAL COMMUNICATION UNBOUND

Series editors: Nikki Usher, The University of Illinois Urbana-Champaign, and Daniel Kreiss, University of North Carolina at Chapel Hill

Journalism and Political Communication Unbound seeks to be a high-profile book series that reaches far beyond the academy to an interested public of policy-makers, journalists, public intellectuals, and citizens eager to make sense of contemporary politics and media. "Unbound" in the series title has multiple meanings: it refers to the unbinding of borders between the fields of communication, political communication, and journalism, as well as related disciplines such as political science, sociology, and science and technology studies; it highlights the ways traditional frameworks for scholarship have disintegrated in the wake of changing digital technologies and new social, political, economic, and cultural dynamics; and it reflects the unbinding of media in a hybrid world of flows across mediums.

Reckoning

Journalism's Limits and Possibilities

CANDIS CALLISON AND MARY LYNN YOUNG

Oxford University Press is a department of the University of Oxford. It furthers
the University's objective of excellence in research, scholarship, and education
by publishing worldwide. Oxford is a registered trade mark of Oxford University
Press in the UK and certain other countries.

Published in the United States of America by Oxford University Press
198 Madison Avenue, New York, NY 10016, United States of America.

CIP data is on file at the Library of Congress
ISBN 978–0–19–006708–3 (pbk.)
ISBN 978–0–19–006707–6 (hbk.)

For our daughters and our students.

CONTENTS

ACKNOWLEDGEMENTS

Our first thanks goes to the journalists we interviewed, whose names and quotes appear throughout this book. We are deeply appreciative of everyone who took time out of their busy schedules not only to be interviewed but to later read transcripts of their interviews and then read drafts of chapters. We are also thankful for those journalists who publicly shared their personal stories in a variety of ways and formats, some of which we have drawn from to chart the digital reckoning taking place.

Our enormous thanks also goes to Artist and Photographer Fazal Sheikh for the book's cover image:

41°13'0"N / 112°31'35"W

October 17, 2017

The aerial photo depicts a portion of the Southern Pacific Railroad causeway, built in 1959, which bisected the Great Salt Lake, reducing the influx of fresh water to the northern section and increasing the salinity. This image captures the ways in which roads, long associated with communications infrastructure, enables some kinds of circulation (goods, materials, bacteria) and restricts others (fresh and salt water). We're grateful for this image which gestures at how worlds are built, assembled, and impacted by infrastructure perhaps more profoundly than words. The image is part of a new body of work, *The Exposure Trilogy*, in the Southwestern United States that continues Fazal's award-winning work with communities and representations of land, water, and the deeply intertwined relations between humans and nonhumans.

We are grateful to the many reviewers who generously shared their time and expertise to read and provide feedback for chapters and earlier versions of this manuscript. They include: Chris Anderson, Carrie Ching, Alfred Hermida, Daniel Justice, Michael M. J. Fischer, Kirk LaPointe, Minelle Mahtani, Erin Millar, Robert Picard, Jim Rankin, Tanya Talaga, and Jesse Wente.

Thank you to series editors Nikki Usher and Daniel Kreiss for repeated and close reads, comments as well as their deep commitment to this project. Thank you to our three sage and discerning anonymous reviewers. We also greatly appreciate the skillfulness and dedication of Angela Chnapko and the OUP team.

Thanks also to our research assistants: Zoe Tennant, whose early research and contributions helped us to develop Chapter 3, as well as Emily Blake, Mascha Gugganig, Brenna Owen, and Anya Zoledziowski. And thank you to students who participated in our first class at the University of British Columbia on themes central to this book, as well as to all of our students that we've taught over the years at UBC and for students Candis taught at Princeton. We are writing this book because of the many essential questions you have raised about journalism, power, and social justice.

We are also deeply appreciative to those who participated in the International Symposium on Climate Change and Indigenous Communities in 2018 at Princeton University. The Symposium functioned as a kind of paraethnographic space for us where journalists we quote and interview came into conversation with each other and Indigenous scholars. Our thanks to Simon Morrison who suggested Candis come to Princeton and co-organize a conference like this that brought together Indigenous scholars and journalists.

Candis also wishes to thank the team that makes up *Media Indigena*: Rick Harp, Kim TallBear, Brock Pitawanakwat, and Kenneth T. Williams for the many conversations we've had about how mainstream journalism and Indigenous media cover and report on issues related to Indigenous lives, history, and experiences. A few of those conversations have made it into the book, and many of them inform how we thought about issues discussed in the book.

Thanks to the panels and conference papers at Montreal AEJMC in 2015, Barcelona 4S in 2016, International Journalism Festival in 2018, Boston 4S in 2018, Iceland NORA 2019, and the scholars and journalists who provided us with early feedback throughout the life of this research project. These conference panels and audience feedback helped us get on the right track and to know when we'd hit our stride, too.

Thanks to our colleagues and administrative support at the Journalism School, especially Alfred Hermida and Lee Yupitin.

All mistakes are ours, and we appreciate the efforts to help us minimize those inevitable errors in a project of this size and duration.

Our wholehearted thanks to our families, especially our daughters, for their patience and support as we worked on this book. We hope that this book contributes to a future in which multiple journalisms thrive and continue to transform the profession and the worlds inherited by future generations.

Reckoning

Opening up Journalism's Crisis

WE ARE WRITING THIS introduction less than a year after the killing of five journalists at the *Capital Gazette*, a local daily newspaper in Maryland. The suspect was a man who had what the *Baltimore Sun* described as a "long-standing grudge against the paper."[1] The journalists were gunned down in their newsroom while doing their job—putting out a small daily newspaper in Annapolis, Maryland. The *Capital Gazette* can claim 270 years of history at a time when its local news peers are facing closure and decline. In an editorial a week after the mass shooting headlined, "Our say: Please help stop the madness that killed five at *Capital Gazette* newsroom," the paper expressed its anguish and grief as it took on the complexity of gun violence discourse in the United States. It did so with an unconventional uncertainty and humility about journalism's power to assess and impact policy, understand human nature, and effect change:

> Anyone expecting national consensus to come from the death of five community journalists in Annapolis will be sorely disappointed. We can't even agree on the question, let alone the answer. If there were going to be agreement on what to do about gun violence, it would have come after the death of school children in Newtown. If we could reach a common ground that mental health was the problem, we would have found it after the murder of movie patrons in a theater in Aurora, Colorado. If we were going to meet someplace in the middle on assault-style weapons, surely it would have been after the gunfire stopped at a country music festival in Las Vegas. There isn't even concurrence on what language to use to describe the weapons. Five journalists were killed in a rampage that will change forever what it means to be from Annapolis. This can't be undone. We'll be the headline until the next mass casualty. . .[2]

The editorial ends with a call to action to end gun violence, with the caveat that "this paper is not wise enough to figure this out" and calling on politicians—at a time when partisanship (which they recognize) within the political system is a significant concern.[3] This narrative is not the systematic holding power to account and moral certainty journalism of Watergate or the more recent Panama Papers.

The narratives that emerge in the aftermath of this tragic event and the digital reckoning that we follow through this book shows that there is a disquiet among journalists about their reduced capacity to set news agendas in increasingly polarized social, political, and economic contexts. The stakes are high for journalists personally and professionally. Questions are increasing about journalism's epistemological foundations: how journalists know what they know, who gets to decide what good journalism is and when it's done right, whether journalists are experts, and what role they should (and do) play in society?

North American journalism and journalists are responding to a range of serious concerns across an array of domains, many of which have been deemed as "in crisis" by pundits and scholars. Examples include: violence by citizens and police; market failure and labor precarity; sustained criticism of "fake news" by a sitting U.S. president and others; real-time feedback from increasingly participatory, powerful, and diverse publics; newsrooms across the continent that remain largely white; and pressures to stay current with rapid and constant technological change. These forces are shaping what it is to do journalism and marking a distinction between the journalisms of the pre- to early digital eras—when we both were journalists in Canada and the United States—and today.

Yet despite this wide range of concerns, the multiple overlapping crises in North American journalism have been largely circumscribed as stemming from either economic decline and/or technological disruption and change.[4] This narrow lens has limited the possibility for discussion of wider and often prior challenges to the current state of journalism and their solutions. Our motives in writing this book are to bring together these wider conversations about journalism in areas that have been quite distinct and separate. We complicate the notion of crisis, which tends to be seen as a "unitary phenomenon," with limited explanations for both causes and solutions.[5] In contrast, we situate concerns about technology and economics alongside chronic issues related to power, structure, and epistemology in order to analyze gaps and exclusions.[6] Understanding what journalism can and should do—its limits and possibilities—is essential to imagining new contours for how journalism might respond to this digital reckoning taking place at a time when quality reflexive journalism also matters. We open up these discussions to move both beyond and beside a defense of journalism to get at "a deeper set of historiographical problems" in order to understand the current moment in journalism.[7]

We are not alone in trying to understand how we got here, and what kind of knowledge journalism is, as well as possible approaches to the future. Reckoning inevitably means coming to terms with unfinished business, a settling of scores and/or past mistakes. A column by Margaret Sullivan, columnist for the *Washington Post* and former public editor of the *New York Times,* clearly articulated some of the unfinished business in a column following a joint press conference held by U.S. President Donald Trump and Russian President Vladimir Putin in Helsinki in July 2018. She argued that this meeting represented a stark political realignment of five decades of global geopolitics and predicted that coverage moving forward for the "reality based press" will necessitate "clarity and moral force, in ways that we are not all that comfortable with."[8] In this crucial moment, Sullivan locates a main problem and its solution in journalism methods and epistemologies (how journalists know what they know). Journalism must, in Sullivan's formulation, exercise its power, ability, and moral duty to discern allies and enemies: "That job will fall, in part at least, to the American press, which will find itself in the uncomfortable position of calling a spade a spade, with none of the usual recourse to false equivalence or 'both sides with equal weight' coverage."[9]

But what does re-configuring journalism as such a task mean? Did journalism not have clarity and moral force in the past, and/or did it have more? Or did certain journalisms have clarity and moral force, while others didn't? Is there one journalism or multiple journalisms? What is calling "a spade a spade" in a world of complex systems and global concerns such as climate change, which include questions of structure, colonialism, race, gender, and class?

It's on this wide terrain of questions and critique that we envision this book as contributing to both journalism practice and scholarship. Economists regard cultural products such as journalism as an *experience good*, which means that value, and even quality, are determined on consumption.[10] Good journalism then is an iterative process that is both internal to journalism (professional norms and practices in terms of production and identity) and external to journalism (which takes into account the audience experience). The internal discussion has been dominated by scholars, journalists, and professional organizations who have not adequately recognized the representational harms of journalism, journalism's role in social ordering, and the related epistemological limitations of its system of knowledge production. While some have increasingly acknowledged that objectivity—journalism's dominant authority or norm—is flawed, the vast majority have not gone far enough in understanding how legitimizing a "view from nowhere" impacts power relations both internal and external to the profession.

We contend that this disjuncture has obscured multiple ruptures in the fabric of modern journalism. These ruptures, which include chronic representational issues, dissonance for journalists, and alienation for various publics, have been there for a while—all one has to do is pay attention to them. Gans noted as early as 1979 that "news reflects the white male social order." [11] Yet, despite the decades of critique that followed, objectivity, and its milder forms, fairness and balance still justify and ground journalism ideology. In a way, this constancy represents an accomplishment stabilized more by white masculinity than professionalism and aspirational fourth-estate ideals. Given the North American media system's largely commercial context[12] and the genuine difficulties inherent in understanding and communicating to large diverse publics, it's not difficult to see how the paternal professional context has persisted with a limited capacity (or one might wager, desire) by editors and journalists to respond, talk back or transform—until now.[13]

Journalism for Whom, With Whom

The reckoning we find in this book in many ways starts with the audience—journalism's multiple, diverse publics—which have been constructed as part of a virtuous circle of who journalists think they are. Journalists and journalism scholars have, by and large, reified doing things "in the public interest" or "serving the public" in ways that people in the creative world and Science and Technology Studies (STS) have questioned for much longer. In his now well-known catch phrase, Rosen was among the first in journalism studies to question the role of the "people formerly known as the audience" in the late 1990s, even as digital media remained a nascent revolution waiting to begin with the force we now take for granted.[14] Despite the recent "audience turn" more generally since Rosen, we find scholars haven't been asking the more difficult questions: it is not about who journalism serves but *who journalism isn't serving*. This book then is not a rallying cry to repair journalism from the inside but a recognition of the long-standing harms and persistent critiques.

In this book we make these claims: that journalism scholars and journalists have said the most urgent and pressing issues in journalism are about technological revolution and economic crisis—not because they aren't concerns but because their resolution confirms a liberal view of journalism history as progressive. In such a view, digital media disrupts the efficacy and stability of journalism as a public good rather than confronting, evolving, or enhancing it. Journalism scholars have recognized journalism knowledge is constructed and have had ample evidence since journalism ethnographers did their first studies of newsrooms in the 1970s and 80s.[15] But they have not made the turn to recognize how deeply that construction and the authority that it deploys through objectivity have been rooted in power relations, the performance of white masculinity, and maintaining social orders.

In our varied analyses of how journalists are engaging in efforts to repair, reform, and transform, we suggest that certain kinds of journalism are addressing system-wide issues—including its own. Our main research questions ground all of these concerns as they relate to how journalists do what they do and how much power they have—and should have—to do it. We argue, similar to Carey decades ago, that the most common contemporary crisis narratives revolve around "the slow, steady expansion of freedom and knowledge" framed around "industrialization, urbanization, and mass democracy."[16] In such a framework, technology is seen as a disrupting factor that deeply impacts not only journalism but the very functioning of democracy. As we suggest throughout this book, these narratives of decline and crisis *must* be brought alongside persistent critiques related to gender, race, indigeneity, and colonialism.[17] Within journalism studies, the role of journalist has been deeply historicized, but much less attention has been paid to who that journalist is likely to be and what or whose social order has been reinstated and reinforced through works and/or acts of journalism.[18]

In following this thread, we find journalists, startup founders, sources, activists, and citizens holding up a mirror, resisting prior journalisms by using social media and other forms of digital media to reflect, resist, talk back, counter, and refuse to participate in legacy media or journalism conversations. These case studies of journalists and audiences, dealing with the gaps scholars have left underexplored, explain the reckoning in both the internal and external conversations of journalism. We find many journalists responding and struggling with journalism's dominant authority, history, and reckoning at individual, structural, and organizational levels. This book in particular analyzes the contours of this reckoning among journalism organizations that range from women-led startups to legacy media and individuals in loose social and freelance networks like Indigenous journalists. We build on a range of scholarship to argue ultimately that multiple journalisms are emerging for overlapping, diverse publics, built on ever-evolving digital platforms, transmedia configurations for content, civic imaginaries and media, and newer norms and practices for local, national, and global audiences.[19]

For North American journalists working globally, we find evidence of a transition from a modern journalism subject to an increasingly cautionary and implicated journalism subject—similar to the editorial written by the *Capital Gazette* that led this chapter. We conclude there have been limits, as well as deep underlying challenges, to what journalism could and should do. Objectivity and reporting methods are insufficient for journalists to report on complicated events, incomprehensible trauma, as well as its own colonial violence—all while trying to make sense of truth and difference.

The journalistic front line is already crumbling while simultaneously pointing to areas of future possibility. Individual journalists are largely on their own, trying to navigate complicated subjectivities, geopolitics, and history. We find that legacy media, too, are struggling with this reckoning and trying to stem the rupture. Even startups, which are considered on the edge of repair in the field with explicit, well-articulated epistemological interventions, are challenged to contribute in a context that has not been fully held to account for its gendered, colonial, and racist histories. This book brings together ethnographic accounts of journalists and scholarship in order to shed light on questions, experimental practices, and their rationales, as well as gaps in historical consciousness and critiques of professional journalism.

This book intervenes by considering digital media technologies as diagnostics that make visible what has been sutured in legacy media namely that (1) ideals like objectivity and balance are not good enough as rationales for and defenses of journalism, (2) audiences are rapidly transforming and have evolving expectations for what role journalism should and does play, (3) the lack of diversity and whiteness in newsrooms is untenable and indefensible, and (4) multiple journalisms are flourishing that provide experimental paths forward for the profession as a whole. In so doing, we are contending with three strands of theoretical conversations that we suggest haven't gone far enough: (a) journalism studies and the related decades of internal critique of objectivity that also doesn't draw on cultural studies or media studies, critical race, or scholarship on colonialism, (b) feminist media studies and its move to "strong objectivity" that needs to go further to integrate intersectionality and Indigenous feminisms, and (c) the emergence of STS in journalism studies as largely focused on technology and "bright, shiny things" instead of power and societal structuring.[20] We question why journalism studies scholars have not taken up more than two decades of contributions from intersectional scholars on the impact of a journalism defined by various articulations of objectivity as its dominant authority for marginalized groups despite decades of evidence of racism, gendered media coverage, and bias in journalism coverage and the overwhelming whiteness of mainstream media. We argue that this resistance has both negated and neglected the real harm, inequities, and erasure of the experiences of women and marginalized groups as well as the real impact on journalists.

Exclusions of racialized and gendered bodies, land, and non-human actors matter in both structurally broad and specific ways. For example, Rhodes articulated the stakes almost 25 years ago, when she called out U.S. media for their focus on technological and financial accomplishments over responding to their complicity with a system of "racial dominance and control."[21] Similarly, Anderson and Robertson chronicle a harsh past of Canadian media up into the present of reproducing stereotypes and settler-colonial tropes in their coverage of Indigenous peoples, and advocacy for a particular social order where dispossession, state violence, and genocidal practices are affirmed and celebrated.[22] Building on Steiner's lamentation that the wider field of journalism studies has been mostly uninterested in gender studies and/or using gender as an analytical category through which to understand journalists and journalism, we advocate for a widening of scope that accounts for intersectional concerns and critiques rooted in long histories of harm and suffering.[23] Finally, we draw on articulations by journalists like Rick Harp, a longtime Cree journalist based in Winnipeg and the force behind the podcast, *Media Indigena*, who pointed out during a 2018 symposium on climate change at Princeton University that for Indigenous people, "stories literally can be life or death."

Why have questions related to gender, race, and colonialism been so hard to ask in a field that studies a profession whose mission is to speak truth to power? We owe a debt to scholars such as Haraway, Harding, and TallBear who took on science from a feminist perspective accounting for settler-colonial and postcolonial scholarship. They showed us that all knowledge production—whose meaning, method, data, and for what and whose purposes—is always political. Several decades ago, Haraway, Traweek, and Star began challenging scientific norms and authority, arguing that the method of neutral observer or "view from nowhere" is rooted in masculinity's power to disassociate itself from its implicatedness. This distanced "view from nowhere" functioned as a way to situate knowledge claims not as opinion but fact—with the gendered, racialized arbiter able to dislocate difference, silencing representational dissent. We also owe a debt to Indigenous studies, media studies, critical race scholars, and anthropologists working at the confluence of media, science, and technology who have continually pointed out the ways in which structural oppression manifests in representations, storytelling, and the interaction of systems that govern everyday life.[24]

Power and Partial Truths

This book, as a way forward, suggests that journalists think through the systems they are operating within, and what kind of experts they are, as well as what kind of expertise they are deploying. Navigating complex systems and selecting expertise constitute ethical decisions whereby journalists must negotiate double binds and their own situated knowledges in order to shine light on issues of justice and inequality. Jasanoff explores the "social underpinnings of expertise" by articulating a base struggle between the power of "lay expertise" and specialist expertise.[25]

> I have always insisted that expertise is not merely something that is in the heads and hands of skilled persons, constituted through their deep familiarity with the problem in question, but rather that it is something acquired, and deployed, within particular historical, political, and cultural contexts. Expertise relevant to public decisions, I have further shown, responds to specific institutional imperatives that vary within and between nation states. Accordingly, who counts as an expert (and what counts as expertise) in UK environmental or public health controversies may not necessarily be who (or what) would count for the same purpose in Germany or India or the USA. Different bodies of expert knowledge come into being, with their associated markers of excellence and credibility through disparate contingencies of politics and knowledge production in national decision-making settings.[26]

In Jasanoff's formulation of how expertise is rooted in and reflects historical and national contexts lies the crux of the matter for journalism scholars. If expertise responds to institutional imperatives—and bodies of experts come into being—this digital reckoning signals that these settings are changing. This framework exposes journalism expertise for its own location in a certain time, place, and national decision-making context.

We contend that this digital reckoning signifies that journalists are and need to be what we term *systems journalists*, whose greatest value rests in their ability to share and shape public discourse in ways that understand their role and position in a set of complex global systems. Anyone who is in a relationship will know how hard it can be to identify and parse one of journalism's main questions—what happened—by focusing solely on content, without weighing questions of history, family of origin, power, personality, quality of the connection and whether there is a shared direction. It is the origin of the proverbial he/she/they said double bind. Trying to answer the question of what happened is messy and inevitably involves perspective and subjectivity of which we all have varying degrees of capacity for seeing, hearing, and communicating. In addition, the roles and responsibilities of observer and storyteller vary culturally and in their time and place. Valid and reliable methods, shared goals, meaningful connections, shared experiences, epistemologies, and relations are some of the ways we navigate difference, generate understanding, and share stories and truths.

Digital media have thrown many questions about journalism and the knowledge it produces onto a new terrain. But that doesn't necessarily mean the questions change: rather, in some cases, these questions are amplified and more urgent. Lewis and Westlund identify journalism as "among the most influential knowledge-producing institutions of the modern era."[27] They walk us through a history of journalism epistemology referencing Tuchman and others on journalists' propensity to use routines and habits such as getting both sides of stories, objectivity, and multiple sources.[28] In such a framing, these routines and methods then become much more powerful and should be open to questioning as they undergird professional identity and ultimately an ability to make knowledge claims.

Here, not surprisingly, journalism methods and literary edges have not fared well as part of the emergent data and risk society as Ericson predicted in 1998. He identifies a range of truth regimes in journalism—from a journalism of "literary properties" that "blur distinctions between fact, value, information and knowledge" to systematic social science methods and more recently data science.[29] Similar to Borges-Rey, he suggests these regimes complicate the terrain of what kind of knowledge journalism is and how to assess its validity. At the same time, he questions why one would even expect a cultural product such as journalism to reflect reality, such as facts about crime and other domains, when even police statistics "do not mirror the reality of crime but are cultural, legal and social constructs produced by the police for organizational purposes."[30] Statistics measure arrests, not crime—most of which goes unreported.

That journalists have both been presented as a way and *become* a primary way for society to understand itself outside of its own organizational norms is an accomplishment, and perhaps a particular accomplishment for a particular era of modern journalism. But what if, as our earlier questions related to Sullivan's prescriptive indicate, the story journalists and journalism scholars have told themselves about their methods has long reinforced journalism's aspirational and ideal typical goals while it largely neglects its own exclusivity, harm, and methodological looseness with respect to colonial, racist, and gendered structures and power relations—and relations between human and non-human actors?[31] What if objectivity, in particular, is heavily and cogently criticized and dissected by professional journalists and scholars—but *not* for the role it plays propping up intersectional relations, dominant social orders, the "pillars of whiteness," white fragility and other ways that journalists have told themselves there can be fairness and balance without considering subjectivity, structural concerns, and histories?[32] That the scientific method, as STS scholars have argued, is historically rooted in and dependent on a performance of white masculinity sheds light on how journalism's loose methods have held together for so long and become paradoxically rigid in some respects.

How does journalism then become Sullivan's moral force if it has a difficult time discerning its own gaps and recognizing and acknowledging the historic violence of prior journalisms? Moral force changes in time and place as do definitions of journalism; yet journalism in this formulation retains an ability to adapt or a timelessness—it's not entirely clear which one Sullivan might be implying.[33] Sullivan is not the only one suggesting moral and ethical shifts to shore up relevance, credibility, and interventionist possibilities despite past failings. As we detail more in Chapter 1, *National Geographic* issued an apology in 2018 with the headline that "for decades our coverage was racist. To rise above our past, we must acknowledge it."[34] Yet, good intentions and mea culpas are never enough to shine a light and represent the subaltern, nor are internal to journalism critiques, ethical models and accountability when "speaking for" is a primary epistemological orientation.[35] Byrd draws on Spivak in order to ask a newly configured question that aptly moves this forward and reflects the terrain of this book: "The question has now become how, and by what and whom, is the subaltern silenced."[36]

This question becomes more complicated when journalists (and audiences) use bias, which is a tricky thing to define. It is the jab most often directed at news organizations and reporters (i.e., that they're "biased" and therefore must be read appropriately, lack credibility, and/or should be ignored completely). Often, "bias" is a code for difference among journalists—and not, as we argue in this book, a recognition of situated knowledge or expertise. It's that much more complicated when publics weigh in, told as they have been that journalism, in order to be informative and useful for democracy, is or should be objective, unbiased, and/or free from opinion. In 2018, Gallup's lead into their report on public perception of "news media bias" indicates that "Americans' perceptions of news media bias have increased significantly over the past generation":

Thirty-two percent believe the news media are careful to separate fact from opinion, well below the 58% who held this view in 1984. Meanwhile, 66% currently agree that most news media do not do a good job of letting people know what is fact and what is opinion, up from 42%.[37]

It's worth noting that in 1984, the constellations of power relations were changing from a time when fewer sources and platforms for news often likely stood in for more unified accounts of events, scandals, and problems given well-documented instances of competition and hierarchy among news organizations. Beyond the time factor—there is something much more fundamental in play here. The notion that fact and opinion can be separated is foundational to journalism's method and internal professional valuation—by this, we mean that journalists do not want to be considered biased, nor do news organizations. Hence, even the fiercely and proudly partisan Fox News long marketed itself as "fair and balanced," which has recently morphed into "most trusted, most watched." Interpretation, meaning making, and other essential aspects of carrying out the job of journalism stand alongside formulations of trust, fairness, bias, balance, and objectivity. However, the complexity of these tasks—and their high stakes—are much less discussed even in journalism education. Objectivity tends to play a performative role, suturing over questions about how journalism reflects particular social orders.

Journalism legitimizes, amplifies, and reinforces some experts, views, and perceptions of events and problems in the world—and their potential range of solutions—over *other* experts, views, and perceptions even while they obscure how it is they arrived at their own perceptions.[38] In asking questions about the systems of knowledge and social order that journalism is a part of, we are purposefully creating new spaces for interventions that we hope other scholars and journalists will build on: asking why and how a reckoning with journalism is emerging and what repair, reform, and transformation might look like in both the study and practice of journalism. In so doing, we are contending explicitly that other journalism studies scholars and feminist media studies scholars have not gone far enough in questioning the relationship between methods, stance, power, and accountability in journalism.

When technologies, their adoption, and envisioned uses are used as a diagnostic, the role and methods of the journalist open up, exposing how the normative paradigm that positions journalists as essential knowledge producers is bound up in its professional logic and aspirations as a fourth estate—and not in its locatedness. There is inevitable tension as journalism's methods, logic, and aspirations can be and often are contradictory. It is also not surprising then that multiple content analyses and studies from a variety of disciplines indicate that journalism for the most part reinforces the status quo and does not perform the watchdog function idealized in conceptualizations of the fourth estate. As Chapter 2 argues in detail: when race, gender, and colonialism—and the history of media getting it wrong on all counts—are considered essential to navigating information, facts, and interpretations of events in mainstream media, the rise of digital media looks less like a crisis and more like a long overdue corrective for mainstream media.

We would be remiss in focusing solely on critique. Journalism is and has never been only a tool of oppression or handmaiden to gendered structures and colonialism in terms of its ability to foster and enable particular civic imaginations. It is and can be an important tool for resurgent counter-narratives, accurate representations of, and insight into counter-publics. Journalism has contributed to structural transformation and policy impact in many forms and periods, from 19th-century Indigenous newspapers in Hawai'i and the Cherokee homelands to social media hashtags of contemporary social movements, and systematic and long-form genres such as investigative journalism, to name a few. A recent study shows that more than 20% of data journalism stories addressed issues of race, gender, and class.[39] While multiple journalism awards globally indicate the power of long-form journalism to support structural interventions. Anishnaabe journalist Tanya Talaga's award-winning book *Seven Fallen Feathers* on the unsolved deaths of seven Indigenous youths in northern Ontario, which extends from her work for the *Toronto Star*, is just one example of how journalism has exposed ongoing colonial violence setting Indigenous relations with land, waters, humans, and non-humans at the core of its narrative.

Yet despite these examples, the structural subordination of racialized, gendered, and Indigenous groups is deeply embedded in 20th-century journalism's aspirations, business models, and meta genre of holding power to account. Journalists often speak for and about the historically marginalized in ways that often maintain and reinforce existing power relations.[40] In this moment of major, global challenges like climate change, ocean acidification and pollution, species loss, and other problems, how, when, and where journalists locate themselves is only becoming that much more important. Climate change, for example, is also potentially a story of resilience and reckoning.[41] If you look into the deep geological past and Indigenous stories of survival, it includes adapting to climatic changes in the past. Indigenous knowledge in this sense provides an additional resource both in the recent and deep history embedded in Indigenous peoples' relations with land, water, non-human relatives, and other humans. Adaptation involves reckoning with colonial systems, varied expertise, geopolitical maneuvering, commercial ventures, and victim/hero narratives. Methodological questions that might emerge within such a framework that locate journalists as in relationship with lands, waters, humans, and non-humans include: How do you tell the stories of where you are and what methods inform your choice of experts? What is the basis for your situated knowledge and expertise? Who is your audience and how might they participate? What are your obligations to human and non-humans, to land and waters?

If journalism is understood as part of larger systems and connecting ideas, concerns, publics, polities, and experts—as well as defining them— then the role that journalism and stories play might also be considered differently. Indigenous knowledge is generative here as it makes a distinction between knowledge as something to attain, acquire, and/or consume versus its role as an aspect and reflection of relational frameworks, potentially becoming transformative of systems. Questions proliferate when considering both knowledge and the systems and social orders within which knowledge is produced, valued, and mobilized. This work of locating oneself and one's knowledge we suggest is necessary, if not crucial, to how journalism might consider its work in this era of digital reckoning.

Fieldwork and Methods

Our methods and fieldwork reflect our disciplinary backgrounds in anthropology (Candis) and journalism studies (Mary Lynn), as well as our interdisciplinary backgrounds in gender studies, media studies, STS, and Indigenous studies. We use several research methods in this book: ethnography, semi-structured interviews, content analysis, and social media analytics. Each chapter maps out what research method and data is being used. We use multiple methods and entry points in order to get to questions about what journalism is, what it could do, and how it must change and adapt to a more collaborative means for doing journalism—one that takes into account technological shifts, new articulations of social location, multiple perspectives, and its history of misrepresentational (and poorly representational) practices.

With the use of multiple methods, interdisciplinary frameworks and theories of media, we have sought to create a point of intersection that offers varied views of how journalism has been constructed as a set of ideals and interpretive communities.[42] As former journalists, journalism professors and scholars, we come to this research with a substantive interest in not just critiquing but in trying to understand the vast changes underway in the industry. Our hope is that by creating this intersection point, we can continue to support journalism and journalists to do better by, to quote Felt, understanding "who has a voice to make legitimate knowledge claims, who defines what matters, or who participates in imagining and shaping the future."[43] In this sense, we are interested in inherent and often unspoken ways in which knowledge, power, and discourse are deeply related. However, we also take media to be fragmented and diverse in terms of its economic and social organization, and this text deeply considers potentialities to enable or challenge these power/knowledge relations.[44]

Our ethnographic methods are drawn from anthropological approaches to studying media, science, and technology. There is also a long history of ethnographic approaches used by media scholars to study journalism organizations, newsrooms, agency, and identity.[45] However, rather than situating ourselves in one newsroom, we look at a mainstream media newsroom, a start-up, and talk to varied freelancers that reflect the variety of journalistic practices and opportunities available in a rapidly casualizing workforce. We follow multi-sited ethnographic practices that operate within what Marcus and Fischer consider to be an "open system" where investigators must seek to understand the complex, layered social processes at work in a vastly interconnected and increasingly global web of social realities.[46] Media as a techno-social enterprise is, as Fischer has pointed out, part of an interdependent world made up of "emergent forms of life" where mutating perceptions, institutions, and global events give way to "ethical plateaus."[47] In Fischer's view, such forms of life require new modes of analysis and research that are multi-sited, multi-vocal, multi-audience, and rework traditional comparisons, recognizing the traces and sedimentations of other analyses. This book is thus informed both by our discussions and interviews with journalists and by interpolating this data with scholarship, teaching, contributing, and working in a colonial and media context in Canada. While much of our ethnographic fieldwork has been with varied Canadian media organizations, the similarities between the U.S. and Canadian media contexts, scholarship, and professional discourse are significant. Even with national and regional differences, we see overlap in terms of journalistic methods, language, and practices—as well as the impact of technology and crises in news organizations.

As journalism professors teaching in one of Canada's several major cities, our social and professional overlap with many of the organizations and individuals we interviewed is not insignificant. Fischer's term "ethical plateaus" is helpful here and something that we continually encountered. Fischer reminds us that culture is fluid, and when giving grounds or providing explanations comes to an end, emergent forms of life produce ethical plateaus where we must sort through our relations, approaches, principles, and research goals. For us this means that not only have students we supervised and taught worked with the organizations we have studied, but so do or have our colleagues and their family members, and we attend many of the same media industry events and have invited some of the journalists we've interviewed to speak in our classes. We've also been asked to sit on panels or speak publicly with those we've interviewed. Wherever this is the case, unless anonymity has been granted, we have been careful to state our relations and activities with those we interview. Journalism often feels like a small town, and we see our research and book as both being accountable to those with whom we share a professional and personal community and to the wider publics whom we all serve in various direct and indirect ways.

For this "small town" aspect in particular, we relied on approaches to paraethnography, which Marcus describes as collaborations among anthropologists and "other sorts of experts with shared, discovered, and negotiated critical sensibilities."[48] Many anthropologists who work with scientists and other educated and often powerful individuals have employed paraethnographic practices in order to deepen their conversations and collaborations with those they interview and analyze in their research. Theoretically, this entails studying "how culture operates within a continuously unfolding contemporary and where everyone, directly or indirectly, is implicated in and constituted by complex technical systems of knowledge."[49] In practice, this has meant for us that we are actively contributing to the journalism landscape with our research. Those who were interviewed for this book had access to their transcripts, and saw what was quoted from their interview in its context before it was published. This is a commitment we make as anthropologists working in an academic environment with research ethics oversight, but it's also a stark departure for nearly all of the journalists we interviewed. Journalistic practices are quite literally the polar opposite of anthropological practices and this created a generative terrain where we watched as some of our analyses contributed to a shift in practices, for example, with the way the startup we write about in Chapter 5 later began to identify as woman-led and hired Indigenous journalists.

The View From Somewhere

Our personal stories are deeply related to this book project. One of us (Candis) is Indigenous—from the Tahltan Nation located in what is now northwestern British Columbia, and raised in the southern city of Vancouver. One of us (Mary Lynn) is a white settler and raised in southern Ontario. We situate ourselves as gendered, racialized, and as in relation to communities—professional and personal—because this book is also asking journalists to do the same. This book asks journalists to locate themselves such that, to quote Haraway and Harding, a stronger objectivity and a better accounting of the present might emerge, and moves toward justice might be imaginable. Locating oneself as a journalist, we argue, is essential not only for the doing of journalism but also because socialization is such a huge part of the process of professionalizing as a journalist.[50]

As many scholars of knowledge production have shown, facts don't just appear or emerge.[51] They are actively produced by a myriad of "seekers of truth"—seeking truth being one of the prime functions of journalism according to many codes of ethics—and a result of interpretation in support of social structures. In this respect, journalists have much in common with scientists. Yet, as Dumit has pointed out with regard to scientists:

Social histories enable and constrain science at every level of fact, conception, experimentation, publication, and dissemination and reception, but, this does not imply that science is culture. Science produces facts in spite of and, because of these constraints—laboriously, continuously, and creatively. And we, fashion our objective-selves with the fruit of this labor in the form of received-facts, in our own continuous and often creative manner, no matter how skeptical we are. This way of living with and through scientific facts is our form of life.[52]

The same can be said of journalism, predicated as it also is on observable facts and the analysis of experts in order to tell us what happened or is happening in relation to a particular event, policy, or issue.

Living with and through journalistic facts has largely excluded and/or abstracted audiences and their interventions and critiques until recently. At the 2018 International Journalism Festival in Perugia, Italy—attended by a robust mixture of journalists, digital media platform staff, and scholars—Jay Rosen, who we referenced earlier with respect to his early questions and research on journalism's multiple publics, pointed out at that the "people formerly known as the audience" require "radical transparency and real diversity" and that journalists need "to do something better than objectivity." But what that looks like in either journalism scholarship or practice is still an open question.

In order to better understand what's at stake, it's worth a quick look inside newsrooms in North America, where mainstream journalistic methods are similar even with regional and national distinctiveness. Long-term statistical reports tell us that newsrooms remain largely white in both the United States and Canada, and while some gains have been made that move toward gender balance, the editorial positions and executive suites are still largely filled with white males. Indeed, much attention has been paid to the few diverse editors and anchors who have ascended to the top of newspapers and television shows. However, in the United States, the Pew Research Center laid out the bigger picture rather starkly in 2015:

Although minorities [including Black, Hispanic, Asian American, Native American and multiracial populations] make up over a third of the U.S. adult population (35%), they make up only 22% of the local television news workforce, according to a study by the Radio Television Digital News Association. The figure is even lower for daily newspapers, where only 13% of newsroom employees are minorities, according to an annual survey of newsroom employment by the American Society of News Editors (ASNE). These figures have changed little over the past two decades.[53]

The topline numbers paint one kind of picture, but the report goes on to show what this means on multiple layers. Racialized young journalists are 17% less likely than white young journalists to get a steady job within a year of being on the job market.[54] And as the economic crisis in commercial journalism continues (in this case: declines in ad revenues, downsizing, and restructuring of news organizations), the percentage of minorities across news organizations is beginning to decline. As of 2013, minorities made up 10% of newsroom supervisors and the number of minority interns has fallen to about 26%, near the same levels as in the late 1980s.[55] As well, small market media are likely to have less minorities in their newsrooms.[56]

Working minority journalists in Canada and the United States have increasingly pointed out how problematic their under-representation is particularly in the United States, in the wake of coverage of 2017 protests in Charlottesville and the 2014 protests in Ferguson that became nationwide and saw the emergence of the social movement, Black Lives Matter. In Canada, the 2012–2013 protests related to Indigenous-led Idle No More and the 2018 protests related to the deaths of Indigenous youths, Tina Fontaine and Colten Boushie, were similar events that reflected a long-term reckoning with media representations of Indigenous peoples. In the wake of a visceral documentary from Vice media on Charlottesville, CNN's *Reliable Sources* hosted by Brian Stelter interviewed *New York Times* journalist Nikole Hannah-Jones and CNN journalist Tanzina Vega on August 20, 2017. Both are racialized women journalists, and they suggested that *who journalists and editors are matters* in deciding when and what is news and what stories are worth telling.[57] Vega explained it this way:

> Race is often treated as something that's a trend. It's something where you see journalists and newsrooms and editors saying, 'Oh my God, we've got a Nazi rally, we've got Black Lives Matter, we've got to jump on this now,' when it's not a trend. Race is something that people live every day and we have to treat it as a part of a fabric of our society.

Hannah-Jones responded even more pointedly later in the interview:

> The notion that the only people who experience race in this country are people of color and who report through the lens of race are people of color

is, of course, absurd. White Americans experience race as well and their reporting, what they choose to cover or not to cover is heavily influenced by
how they have experienced race in this country.

Canadian newsrooms also reflect a "persistent whiteness" as we argued
in an op-ed for *The Conversation*. We marshalled the latest statistics, and
they are in fact worse than American newsrooms given that Canada's
diversity is similar to the United States but with a proportionally larger
Indigenous population.

A 1998 study by scholars David Pritchard and Florian Sauvageau . . .,
showed that the vast majority (97 per cent) of journalists in Canada were
white from a survey across media. A 2006 study of diversity at Canadian
newspapers by John Miller at Ryerson University found that visible minority journalists accounted for 3.4 per cent of the workforce. A 2011 study
of journalists and diversity in the major journalism organizations (text and
broadcast) in the Toronto GTA by Wendy Cukier, John Miller, Kristen
Aspevig and Dale Carl found that 4.8 per cent of media decision-makers
were visible minorities. The CBC's 2016 employment equity annual report
identified that Indigenous employees accounted for two per cent of permanent staff, while visible minorities were 10.5 per cent.[58]

Looking only at gender doesn't prove to be that much of an encourage-
ment in terms of representation. In the United States, women make up
34% of newsroom supervisors and have not reached over 38% of the newsroom.[59] And while most journalists and journalism students are generally
willing to agree that newsrooms should reflect the publics they serve, the
question lurking behind and around these statistics is whether it matters,
and if so, *how* it matters.

Overview

This book begins with a theoretical and conceptual chapter to do as Carey
suggests and reorient our historical assumptions.[60] We explore a number of
ruptures in Chapter 2—dissonance for journalists and malcontent attitudes
for audiences that have been there for a while. Chapters 3 to 6 are organized as a series of case studies that articulate and explore how journalists
are both responding to and rearticulating in practice this internal and external to journalism reckoning. A summary of each chapter follows.

Chapter 1 lays the conceptual groundwork for the rest of the book and supports the claims we make in the introduction, bridging histories of journalism and science with particular attention to journalistic stance and objectivity and representational harms. In this chapter, we start with why and how this fallen/tarnished ideal of objectivity—the view from nowhere—is still doing so much work, heavy lifting (and harm) despite decades of cogent internal critique. We argue that both the critique and its responses have focused on individual, ethical, and front-stage professional reputational concern more than as foundational to journalism's claims to speak truth to power—and its ability to talk about methods, expertise and make valid and reliable knowledge claims. We suggest that this focus has allowed journalists to deny their personal subjectivity and professional context as a white dominated profession, which has left journalism open to growing critique. Newer forms of storytelling and diverse sources as well as audience pushback and derision are now widely available online. We also explore how journalism studies as a field has failed to address questions of power and decades of persistent content critique from media studies, critical race studies, STS, and feminist media studies. Our approach counters this scholarship by using digital technologies as a diagnostic as opposed to object, such that technology is less about a future with "shiny things" or emergent business models and more about the ways in which our development and use of new media technologies continue to elide, ignore, and/or reproduce inequities and harm.[61]

Social media has shifted the terrain for monetizing journalism, distributing journalism, and altering audience attention spans. It has also offered a platform for counter-narratives, alternative views, and broader expertise. Chapter 2 identifies the digital reckoning by examining a number of prominent hashtag conversations to explore how mainstream media has been steadily supplemented and increasingly supplanted by citizens able to witness, record, and distribute their experiences, observations, and analysis in parallel and sometimes providing correctives to mainstream media narratives.[62] We focus on the social media response in three specific cases: (1) two separate trials for the murders of two Indigenous youth, Colten Boushie and Tina Fontaine, in central Canada—a scenario where the two white men accused in their homicides were acquitted within a month of each other in early 2018; (2) the 2015 civil trial and discrimination case brought by Ellen Pao, a Silicon Valley venture capitalist, who was forced out of her position; (3) a 2016 #MeToo-related moment in which writer Kelly Oxford asked women to share their stories through #notokay. In response to modern journalism's hoarding of the mic, we find a "battle for the story" that plays out in a range of ways from a refusal to participate in legacy media to talking back through hashtags, subtweets, media, to feminist critique and reflexivity by exploring newer decolonizing conversations about journalism methods and subjectivities.

Chapter 3 explores how American and Canadian journalists are struggling with their own personal reckoning and existential crises with respect to issues of truth, subjectivity, and power and how to narrate oneself in a global journalism landscape with multiple colonial histories. We turn the tables from audiences back to journalists to examine how journalists are narrating their own professional identity through real-time "speculative" memoir fragments. We analyze a range of memoir fragments beginning with a series of behind-the-scenes first-person animated videos titled *Correspondent Confidential* that ran on Vice Media—identified as one of the few financially successful global digital journalism organizations—to "quit lit" (where journalists publicly explain their rationale for leaving journalism or doing it differently).[63]

We argue that these stories are an emergent ethical meta genre of how journalists are dealing with the view from nowhere in a global journalism context that is calling for increasing location of identity and interests. These conversations have historically taken place at the dinner table, in bars, in newsrooms and/or other insider professional contexts—and more commonly in the pre-digital era, such articulations came out in published memoirs released long after a journalist's career had been solidified (or when a career was near or at an end). Indeed, the ways in which journalists, in practice, synthesize ways around, through, and with professional norms and obligations have been largely internal discussions for internal audiences in the past. Digital platforms now afford journalists the opportunity, space, and (still precarious) freedom—given labor challenges in the industry—to begin to co-articulate in near real time, however unevenly, previously internal debates, challenges, and negotiations with professional journalism's norms, ideals, and obligations.

In Chapter 4, we examine efforts to address reckoning at one of Canada's most respected legacy journalism organizations, the *Toronto Star*. Methodologically, we draw on public and policy discourse about the journalism crisis in Canada, recent events related to race and gender at the *Star*, and ethnographic fieldwork and interviews with journalists at the *Star* regarding the development of one main stream of digital innovation: data journalism.[64] Our analysis generates questions about how journalism is wrestling concurrently with persistent structural critique and technological transformation in a diverse city. The gender, race, and colonial reckoning that we find in other chapters, we see internally at the *Star* with the tragic death of a woman-of-color journalist and the serious questions it raises about journalism culture, as well as the repudiation of a prominent Black journalist who critiqued journalism methods. Both expose long-standing issues with "the view from nowhere," the challenge of closed systems of journalism and legacy organizations' openness to change while contending with issues such as interpretation, journalism's colonial history, and its systematic whiteness and exclusion of minority journalists.

Chapter 5 shifts the terrain to *the Discourse*, a prominent women-led journalism startup that is working on repair and reform of journalism practices while coming to terms with its contributions within an innovation context that has prioritized technological change over social structures and transformation. Our research question going in was this: What happens when a journalism startup is both mostly female and has been identified as a digital and data journalism innovator/leader in North America? The chapter addresses a number of themes related to emergent studies on innovation, startups, and repair and reform.[65] We suggest that STS frameworks for thinking about repair are necessary to explain how this commercial startup is not just innovating for the sake of saving journalism but also to improve journalism as a tool for intervention and responsibility: In the words of one employee, to "move the needle" on what kinds of work journalism is able to do.[66] We see these kinds of commitments playing out particularly in fieldwork related to these three aspects: ownership and structuring, professional identity and innovations related to collaboration, and deliberate focus of the startup on reconciliation as a public good in a settler-colonial society and media in Canada. Here we complicate the emerging focus in journalism studies on repair and reform as largely a function of the nonprofit and philanthropic journalism sector.[67] However, even with an overarching commitment to community accountability and public service journalism, efforts to repair and reform still present an array of challenges.

Chapter 6 draws on ethnographic fieldwork and interviews with Indigenous journalists in Canada and the United States who have been addressing colonialism, race, and gender in their journalism all along. This chapter provides a bookend to Chapter 1 by suggesting that Indigenous journalists have exposed journalism's deep fault lines as they undertake a differentiated set of approaches that draw on journalism ideals and get at deeper problems structurally. Their work offers instances of where and how transformation within journalism might be possible in terms of profession, identity, and method. Indigenous journalists provide a pathway into discussing not only new bases for ethical considerations but also an example of some of the multiple journalisms available through digital and social media. Indigenous journalists articulate the challenges of working in and among mainstream media that has largely erased and misrepresented Indigenous voices, communities, and concerns on a range of issues. This chapter explores how Indigenous journalists are using digital tools/media to transform journalism methods decolonizing "fairness and balance" by drawing from Indigenous knowledge and relational frameworks.

In conclusion, we find a reckoning of journalism's "view from nowhere" and persistent misrepresentations with digital technologies exposing and offering journalists, citizens and sources an opportunity to hold a mirror up to journalism practices and positionality. From journalists experimenting with speculative memoir fragments to Indigenous journalists exploring "radical relationality," digital technologies are exposing and providing platforms for multiple journalisms and their audiences. We suggest that a turn to systems journalism that recognizes the complexity of global relationality, subjectivity, structures, and challenges. Doing so, we conclude, requires opening up journalism crisis narratives, contending with persistent critiques related to intersectionality and settler-colonialism, and re-evaluating to whom and what social order journalism is contributing.

CHAPTER 1 | Reckoning with the "View From Nowhere"

Introduction

The challenge inherent in considering a "reckoning with" journalism is that, as a practice, it is predicated mainly on good intentions *and* unexamined, power-laden, gendered, racialized, and colonial relations. Even while delivering what is considered vital information in democratic societies, journalistic representations often fail to consider the harm they have done to peoples and environments, historical shifts in the cultures of journalism, and the colonial contexts for the practice of journalism. Instead, what gets substituted for self-examination by journalists and journalism educators working in a North American context is still a kind of paean to the role of the so-called fourth-estate functions, the need for watchdogs and accountability, and the power of storytelling to bring justice and to speak for those who cannot.

This self-examination largely occurs under the umbrella of a journalism ethics specific to North American journalists and journalism. Professional journalism ethics codes advocate for fairness and accuracy, caution, balance, and minimizing future harms, and are still largely operationalized methodologically through the broad epistemological lens of objectivity despite decades of cogent intellectual critique within journalism studies and beyond. Feminist and postcolonial scholars began critiquing the "view from nowhere" more than 20 years ago, alongside increasingly rigorous and interdisciplinary approaches to journalism studies scholarship and commitments to deepening journalism practice and expertise.[1] This book and first chapter specifically shed light on why and how this fallen/tarnished ideal, value, and method is still doing so much heavy lifting (and harm) despite extensive critique, the field's growing interdisciplinarity, and chronic ruptures and crises in journalism that point to its deficiencies.

In claiming objectivity, journalists have been doing more than merely advocating for an "impartial" ethical stance and approach to method. They are, according to Schudson and Anderson, bolstering their own ability to make knowledge claims:

> US journalism's claim to objectivity—i.e., the particular method by which this information is collected, processed, and presented—gives it its unique jurisdictional focus by claiming to possess a certain form of expertise or intellectual discipline. Establishing jurisdiction over the ability to objectively parse reality is a claim to a special kind of authority.[2]

This "authority" or expertise has developed as an implicit—or at the very least, not fully transparent—pillar of North American journalism over the course of the past century. Yet journalists aren't supposed to be experts. They are stand-ins for the public: the average citizen as witness to important events on behalf of the collective. They don't often claim to be experts in any particular knowledge area but rather of the practice or craft—the forms and styles of journalism. Good storytelling and "solid" journalism are often indicated by peers, industry awards, and/or audience acclaim; and it's not uncommon for journalists to point to societal or policy impacts that have resulted from their journalism as a kind of gold standard.

This gold standard of journalism is exactly what has been under attack both because of new sources and newer forms of storytelling, and because of counter-narratives and refusals from multiple publics that are widely available online. The "why should we listen to you" and "who is speaking" now matters as much if not more given the problematic business case for news and journalism. How facts are established and what kinds of stories get told about how reality can be interpreted are held up for scrutiny and comparison across multiple, varied sources for news and information.[3] Early hype about a freedom of mind espoused by cyberutopians have given way to a world where journalism's credibility and authority are seen to be under threat, along with its commercial economic models—and hence, democracy as we've known it.[4]

In this chapter, we first explore how journalism studies scholars have wrestled with journalism's "special kind of authority" as individual, ethical, and front-stage professional reputational concerns. By contrast, we argue that this authority is foundational to journalism's claims to speak truth to power—and its ability to talk about methods, expertise, and make valid and reliable knowledge claims.[5] We further contend that North American journalists have been able to deny their subjectivity and their locatedness as a white-dominated profession (and the broader impact of this) in part because of how this authority and expertise came into being alongside ongoing colonialism and commercial media systems specific to North America.[6] As these interrelated systems are exposed through numerous contemporary social movements and market failure, journalism is open to growing critique in general, and critique specifically related to its underlying methodological looseness and rigidity of approach to stance, interpretation, and validity.

By starting with scholarship, we lay a foundation that informs the case studies on journalistic practice and digital reckonings in the chapters that follow. This first chapter identifies disciplines from media studies, feminist media studies, and Indigenous studies to postcolonial STS, which have critiqued journalists, journalism studies scholarship, and journalism representations and methods for not addressing power relations and representational harms. We explore how objectivity has been identified as a guise for the performance of a certain kind of white masculinity that claims its power through ignoring and denying its locatedness. We go on to consider how journalism studies, even with the injection of STS and the current flowering of multiple journalisms, continues to largely ignore structural concerns and multiple publics and their histories. Our approach in countering this scholarship is to use digital technologies as a diagnostic as opposed to object.[7] In this way, technology is less about a future with "bright, shiny things" and more about the ways in which our development and use of new media technologies continue to elide, ignore, and/or reproduce inequities.[8] Finally, we end by suggesting that feminist approaches to journalism's dominant authority, while an important starting point, haven't gone far enough in integrating intersectional and postcolonial critique.

Objectivity's Embrace, Rejection, and Critical Reappraisal

The Early Years

In April 2018 Susan Goldberg, the self-described 10th editor of *National Geographic* since its founding in 1888, and the first editor who is both Jewish and a woman, made headlines around the world with her editorial acknowledging the award-winning magazine's racist coverage titled, "For Decades, Our Coverage Was Racist. To Rise Above Our Past, We Must Acknowledge It."[9] The editorial begins by describing the coronation coverage of Ethiopian King Halie Selassie in 1930 (14,000 words, 83 images). It is followed by musings about how similar coverage of a Black leader in the United States might have played out at that time in then-segregated Washington, DC—a segregationist context that included *National Geographic*'s own lectures where Black men and women would have been denied entry. Despite decades of critical feedback from many communities of color, Goldberg only acknowledged the magazine's dubious past after hiring a historian to analyze *National Geographic* coverage over time.

The Twitter response and coverage by mainstream media was enormous and global, with Goldberg's admission greeted by surprise, mock surprise, and yet more critique. The *Washington Post* described Goldberg's editorial and then turned to excerpts from an editorial by Breanna Edwards, news editor from *The Root*. In the excerpt, Edwards expresses concern about balancing appreciation of the apology with expectations of just behavior:

> Bluntly acknowledging its own past in this way is indeed powerful, but it is not necessarily something, I think, that we should applaud, as much as we should expect . . . especially at this time in our lives when race and discussions of racism and even general cultural insensitivity can be volatile, tense and perhaps even deadly.[10]

In its excerpt, the *Post* sidesteps the biting sarcastic tone Edwards begins her editorial with: "This may come as a surprise to no one, but [*stage whispers*] *National Geographic* (along with many other publications) used to be *hella, obviously* racist. Shocking. I know."[11]

Gene Demby, co-host of the National Public Radio podcast *Code Switch*, similarly offered up a sarcastic response when tweeting: "Is Nat Geo's cover story finna be the shocking revelation that race is socially constructed?"[12] His next tweet responds to his own question: "Sigh. Turns out that IS the big revelation." He goes on in his tweet thread to state: "It would be great that if, upon stumbling upon the idea that race is not a biological reality but socially constructed, people didn't immediately proceed to presume that that means it can just be waved away. Money is socially constructed. Nation-states are socially constructed." And drawing on a prior Twitter conversation, Demby cites BU PhD student Dan Hauge's point: "I think one issue is we whites imagine the endgame of anti-racism as harmonious relationships rather than equal power to shape society."[13] Demby, Hauge, and Edwards's responses reflect what scholars have been pointing out for some time. Race and racism can't be talked about as something without real-time consequences or without historical consciousness and awareness of the power relations and societal structures that have been put in place as a result of structural inequities.

TallBear, an Indigenous scholar who has written about *National Geographic* in her book, *Native American DNA*, argues that the challenge now is not only recognizing the history of harmful representations but "embedded old school notions of race that are harder to see now."[14] For example, the *National Geographic* apology edition of the magazine focused on coverage of Black and white relations, mostly ignoring Indigenous people, except for a short story on previous racist coverage of Pacific Islanders. This approach ignores and reinforces the persistence of erasure of Indigenous people in U.S. media. TallBear pointed out in response to the apology that while *National Geographic* does photography and glossy media very well:

> Their narratives really haven't moved on a lot in the last hundred years. They just get re-combined with these kind of more multicultural 'let's all get along,' 'we're all related,' 'can't we just all love each other' kind of narratives, but the old school race narratives that are dependent on hierarchies of races, that are dependent on portraying Africans and Native Americans as always part of the past not as contemporary peoples. Those are things that we still haven't done away with since the nineteenth century.[15]

Over a century's worth of journalists in North America—130 years at *National Geographic* alone—have participated in these kinds of narratives and representations from which harms still reverberate, as the apology and responses to it demonstrate.

We begin the chapter with this storied journalism organization's acknowledgment of racist coverage and some of the responses because the example offers insight into and evidence of the reckoning well under way within journalism. It produces questions for scholars about how to come to terms with gaps in scholarship and attempts by journalists to redress a past riven with harm and complicity despite varied and evolving articulations of professional objectivity, fairness, and truth-seeking. It has only been in the past two decades that journalists have begun to think about harm as a part of professional journalistic codes.[16] Harm, in the case of *National Geographic*, continues to impact ongoing representations of many non-Western and non-white peoples, creating and adding to an early sedimentation of representations that all journalism thereafter must contend with in some way. As Goldberg writes: "I hear from readers that *National Geographic* provided their first look at the world. Our explorers, scientists, photographers, and writers have taken people to places they'd never even imagined; it's a tradition that still drives our coverage and of which we're rightly proud."[17] Herein lies the gauntlet: These publications still exist and are motivated by similar editorial *and* audience desires, having cultivated a sense of knowability that might be met by more accurate, more "authentic" portrayals even as dominant frameworks of othering and essentializing persist. Crucially also, these publications persist even as such portrayals remain largely disconnected from commentaries and analyses that might shed light on cultural ways of being and becoming, global and national structural inequities, and other aspects of contemporary erasures and "social situations."[18]

Both harm and the dominance of stereotypical frames and narratives that erase histories of colonial violence and ignore, criticize, or blame minority communities have rarely been tackled by journalism studies scholars. The focus of critiques has instead been mainly on the professional commitment to objectivity: a commitment that arguably, if actionable, should absolve journalists of charges of misrepresentation or even of acting within the cultural contexts of their time. Few of the ways in which objectivity as an ideal has structured practice and supported not only approaches like *National Geographic*'s but a persistent lack of gender and racial diversity in their newsrooms and others have trickled into journalism studies scholarship. This is all the more troubling given that beginning in the late 1970s, major scholars like Said and Hall introduced analyses that have transformed scholarship related to media, representations, and Western institutions broadly speaking.[19]

Instead of embracing and incorporating such critiques during the late 20th century, journalism studies scholars have spent decades developing an internal critique of objectivity in response to its growing dominance as the defining 20th-century method for journalists. Reaching as far back as 1972, Tuchman observed that objectivity's function in journalism is more of a "strategic ritual" rooted in social and organizational needs than reliable method:

> The newsmen view quotations of other people's opinions as a form of supporting evidence. By interjecting someone else's opinion, they *believe* they are removing themselves from participation in the story, and they are letting the 'facts' speak (*emphasis added*).[20]

Following Tuchman, scholars have found fault and/or attempted to understand and advance objectivity's contingent role in journalism from a number of perspectives.[21] Carey, for example, found newsrooms key sites for "sizing up situations and naming their elements"—and "in a way that contains an attitude toward them."[22] As part of their critique, many scholars have argued both for a renewed commitment to truth and the retention of objectivity in an albeit contingent, adjusted and/or reflexive form.[23] For example, Ward's aptly termed "pragmatic objectivity" for journalists suggests that the current practices of journalism could be evaluated based on three aspects: the moral stance of the journalist, the methods used by journalists, and the accountability mechanisms for the application of these methods. Ward has further argued that a "commitment to truth is also a commitment to objectivity, ontologically and epistemologically."[24] That said, Ward is careful to point out that journalism is an "active, interpretive, cultural activity."[25] He stakes out a nuanced position in rejecting what he terms "traditional objectivity" in favor of "multi-dimensional objectivity" (alternatively, he also calls this "pragmatic objectivity"), which offers a "fallible but important method for testing interpretations."[26] Much rests, as it always has, on the individual journalist to, as Ward puts it, check their "cultural baggage" and use a more "holistic method for testing interpretations."[27] This approach promotes journalism's main ethical principles (accuracy, fairness, transparency, accountability, minimization of harm) and journalism's main task, according to ethical codes: truth seeking.[28]

Ward is not alone in offering alternatives for thinking through, with, and about objectivity in more nuanced terms. Deuze, drawing on Ryan, suggests that "objectivity may not be possible but that does not mean one should not strive for it, or redefine it in such a way that it in fact becomes possible."[29] Deuze reviews the broad critiques of objectivity and concludes that "the embrace, rejection as well as critical reappraisal of objectivity all help to keep it alive as an ideological cornerstone of journalism.[30] So, even with efforts to improve journalistic methods, most scholars and practitioners still rely on the story journalism tells itself of good intentions and reliable methodologies for assessing the internal validity of knowledge. Yet all the while this story largely leaves aside the ways in which, as Ericson argues, facts are open to epistemological interpretation. The *National Geographic* apology hammers home Ericson's observation by showing how cultural and historical contexts, the imperatives of colonialism and imperialism, and changing notions of who is an "other" and an "us" over time should also be considered in any analysis of journalism's epistemic commitments.[31] TallBear's point speaks to the durability and malleability of stereotypes even as they get re-coded otherwise and suggests that these commitments must be continually reevaluated against powerful meta-narratives.

Among journalism historians and scholars, there is a general consensus that objectivity emerges as a stable aspect of method and as a value in journalism in North America over a century ago, in the 1910s and 1920s. Schudson points out that objectivity wasn't an inevitable development but rather one that springs from historical events and heavily circumscribed contexts that coincide with the need to articulate journalism as a profession that could produce facts vital to the functioning of Western democracies.[32] These events were influenced heavily by the credibility ascribed to scientific methods and the need to professionalize journalism through the instantiation of similar methodological imperatives.[33] According to Ward, in the earliest U.S. codes of ethics, journalists were advised explicitly to "keep yourself out of the story" and objectivity was seen as the chief corollary to truth seeking.[34] Ward points out that the connection of journalism to democracy was an essential rationale in this move to more credible methods:

> Objective reporting, it was argued, was crucial to egalitarian democracies. Commentary was not enough and biased [or manipulated] reporting tainted the information supply. Citizens needed objective news about their government to make political judgments about themselves.[35]

He goes on to suggest that "traditional objectivity advanced a strict, reductive form of objectivity that reduced objective reporting to one dimension of good inquiry—reporting facts."[36]

Even while it's been instantiated in codes and notions of professionalism, journalists have periodically struggled with and pushed against objectivity. As Henry Luce, the founder of *Time* magazine, stated in the 1920s: "Show me a man who thinks he's objective and I'll show you a liar."[37] Broadcast media such as early current affairs television in the United States, as well as new journalism and forms from the era of digital media that we address in later chapters, have tended to emphasize interpretation, point of view, and the personal.[38] Yet, objectivity remained well ensconced in ethical codes until the 1990s. In 1996, the mostly widely used professional code of ethics for the Society of Professional Journalists (SPJ) was revised to remove the word "objectivity." The previous code, accepted in 1973, had referred to objectivity as "a goal which serves as the mark of an experienced professional," and as a "standard of performance toward which we strive," noting that "we honor those who achieve it."

Schudson argues that even in the early 2000s, objectivity remained a dominant norm that sets American journalism apart from European journalism. He describes it this way:

> The objectivity norm guides journalists to separate facts from values and to report only the facts. Objective reporting is supposed to be cool, rather than emotional, in tone. Objective reporting takes pains to represent fairly each leading side in a political controversy. According to the objectivity norm, the journalist's job consists of reporting something called 'news' without commenting on it, slanting it, or shaping its formulation in any way.[39]

Indeed, despite the long-standing critical reappraisal, most journalism scholarship still tends to unpack objectivity as journalistic ideal/practice and journalism as a democratic good.[40] Such analyses shed little light on journalism's impact on diverse publics, and even less attention is paid to who is (and has been) in the newsroom offering meaning making and critical insight, producing knowledge and interpretive frameworks, and solidifying consensus.

Like a good virus, objectivity as a notional good has mutated and now obliquely comes in a range of diluted yet co-existent stand-ins, such as distance, impartiality, unbiased reporting, and independence. Deuze similarly suggests that "academics and journalists alike revisit this value through synonymous concepts like 'fairness,' 'professional distance,' 'detachment,' or 'impartiality' to define and (re)legitimize what media practitioners do."[41] Maintaining these attributes has become both increasingly important and contentious in this era of protecting journalism through this period of "crisis" and with good reason given the challenges to the profession, its methods, and its economic viability. But herein also lies an embedded challenge. It isn't just that objectivity is an impossibility or the default that won't go away but rather that it serves a larger societal purpose. The role of the journalist, in other words, has been deeply historicized but much less attention has been paid to who that journalist is likely to be and what or whose social order has been reinstated and reinforced by journalism and journalists.[42]

It's this intention to represent social realities adequately and accurately, to ascertain and uncover matters of fact and "the truth" that animates journalism and confounds it at the same time. In memoirs, journalists have often discussed their struggle with this aspect of their professional role.

We address some of this in Chapter 3 through an analysis of graphically animated memoirs where journalists examine what kinds of realities they couldn't represent—their own and those whose stories they told. In his look at recent journalism memoirs, Broersma suggests that journalism has limits to what it can and can't do with respect to truth claims, such that it is more of a performative discourse than a descriptive one as it claims.[43] He contends that in adhering to professional routines and conventions, journalists mask their own subjectivity and news selections in order to convince their audiences that their interpretations are truth and reality—and must be acted upon. Broersma further suggests that journalists should be transparent about these limitations and introduce a kind of "structural ambiguity" into their writing such that audiences are aware that other interpretations are possible.

Transparency has, in the digital age, often been added to the lofty list of ethical goals for journalists and news organizations.[44] But what Broersma is suggesting is an order of differently configured magnitude where the long-sought goal of credibility might be relinquished by pulling the veil off journalism as a performer of forms and styles that describe to convince with hard-won, expensively produced and distributed facts. This has left journalism open to growing critique because of backstage methodological looseness and paradoxical rigidity even while journalism's forms and styles have presented professionally sutured front-stage accounts of events, problems, processes, and people. Zelizer argues that the stakes are even higher however. It is not only the matter of credibility but also journalism's role in maintaining social order.[45] On this point, STS provides an additional helpful set of analytical tools not least of which is because, as Schudson and Ward point out, the roots of journalism's credibility lie in throwing its lot in with science and objectivity. In this sense, journalism and science are both involved in the production and generation of knowledge, which as Shapin and Schaffer argue in the case of early modern science, is based on solving the problem and subsequent structuring of social order.[46]

"The Culture of No Culture"

Epistemological Scrutiny And Feminist STS

That journalists are open to epistemological scrutiny similar to scientists is a terrain yet to be explored by journalism studies scholars. This book marks what we hope is a new direction for integrating STS and journalism studies scholarship that draws on broader and more diverse critiques, problems, and analyses.[47] STS, and feminist scholarship as well as modern journalism, and its critics have added to and substantiated skepticism about the possibility of achieving objectivity. Beginning in the 1980s, feminist science studies scholars such as Donna Haraway, Sandra Harding, Sharon Traweek, and Leigh Star destabilized objectivity in scientific methodologies as being less about transcendent facts and methods, and more about masculinity, whiteness, and cultural/social contexts. These moves had consequences for the field, ultimately supporting a growing and robust area of feminist and postcolonial STS.[48]

Yet despite increasingly rigorous attention to objectivity, what might be considered a general commitment to liberal Western democracy and the prized role given to journalism among journalism studies scholars has prevented them from making similar critical intellectual turns—or at least, this is our most generous read. These next sections explore why similar accountability conversations have not become central to journalism studies as the practice of journalism increasingly comes face to face with wide, sustained criticism and crises.

How facts are produced, who produces them, and what role social structuring and institutions play are vital to understanding epistemological stakes and ethical plateaus for journalism as it continues to evolve as practice and profession, and as it is replicated by citizens performing "acts of journalism." As we mention earlier, historians have pointed out the influence of scientific methodologies and norms in the rise of the professionalization of journalists; however, the influence of the history and culture of science have not been applied to analyses of journalistic norms and practices.[49] In the wake of social movements, such as #ArabSpring, #BlackLivesMatter, #IdleNoMore, #JusticeforTina and #JusticeforColten, #MeToo, #NoDAPL, #Occupy and #StandingRock, race, colonialism, and gender can no longer be relegated to sidebar analyses given the role that journalism has played in creating knowledges that are almost always structurally unable to intervene on behalf of a "public."

Looking back at the longer history of science helps to excavate some of the roots of journalism's problematic commitment to objectivity. Shapin and Schaffer's seminal book on the history of modern science sets up 17th-century scientist/philosophers Robert Boyle and Thomas Hobbes as protagonists at a specific period in which knowledge and social order were in flux.[50] Each proposed a "form of life" or a social order in which to produce, validate, and distribute knowledge. As Haraway has pointed out, it was a question of "what could count as knowledge."[51] In Hobbes's case, the answer was predicated on absolutist enforcement of truth, corporeal knowledge, and causality. Boyle shifted the field of vision, practice, and accepted knowledge instigating an experimental form of knowledge with an accompanying social order. Boyle's method introduced the role of witnessing and the use of three technologies: material, social, and literary. Each of these "technologies" encapsulate the establishment of boundaries around what was determined to be "factual" through the use of virtual witnessing, the creation of a community of experimentalists, the disciplined space and materials of the laboratory, and the new rules for engagement (resolving dissent, restricted access to the lab)—much of which we still think of as good scientific practice.

While interrogating Boyle's practice, Shapin and Schaffer also seek to rehabilitate Hobbes's contributions by demonstrating that facts are politically manufactured "social conventions," and that the methods we use to produce facts support the structuring of an enduring social order. Haraway, drawing on Shapin and Schaffer, has argued that what emerges in this order is a "modest witness" who inhabits as Traweek so famously put it in her study of physicists, "the culture of no culture."[52] Boyle's experimental order set scientific inquiry as outside culture and society, where:

> The modest witness is the legitimate and authorized ventriloquist for the object world, adding nothing from his mere opinions, from his biasing embodiment. And so he is endowed with the remarkable power to establish facts . . . His subjectivity is his objectivity. His narratives have magical power—they lose all trace of their history as stories, as products of partisan projects, as contestable representations, or as constructed documents in their potent capacity to define the facts.[53]

These observations are applicable to journalists as well. They can be found embedded in common critiques of journalism, which include: lack of context and/or historical consciousness, agenda setting as rooted in subjectivity and/or ideology and not a reflection of external news events, the suppression of opinion, and the ways in which journalism circulates as commodified story and "contestable representations." But the rabbit hole goes deeper. Haraway points to the co-development of a " 'naked way of writing,' unadorned, factual, compelling . . . Both the facts and the witnesses inhabit privileged zones of 'objective' reality through a powerful writing technology."[54] For Haraway, that writing technology is the modest witness rooted in masculinity, a maleness that "guarantees the clarity and purity of objects . . . The narratives become clear mirrors, fully magical mirrors, without once appealing to the transcendental or the magical."[55]

That women, racialized bodies, technicians, and lower-class bodies were excluded in science is hardly surprising given the time, but the ramifications are powerful because of the ways in which some of these exclusions persist in journalism. As Haraway argues, gender, race, class, and sexuality were made and continue to be re-made through "the constitutive practices of technoscience themselves."[56] What sounds like fact and news in newsrooms is more likely related to what and who is considered to be rational, able to report, and/or distanced enough as numerous feminist media scholars have pointed out.[57] The corollary for journalism is, as Haraway eloquently puts it, "struggles over what will count as rational accounts of the world are struggles over *how* to see."[58] One only has to look at the critical reaction to the *New York Times'* decision to run graphic photos of dead bodies after a 2019 terrorist attack in Kenya to see how prominent journalists and journalism organizations are seeing race and colonialism, as well as the problems with their view.[59] One can also see how, despite an emphasis on journalism in service of society, scholars of objectivity (as well as journalists themselves) have largely not integrated this critique, nor any of the additional concerns related to gender, race, and colonialism that emerge from decades of representational analyses in media studies. And that is surprising given the times—and claims of the profession and industry being in crisis.

Decades of Scholarship on Representational Harms

Despite its relationship to larger disciplines such as media, cultural, and communication studies, journalism studies has more often than not focused on the emergence and maintenance of the role of the professional journalist—and less on exclusions, broad contexts for production and knowledge creation, power, representational harms, and audiences. In our analysis, objectivity remains the putative stance of a high-stakes method that validates journalists as credible, reliable producers of knowledge and facts but removes them from the perception of messy entanglement in which material and social elements are constantly in shifting, contingent, culturally informed relationships.[60] This general disconnection of journalism from its context was recognized in a special issue of *Journalism Studies* in 2000 edited by Zelizer, which advocated for "a world of journalism studies that might consider its past alongside its future" and "its texts and their connections with its contexts."[61]

Media studies, feminist media studies, communication, and critical race scholarship instead have focused on these perspectives and how they do or don't wend their way into mainstream media.[62] They have engaged with questions that include: what is knowledge in news and journalism and how is it produced, in whose interests is it produced (including what is the political economy and ideologies of news production from various approaches such as Marxism and institutional theory), as well as a large body of literature on representations and how racialized and gendered groups are represented.[63] These critiques have articulated how journalism knowledge supports certain powerful interests over others and found that media representations tend to reinforce structural inequities and identities, such as gendered and racist stereotypes,[64] violence against women,[65] social control,[66] white supremacy,[67] and settler-colonialism.[68]

The North American scholarship is extensive and damning. One of the early important contributions includes Rhodes's powerful critique of journalism and media depictions.[69] Writing almost twenty-five years ago, Rhodes called out U.S. media and scholars for their complicity with a system of "racial dominance and control."[70] This system, she argues, has played out in the "struggle between the transmission of racist ideology and dogma, and the efforts of oppressed groups to claim control over their own image" in the process generating an under-examined historical legacy for journalists as a "national institution encumbered by a racist past."[71] In supporting her argument about the centrality of race to journalism history, Rhodes begins with how the development of the penny press in the United States both "served the agenda of asserting racial superiority" and was linked to the origins of the Black press.[72] She identifies how there was little discussion of Black or Indigenous peoples in popular discourse of the period, and what was there "served as a powerful agent of control, encouraging the dominant group to assert their authority and constantly reminding the subordinate groups of their fragile and oppressed status in society."[73]

According to Rhodes, the early Black press emerged in response to the "racist discourse in the nation's press and sought to present a distinct racial identity and agenda."[74] Further she argues:

> The impulse to establish an alternative medium in response to oppression from the mainstream served to improve communication to a smaller audience, in this case, other Blacks and white abolitionist supporters.[75]

Yet, instead of an historical reckoning with journalism's harms, she concludes that late 20th-century media discourse focused "on the celebration of technological achievement and financial success"[76] which is consistent with the historiography we are trying to reorient more than two decades later.

Similarly, in Canada, a 2009 retrospective by Jiwani charts the long history of Canadian research on race and the media, narrating how it emerged in the late 1980s and early 1990s initially from activist organizations and social movements. Successive waves of research followed from scholars who tended to focus on the growth of a sophisticated form of "modern"[77] and/or "inferential racism"[78] largely through methods of discourse and content analysis. Jiwani suggests in retrospect that context and connection to community matter:

> It would seem necessary to heed community concerns if we are to mindfully address issues of representations in terms of their material and social implications. In that regard, it is well enough time to stop debating the relevance of race [especially in this climate where the current ethos is one of society as being 'post-race'] and instead deal with questions of power—power that is grounded in a racialized and gendered economy and reproduced in mediated landscapes that surround us.[79]

Squires's recent work deconstructing the notion of a "post-racial" United States also raises "questions of power." She touches on themes and disjunctures that we engage with in this book; how post-racial media constructions are limited, ahistorical, damaging, and "not all bad."[80] In exploring the wide gaps between "the aspirational post racial discourse and the brutal realities of poverty, police profiling, anti-immigration vitriol, and mind-boggling incarceration for Blacks and Latinos/as," Squires finds these discussions "inherit a lot of the same elements of past articulations of how to solve the colour line in ways that are seemingly oblivious to the critiques and contributions of people of colour and their allies to rethinking race and racism."[81] We find a shared general refusal to acknowledge the multiple ways that power relations affect what we understand as contemporary journalism and its role. As we argue in a 2018 op-ed with respect to media coverage of Indigenous peoples in Canada:

> Canadian media have—since before Confederation—continually reproduced stereotypes in which Indigenous people are found wanting morally, physically, mentally, historically. This 'othering' helped to 'promote a nation,' an 'imagined community' of Canada, in Benedict Anderson's

terms, in which Indigenous people are seen as on the margins and the brutality of settler colonialism is seen as natural and normal.[82]

However, journalism is certainly not only a tool of racial oppression or handmaiden to colonialism in terms of its ability to foster and enable particular civic imaginations: it can be an important tool for resurgent counter-narratives and accurate representations of and insight into counterpublics.[83] Silva points out that journalism historically has acted in a transformative decolonizing capacity such that Kānaka Maoli journalists were able to play a role in resisting colonization in 19th-century Hawai'i.[84] Historians are also beginning to look more closely at other Indigenous newspapers such as the *Cherokee-Phoenix*, the first Indigenous newspaper in the United States, which was founded in 1828. More recently, the rise of Indigenous journalism outlets in northern Canada beginning in the 1970s, as well as the launch of APTN in Canada, similarly situate Indigenous journalism as offering a much-needed counter-narrative to mainstream media.[85] More scholarship is needed on these efforts and others such as the re-launch of U.S.-based *Indian Country Today* and on-demand video like Oiwi TV in Hawai'i that offers programming in both Hawaiian and English languages. Chapter 6 explores some of these conversations in fieldwork and interviews with Indigenous journalists.

Scholars have also contributed to a broader understanding of how media have functioned and continue to function for Indigenous communities. Daley and James in their study of Alaska Native media draw on Valaskakis who developed the concept of "resistance as cultural persistence" in order to point out that the use of media among Indigenous groups can be "understood as a set of cultural practices that reinforce and amplify the group's own creative roots and dynamism."[86] They look closely at the work of William Paul in the 1920s, the Tlingit editor of the *Alaska Fisherman,* who articulated his rationale for countering hegemonic mass media of the time this way: "A group of people without the power of telling what they have done can be robbed."[87] They also suggest, drawing on a group of Iñupiat students in Barrow, Alaska, that "the western journalistic paradigm of objectivity" reflects its own "cultural pain and dislocation."

Interrogating Western news values from an Indigenous perspective, they began to see objectivity as a poseur—a masquerader hiding a storyteller's perspective as if its teller were everywhere and nowhere. For Alaska Native storytellers, the important point is to narrate stories from those places where their understandings of nature are part and parcel of their cultural milieus.[88]

Indeed, Alia and others have pointed out that Indigenous media has grown out of and adapted to new forms of media precisely because they weren't well represented and they saw the potential for self-representation and self-determination. Duarte's work on the development of ICT's echoes a similar sentiment when she says:

> Understanding how Native and Indigenous peoples use analog and digital systems to share knowledge toward self-governance and self-determination—by talking story, by sharing information and data with one another—gives us insight into the subversive ways that Native and Indigenous peoples apply digital technologies towards creating spaces for Native and Indigenous forms of resistance, endurance, and liberation.[89]

Further, Brooks points out that stories of resistance are necessary precisely because they open up a space for collaboration "even across previous geographical and political chasms."[90]

Looking at specific examples of what might be considered alternative media, both in the past and present, is a reminder that de Certeau's notion of "making do" is a useful framework for understanding mainstream and legacy media's claims to supporting democracy.[91] Jenkins has adapted de Certeau's ideas to understand how publics make do with the media provided to them—and develop tactics to cope, respond, and resist.[92] Indeed, many minorities in Western democracies aren't likely to have seen or currently see themselves well represented, and in part civic media projects reflect not just activism but the partiality of mainstream reporting on events.[93]

New media platforms provide new avenues with which to make do, and improvise new tactics to self-represent. Consider the film, *Democracy Now,* which was among the first to use crowd-sourced video to show how activists at the 1999 demonstrations against the WTO in Seattle were intentionally and persistently misrepresented by mainstream media.[94] There are a myriad of similar small and big examples that have proliferated with digital media platforms. The challenges laid at the feet of mainstream media reflect a long-term set of disaffected diverse publics that have often sought out newer technologies in order to self-represent their experiences at events, at the hands of institutions, in politics, and with technologies. We will return to this again in the next chapter to discuss the reckoning well underway with diverse publics and counterpublics. First, we turn back to journalism studies and the response and lack thereof to these critiques even as the digital era presents such a reckoning—and opportunity, we argue, to assess journalism's limitations and possibilities.

Doubling Down on Tech

Breathing Life Into Dominant Normative Approaches

Instead of a sustained structural rethink in light of a few decades of this representational and post-objectivity critique, journalism studies scholarship has mainly focused on technological changes to the practice of journalism. This focus on digital technologies as the object(s) of study—as actors, processes, affordances, economics, materiality, innovation, economic disruptors, savior—is remarkable for its rigorous contributions to the discipline (and at times, magical thinking) on the potential of technology to improve journalism without also centering wider structural forces. While we make special note of the extensive and significant contributions of STS scholarship to the sociology of journalism knowledge production, we are writing against its general disregard for questions of power, identity, and representation, which is also reflected in the whiteness and masculinity of the scholars themselves.[95] Specifically, we contend that while this digital journalism scholarship advances early critique of the contingency of objectivity and the notion that there is an objective knowledge in journalism, the emergent canon still breathes life into normative understandings of a dominant approach to journalism.[96] In addition, there is an underlying technological determinism in some of the studies that we address later in this chapter.

Brennan and Kreiss's essay on digitalization is useful to draw from with respect to some of the gaps in journalism studies of technology scholarship.[97] They define digitalization as "the way in which many domains of social life are restructured around digital communication and media infrastructures."[98] They base their definition of digitalization on *social life* and reference studies from other disciplines such as law and legal studies that integrate larger structural and other disparate forces in understanding the effects of digitalization on specific domains. This wide remit provides some context for comparison to journalism studies scholarship on technology, which has taken a narrow slice of social life to explore the impact of technology on practice—largely ethnographies of legacy journalism organizations. Such ethnographies are intended to make logical generalizations across the journalism industry; and while they do shed light on practices and routines, they don't also engage or analyze how journalism is implicated in propping up social orders, what kinds of knowledge it privileges and produces. Nor do such studies address challenges related to dominant social structures and contemporary erasures in newsrooms. Boczkowski's 2004 seminal study on the digital turn in three newsrooms is a case in point. It set a methodological orientation for much of the literature that follows in its focus on two large legacy U.S. newsrooms (*New York Times* and *Houston Chronicle*) out of three in the study.[99] In addition, STS research that also considers journalism has for the most part glossed over or ignored core STS approaches that account for critique related to race, gender, and power.[100] This is in addition to the major contributions suggesting the wider commitments and concerns of publics have been erased or discounted in efforts to democratize science.[101]

Two recent contributions to journalism studies of technology serve as examples of how this scholarship while generative to a number of conversations, such as extending the historical periodization of questions about journalism authority to a predigital era, and adding a more complicated understanding of publics and audiences, still animate normative orientations to journalism methods.[102] Anderson makes a significant turn by exploring how journalists have been trying to deal with uncertainty and improve their credibility since long before digitalization. Anderson's goals were in many respects similar to our research questions going into this book about the nature of journalism inquiry in this moment of multiple crises. He set out to both historicize and explore "the values that lie beneath the drive to separate facts from values," and the relationship between "objective knowledge" and a number of crises, which for him include "political crises, epistemological crises, and the reaction of journalism to these crisis moments."[103] He found that professional journalists have gained "increasing confidence" to make "contextualized truth claims" by actively trying to make their claims to knowledge more certain and explanatory since the mid-20th century.[104] He concludes that journalists' own growing certainty is an effect of (and contributes to) political discourse, which has struggled to deal with uncertainty.

In comparison, Ananny's recent book on networked press freedom sets out to explore the myth of journalistic independence and expose its limits in a digital age by rebutting the key journalism ideal: "If we just get out of the way of good journalists and let them tell truth to power, they will produce the information that vibrant democracies need."[105] He argues in favor of an extended and networked press freedom, which he distinguishes from traditional press freedom as a "system of separations and dependencies among humans and nonhumans that helps to ensure not only journalists' right to speak *but publics' rights to hear*" (*emphasis added*).[106] This emphasis on publics and "versions" of the public is important in Ananny's conceptualization of a modern press freedom as it suggests not just "journalists breaking free to tell truths to the publics they imagine," but a "subtler system of separations and dependencies that *make* publics, then we might see each era's types of press freedom as bellwethers for particular visions of the public."[107] He uses press freedom as a diagnostic to generate questioning about how the press in general, and the contemporary technologized press specifically—"journalists, software engineers, algorithms, relational databases, social media platforms, and quantified audiences" create a hierarchy of publics in their deployment of independence.[108] His prescription is that by exposing these systems and a more nuanced understanding of networked press freedom, we can start to reposition a public's "right to hear" alongside a journalist's right to speak.

Both works address key conversations that we engage in—the role of technology, journalistic practices, epistemology, authority, and ideals as they relate to methods for establishing facts, professionalism, and publics. They also replicate gaps and underdeveloped questions about power in journalism studies scholarship as a whole in that they fail to narrate how and why some facts, stories, experts, publics, and knowledge matter, and others don't. Specifically, how an aggressive deployment of a technological professional identity is able to shape scholarly and industry agendas in part because it is rooted in the performance of a white masculinity so foundational to modern journalism methods. We take a different approach bringing into view both the underlying epistemological stakes of journalistic methods and the power relations of larger programmatic ideals. We address, for example, ideals such as "giving voice to the voiceless" and how these are intertwined with the mission of concepts of objectivity and independence—and social order. Indeed, our contention in writing this book is that journalistic authority and expertise have not been fully examined historically, as scholars have tended to focus on its fourth estate and professional functions over its materiality and embeddedness in webs of structures and histories.

We began our research by decentering technology, using it in the traditions of STS and feminist scholars as a diagnostic and an antidote to the primacy of its location in this literature.[109] STS scholars have long argued that technology reflects and maps onto our beliefs, ideals, values, and webs of practice—in other words, that technology by itself doesn't change anything and media are no exception in this regard.[110] Instead, technology serves as a diagnostic and an element of co-production that helps assess how and what journalists are doing in the world, and what kinds of knowledge are being co-produced by journalists and for whom.[111]

Here we contend that technology offers a diagnostic to understand much deeper, persistent, and structural problems confronting journalism—and that technology has only served to amplify these problems, making such problems more visible to those who choose to ask questions about power, representation, and social order/structure.

For example, technology has effected small and big transformations on the doing of journalism, the running of news organizations, and the participation of "the people formerly known as the audience."[112] But it also provides a diagnostic for understanding what role journalism has played and for broader imaginations of what role it might play in civic society given its differently configured and rapidly evolving role of being in relationship with diverse publics.[113] However, journalism's focus and forte of elevating what anthropologists would call "the particular" through its focus on news events, and its implicit and often unacknowledged claiming of the universal—such as the dominance of a performance of white masculinity—has made it more difficult to make meaningful larger claims and observations.[114] It's more difficult for journalists to reflect and name structures and contexts such as colonialism in their reporting as well.

Drawing on the particular and implicit universalizing power of whiteness and masculinity means journalism hasn't had to consider what role it plays, whom it supports, or who benefits from its methods and outcomes. Nor has journalism had to consider how methods for naming and framing, and its event-centrism effects a particular view with consequent limitations for understanding how worlds are structured and peopled historically and in the present—and part of larger systems of governance, articulations, and communality.[115] In a rapidly globalizing world, we build on Choy's argument about transnational environmental politics where he argues that universality and particularity are not contradictory but constantly and equally deployed.[116] New technologies, we argue, demand that journalists account for what kind of experts they are, what kind of knowledge they are producing, and which perspectives, experts, and concerns that they are amplifying. In order to do that, however, journalists, we further contend, must also consider themselves as socially and historically located.

Critique and Moving in the Right Direction

Two feminist journalism studies scholars, Durham and Steiner, in particular, have been arguing to include social and historical locatedness in journalism epistemology for 20 years. Their work has had limited uptake within the larger field and conversations about journalism authority, despite its increasing relevance in a digital era.[117] Durham first raised concerns about the view from nowhere in 1998, questioning the inherent bias in news content that "stem principally from the social location of the reporter, the news organization, and conventional journalistic practices."[118] She argued in favor of a standpoint epistemology or strong objectivity for journalism, which she defines as an evaluative method that recognizes the

> socially situated nature of various knowledge claims as the basis for maximizing objectivity. This involves a reformulation of the term 'objectivity,' taking it away from any notion of eradicating bias toward a method of acknowledging and incorporating bias into the structure of the scientific method.[119]

This approach rests on reflexivity and "the constitution of an equivalence between the subjects and objects of inquiry, that is, the subjects and objects of research are placed on the same critical plane."[120] Standpoint theory thus offers a counter to concerns about impartiality and power relations, as well as the functional role that objectivity plays in supporting the status quo:

> The reportorial canon of presenting all perspectives without any engagement with the political valences of such perspectives effectively prevents any progressive or emancipatory politics from developing out of journalism. As in science, the current-day formulation of objectivity in journalism actually functions as a blocking device, stopping the rigorous and informed examination of power in everyday journalistic practice. The relativism of balance and fairness is thus ultimately regressive in its impact, functioning mainly to preserve the status quo by its stolid refusal to acknowledge or address the ideological bases of various truth-claims presented by supposedly impartial journalists.[121]

Durham draws from STS feminist scholars and feminist philosophers as they similarly sought to move experimental practices toward what Harding calls a "strong objectivity" where technologies, practices, subject positions, and "ways of inhabiting subject positions" must be made "relentlessly visible and open to critical intervention."[122] Haraway's concept of situated knowledge also suggests that journalists must acknowledge their own locatedness even while recognizing location "as always partial, finite, always fraught."[123] For Star, it means recognizing a multiplicity of identities, and having double vision such that relations of power and the technologies that establish "what may count" and how worlds are brought together might make the world more livable.[124]

In a point particularly salient to contemporary journalism, Durham argues that standpoint epistemology "has the potential to lead to a more engaged journalistic praxis—a praxis that recognizes and grapples with issues of ideological bias and the problems of alienation of socially marginalized groups from mainstream news coverage."[125] Steiner, writing in the digital era, goes even further: "If rigorously applied," standpoint epistemology and its related method and concepts would provide journalists with an antidote to the persistent charges of fake news, mis and dis-information, and "enable journalists to refute claims that their work is false, without resorting to the conventional but indefensible idea of objectivity."[126]

In addition to resolving some of the methodological looseness related to journalists' ability to make knowledge claims, placing these subjects and objects on the "same critical plane" would demonstrate the conceit of a journalism authority as an omniscient view from nowhere. It would expose that journalism authority has been about a view from somewhere all along, specifically the performance of white masculinity as the default identity. We draw from Judith Butler and her definition of gender identity as constituted through a *"a stylized repetition of acts"* (italics in original) in order to account for the way white masculinity has also evolved over time as has its performance in the newsroom.[127]

Haraway and Spivak[128] both unpack the ways that the performance of white masculinity has constituted a/the primary authority and knowledge legitimization in both science and intellectual discourse.[129]Spivak, in particular, discusses how alternative modes of thinking in philosophy are both excluded and co-opted such that the speaker is beholden to the frames and logics of primarily white male philosophers, with the subaltern always a project of the intellectual self in service of political and economic representational expediency. Following 9/11, Spivak asked similar questions of journalists, namely: "What response to offer in the face of the impossibility of response." In so doing, she situated media and white masculinity as prefiguring the terrain on which one could speak or respond and in the process enhancing their own reputation and power:

> The stereotype of the public intellectual, from Fareed Zakaria of Newsweek International to Christopher Hitchens, the freelance British gadfly, would offer statements describing US policy, coming out promptly in response to every crisis. This is undoubtedly worthy, often requiring personal courage,

but it is not a response. It enhances the charisma of the white male intellectual and produces in the reader a feeling of being in the thick of things.[130]

The over-representation of white masculinity in North American journalism, from the whiteness of newsrooms to repeated studies about the gender divide in sourcing and their consequences is persistent.[131] Strong objectivity provides an alternate way of understanding and responding to journalism's multiple crises. What makes this approach crucial is as Jasanoff has argued, expertise and knowledge "come into being. . . with their associated markers of excellence and credibility through disparate contingencies of politics and knowledge production in national decision-making settings."[132] To extrapolate then, journalism expertise and its dominant authority have come into being in political and knowledge production settings that have privileged white masculinity.

In addition, societies have various civic epistemologies, ways of ranking and valuing evidence and knowledge.[133] How journalism imagines itself and considers evidence is deeply related to the society it is a part of but also the publics it serves. Credibility directly rests on what and how a particular civic epistemology is elaborated. Not only that, journalism's ideology is also deeply connected to what Baiocchi et al. (2014) refer to as civic imagination—the particular way a society imagines itself, its problems, and its solutions. Given that journalism has traditionally seen itself as herald, gatekeeper, and suggester of solutions, its lack of reflexivity about how its own positionality has been elaborated in relation to diverse publics, technologies, dominant narratives, and social order presents distinct questions that will be addressed in the next chapters.

Finally, while the contributions of prior feminist journalism studies scholars present a meaningful solution to some of the ongoing issues with journalism authority in the form of strong objectivity, they don't go far enough in two areas. They have largely neglected an intersectional and post- or settler-colonial feminist critique (although Steiner starts to raise the importance of addressing intersectional concerns in her recent work).[134] And they don't account for the extensive, material and intertwined/interrelated impact of journalistic representations and power relations that are rooted in settler colonialism. Arvin, Tuck, and Morrill writing on Indigenous feminisms offer a powerful response to why Native feminist theories and decolonizing perspectives matter that has relevance to journalism and the critiques put forth by Ananny and Steiner. Arvin, Tuck, and Morrill argue that "the prevalence of liberal multicultural discourses today effectively works to maintain settler colonialism because they make it easy to assume that all minorities and ethnic groups are different though working toward inclusion and equality, each in its own similar and parallel way."[135] They suggest that in these discourses "justice is often put in terms that coincide with the expansion of the settler state."[136] Specifically that

> while Indigenous peoples do form important alliances with people of color, Indigenous communities' concerns are often not about achieving formal equality or civil rights within a nation state, but instead achieving substantial independence from a Western nation-state -- independence decided on their own terms. The feminist concerns of white women, women of color, and Indigenous women thus often differ and conflict with one another. In other words, within the context of land and settler colonialism, the issues facing Indigenous women, as inseparable from the issues facing Indigenous peoples as a whole, are resolved via decolonization and sovereignty, not [just] parity.[137]

By contrast, legacy journalism has assumed and continues to assume a liberal notion of competing interest groups vying for access and civic engagement, while scholarship suggests that journalism reinforces the status quo. Neither approach addresses the fundamental departures, reparations, and reclamations required for decolonization.

In closing, persistent and unresolved tensions about method and stance remain, which explain some of the backstory for how we have landed in an era of "fake news." This is not to suggest that false information, propaganda, and other forms of mis- and disinformation did not exist in previous eras.[138] We contend instead that the role journalism or journalisms play(s) is increasingly configured differently than in past eras of media, and these changes pose distinct problems for hanging on to the "view from nowhere" and the "culture of no culture."

Conclusion

Our interest in this first chapter is to move both beyond and beside a defense of journalism in order to understand the current moment of reckoning and the rise of technologically fueled *multiple journalisms*.[139] In reading across scholarship, we argue that recent narratives of decline and crisis in journalism *must* be brought alongside critiques related to gender, race, indigeneity, and colonialism such that crises in representation, trust, and credibility might be seen as chronic and persistent.[140] By and large, journalism and its scholars haven't had to deeply consider critiques related to what role it plays in social ordering, whom it supports, or who benefits from its methods and outcomes. This is because journalism and scholarship has largely drawn on objectivity in a way that obscures the particular and implicit universalizing power of whiteness and masculinity. We suggest that journalists and scholars begin to engage with these critiques, recognizing the limits and harms of prior journalisms, and the possibilities of a strong objectivity that acknowledges the social location of journalists and news organizations on a North American terrain of settler-colonialism.

This chapter begins this work by connecting journalism scholarship to broader arguments in STS, media studies, and Indigenous studies that we continue throughout the book. We argue that a fuller accounting is required to understand how long-term critiques of journalism must be part of broader discussions about crises within journalism, new technologies, and multiple reckonings. As we reference in the introduction, media and journalism scholars have been busy defending the fourth estate against claims of fake news and the encroachment of platform competitors, without a recognition of journalism's limitations *and* its role as a means for social ordering. We argue in contrast that journalism is a cultural form that emerged in the 20th century and that new media technologies provide a set of diagnostics for understanding what structures journalistic inquiry. Journalism methods, and objectivity in particular, do not provide a robust way to assess the validity of the knowledge it produces. Finding "both sides" and/or several sources to support a "fact" elides the ways that facts are open to epistemological interpretation and effaces the multiperspectival world we all share. We delve deeper into this in Chapter 3 to account for some of the ways in which journalists and editors recognize the challenge of interpretation for them as storytellers, professionals, and knowledge makers.

In some ways this argument, rather than diminish journalism, elevates its role even while it opens journalistic methods and practices up to more scrutiny, situating journalists as participants in an apparatus for social order(ing). Objectivity as a professional goal and ideal has acted to discount and marginalize the ways in which journalistic practices and methods might and do serve as interventionist. Aside from Durham and Steiner, whose calls to incorporate standpoint theory in journalism have largely been ignored, past approaches to objectivity and its critique don't go far enough in making sense of the implicit and often harmful power relations embedded in assumptions that journalism (like science) can and does transcend the subjective to present the truth. Feminist STS scholars like Haraway, Harding, and Star have been contending with and theorizing these problems in science for decades. More recently, TallBear, Subramaniam, Pollock, Simpson and others have brought this together with postcolonial and settler-colonial critique. Journalism scholars, however, haven't tended to account for the gender, race, and colonial reckoning taking place as sources, citizens, and even journalists resist prior journalisms by using social media and other forms of digital media to talk back, going so far as refusing at times to participate in legacy media or journalism conversations. We draw inspiration from Harding, Haraway, and TallBear, who critique the scientific foundations of objectivity as always rooted in messy structures and power relations that privilege some meanings and someone's meaning over others. As Star puts it: "Power is about *whose* metaphor brings worlds together."[141]

The next chapter records the ways in which digital platforms have allowed multiple publics to speak up, into, and against dominant media narratives and interpretive frameworks. In "battling for the story," articulations from individuals who associate via networks on and offline challenge journalists and news organizations to account for entrenched framing related to race, indigeneity, gender, and colonialism. The critiques, in this case, are not coming from scholars but rather from and through those who are adapting digital platforms to coalesce and move publics with counter-narratives that shed light on journalism's limitations—but also, we would argue, a world in which diverse sources provide accountability and possibilities for journalism's reform, repair, and transformation.

CHAPTER 2 | Battling for the Story

Introduction

When race, gender, and colonialism—and the history of media getting it wrong on all counts—are considered essential to navigating information, facts, and interpretations of events in mainstream media, the rise of digital media looks less like a crisis and more like a long overdue corrective for mainstream media. Digital media is not the cause nor the reason behind reckoning with diverse publics; but it does, we argue, expose the gaps and deep fault lines of journalism's historic and paternalistic relationships with its many public(s). Professional journalists are now liminal, provisional, and authoritative all at once and held accountable for their application of news values as well as what they deem to be fact and "the story." Notions of journalism and its dominant authority are coevolving with publics—including sources—who not only talk back but sometimes take over thanks to a wide spectrum of digital modes and platforms.

Social media, as many scholars have pointed out, serve as connector, amplifier, and on multiple platforms, a forum for crowdsourced critique and consistent calls for structural and systemic societal changes. Consider the range of publics carrying out journalism practices of witnessing in coverage ranging from the 1999 WTO protests in Seattle to more recent social movements like #ArabSpring, #BlackLivesMatter, #IdleNoMore, and #MeToo. Each movement reveals, as scholars have variously pointed out, the necessary messiness created when a range of voices is involved in real-time fact production. In all of these cases, mainstream media has been steadily supplemented and increasingly supplanted by citizens and counter-publics.[1] Picard argues that journalism itself is being fundamentally realigned in a digital landscape with respect to its role as witness:

The transformation under way is not only altering the methods of news production and distribution, but the functions of journalism itself. The traditional functions of bearing witness, holding to account, opinion leadership, and shaming are no longer provided solely by the news media. The bearing witness function—observing and providing accounts of what happened—is being switched to social media and increasingly practised by public witnesses and activists. Holding to account—assigning responsibility and making others accountable for their conduct—is now a function shared with experts, non-governmental organizations, and individuals using the range of digital and social media.[2]

In this chapter, we analyze how gender, race, and colonialism factor into this realignment by looking at the social media responses to three stories that provide insight into how publics, sources, and various historically mis- and-underrepresented groups talk back and engage in a "battle for the story." These citizens and counter-publics are able to witness, articulate, and distribute their experiences, observations, and analysis in parallel and sometimes provide important correctives to mainstream media narratives.[3] The cases we analyze include: (1) two murder trials in Canada involving the deaths of Tina Fontaine and Colten Boushie, and the acquittals of the white men charged with their homicides within a two-week period in early 2018; (2) the 2015 lawsuit and discrimination case brought by Ellen Pao (whose Twitter handle self describes as "ex-reddit reformed VC and lawyer") against her former employer and (3) @KellyOxford, who in 2016 tweeted a request for sexual assault survivors to share their stories following the release of a recording of U.S. presidential candidate Donald Trump bragging about how he groped women. Each of these cases is built around media events, where complex global media with multiple nodes of connectivity influence societies, publics, media, and individuals in multifaceted ways.[4] Media events are also rich sites to study routinized journalistic practices, in these cases, covering court proceedings and elections. In such events, journalists tend to lean heavily on news values such as conflict/controversy, timeliness, emotion, and prominence and often fail to take into account deeply historical contexts for their own practices, methods, and situated knowledges *and* the narratives and stereotypes of the events and people they are covering.

Methodologically, we deploy a network and textual analysis of journalism and social media, specifically Twitter (using Crimson Hexagon's ForSight, an automated content analysis software) to examine how facts were being manufactured and material power relations constructed. We recognize as Tworek suggests that while journalists are using Twitter as a new "vox populi," we must be cautious deploying it as a proxy for the public.[5] However, there is transformation underway as well. The engagements we describe in this chapter and that we draw on from scholarship tend to emerge around event-based news coverage that falls short of considering the deeply problematic ways that journalists have tended to report on gendered, racialized, and colonial subjects. Conceptually, we turn to social movement scholarship to make sense of the cases as it recognizes the ways in which Twitter has served as a kind of tableau in which diverse voices debate and develop articulations with and against one another. For example, Jackson and Welles studied tweets about Ferguson and #Ferguson, finding evidence of counterpublics, marginalized groups using social media to invoke narratives "offering citizens most invisible in mainstream politics radical new potentials for identity negotiation, visibility, and influence."[6] This is not unlike the first case we turn to involving Indigenous publics and Canadian media.

Indigenous Publics: #TinaFontaine and #ColtenBoushie

On February 22, 2018, Indigenous people across Canada were waiting to hear the verdict in the trial of Raymond Cormier, who stood accused of murdering fifteen-year-old Tina Fontaine, an Anicinabe girl from Sagkeeng Nation located northeast of Winnipeg, Manitoba. Fontaine was described by her aunt as "polite and funny, someone who made people laugh all the time."[7] At the time of her death, Fontaine was also struggling to cope with the killing of her father Eugene Fontaine in 2011. His murderers had stood trial and had been convicted of manslaughter in the months before Tina went missing on August 9, 2014. She had sought help to write her victim impact statement while in foster care in the city of Winnipeg. "Foster care" in this context meant being placed in *a hotel* by a social worker, and in the days before her disappearance, she had been in contact with police, paramedics, and Child and Family Services. When her 77-pound body was found in the Red River—which runs through Winnipeg—eight days after she was reported missing, it was wrapped in a duvet and weighted down with rocks. As Mi'kmaw Scholar and lawyer Pam Palmater pointed out in a Toronto magazine op-ed, "Tina died because federal, provincial and state agencies charged with keeping her safe, all failed to protect her. And for that, Canada should stand trial."[8] Hardly any of the media coverage of the trial took into account the role of federal agencies.

It took a year for the police to make an arrest related to the death of Fontaine. Cormier had been one of the last people in contact with the young girl. He made a number of odd rambling confessions to police that ranged from wanting to have sex with the girl to being shocked by her young age. Cormier's legal team offered no defense, but in the days leading up to the verdict in his trial, many Indigenous people active on Twitter began to openly express concern that he, too, would be acquitted in part because many were still reeling from the verdict in a different murder trial several weeks before.

On February 9, 2018, an all-white jury acquitted a white rancher in Saskatchewan for the murder of another Indigenous youth, 22-year-old Colten Boushie. Boushie had been traveling with three similar-aged friends when the vehicle they were in got a flat tire. Boushie was shot by Stanley after stopping to seek help with their vehicle. Stanley was acquitted by an all-white jury—the defense had purposely rejected any jurors who appeared to be Indigenous. The trial, according to an Angus Reid poll from CBC News, left Canadians divided.[9] Indigenous people across the country, however, were shocked and devastated that there was no penalty for the killing of an Indigenous youth. #JusticeforColten became a hashtag that could be found on T-shirts, scrawled on streets, and across Twitter.

In the days and hours leading up to when the verdict related to the death of Fontaine was expected, similar hashtags such as #JusticeforTina and #TinaFontaine circulated occasional tweets—many by Indigenous people wondering if justice would be served. But these discussions, as this tweet from Jesse Wente demonstrates, had begun long before either verdict in response to ongoing media coverage of both Indigenous women and youth.

> Just so I'm clear: After centuries of genocidal policies, violent oppression, slavery, residential schools, prejudicial police, denial of voting rights, and ongoing laws based on ethnicity . . . . It's us who make everything about race? Huh. Cool story.[10]

Wente, a prominent Ojibwe broadcaster and producer with a regular column on CBC Radio, and director of the newly formed Indigenous Screen Office in Canada, is a powerful presence on Twitter.[11] His tweet above was retweeted 453 times with almost 1,173 likes. Indigenous audiences are not alone in pushing back, as this chapter will demonstrate. They are, however, among the most starkly visible both in terms of the impact of media's long history of getting it wrong (i.e., repeating colonial narratives and entrenching stereotypical representations) and the powerful pushback and hashtagged critique on Twitter in particular.

During both trials, Canadian media made missteps in their coverage, particularly horrifying and egregious when it came to what's often referred to as "victim blaming"—treating Fontaine or Boushie as if they were on trial instead of those accused of their murders. One of Canada's two national newspapers, *The Globe and Mail*, offered a weak apology after its headline regarding Fontaine caused an outcry from Indigenous people both on Twitter and in letters to the editor. The initial headline read: "Tina Fontaine had drugs, alcohol in system when she was killed: toxicologist."[12] It was changed the next day to: "Expert tells Winnipeg murder trial he could not determine cause of Tina Fontaine's death."[13] The markedly different headlines for the same story tell its own story about Canadian media and one that stretches back to the earliest days of print media where newspapers were complicit in propping up and advancing a colonial narrative that sought to undermine Indigenous claims to land, rights to resources, and ability to be self-determining.[14]

Whether considering Twitter, Facebook, or online sources such as *Indian Country Today* and podcasts like *Media Indigena* or *Cowboys and Indians*, Indigenous critique and voices provide both a counterpoint and counternarrative *and* a middle ground where differently configured public discourse and expertise can emerge alongside the usual expert voices and interpretations found in mainstream media.[15] In some ways, what social media provides is a map of the omissions, erasure, long histories of misrepresentations, and lack of context that have left Indigenous and other publics frustrated, misinformed, and/or ignorant of the deep structural considerations vital to understanding an event like the verdicts in the trials of Cormier and Stanley. When we talk about a digital reckoning, this is what we mean—that digital media has held up a mirror to mainstream journalists, effectively moving accountability outside the role of an ombudsman or public editor, or even, we argue, the professional code of ethics as some kind of backstop or rationale for routinized practices. Wente, in the aftermath of the headline change at *The Globe* perhaps best summed it up when he tweeted: "We see you Canadian media."[16]

Wente, like many on what's often referred to as #NativeTwitter— Indigenous people who are active, vocal, and identify in their profiles as Indigenous—expressed a range of emotions at the coverage and verdicts related to these cases. And many, like Wente, sought to call media, the courts, and other societal institutions to account by drawing attention to the colonialism and systemic racism and inequities that these cases represent. During the height of the use of the hashtags associated with Tina Fontaine and Colten Boushie, Wente's tweet represented and summed up the sentiments of many using this hashtag:

> If you want to see Canada, look at my mentions and many other FNMI peoples mentions today. That is the mirror to find Canada's reflection.[17]

We analyzed the networks activated by the top 10 retweets of the hashtags #TinaFontaine and #ColtenBoushie (used together) during a two-day spike in the data (see Table 2.1), which occurred between January 31, 2018, and February 1, 2018. The spike of 2,540 retweets on these hashtags followed *The Globe* article with the victim-blaming headline during the Cormier trial, and a *Globe* column critical of the media coverage of the trial by Denise Balkissoon.[18] The retweets are a mix of Indigenous pundits, public intellectuals, activists, lawyers, artists, and journalists from the Aboriginal Peoples Television Network (APTN) seeking to hold media, politicians, and the public to account in the battle for story that we discuss throughout this chapter. The top retweet, referenced earlier in the chapter by Wente is: "#TinaFontaine and #ColtenBoushie are not on trial. We see you Canadian media." Others include a tweet by Holly Moore of APTN calling out the CBC's trial coverage, which was retweeted 190 times: "OK, after seeing the banner under @CBCNews for the tenth time, it is officially driving me crazy. Neither #TinaFontaine nor #ColtenBoushie are on trial here. These are the #geraldstanley and #RAYMONDCORMIER trials."

These tweets are examples of how audiences have tended to use Twitter as a form of accountability.[19] Here, similar to Papacharissi and de Fatima Oliveira, we find a "more vocal stream of opinion leaders emerged, consisting of bloggers, activists, and intellectuals with some prior involvement with online activism."[20] This "stream of opinion leaders" is an overall wider range of Indigenous sources compared to a 2015 network analysis of #IdleNoMore.[21] We also find digital technologies becoming more about the activation of those publics and relationships, with the degree and nature of that activation depending on the stakes for those groups. For example, Max FineDay, who is nêhiyaw from the Sweetgrass First Nation and executive director of Canadian Roots, a national nonprofit organization focused on developing relationships between Indigenous and non-Indigenous youth, tweeted: "To every #Indigenous youth: I value your life,

RETWEET	OCCURRENCES	ORIGINAL AUTHOR
#TinaFontaine and #ColtenBoushie are not on trial. We see you Canadian media. #JusticeForColten #JusticeForTina	710	@jessewente
RT @MaxFineDay To every #Indigenous youth: I value your life, you come from proud people, you are loved. Please remind the youth in your life of that. After the last few weeks, they'll need to hear it. #JusticeforTinaFontaine #justiceforcolten #tinafontaine #ColtenBoushie https://t.co/ sPEcxHBwQf	690	@MaxFineDay
RT @zhaabowekwe Our kids are murdered, the killers walk. As a Native woman, the system says I am expendable. No justice. #TinaFontaine #ColtenBoushie #MMIW https:t.co/0sOj9PWZX9	200	@zhaabowekwe (tarahouska)
RT @christibelcourt Anyway, if you can, remember Tina Fontaine in your prayers. Her family is still sitting in a courtroom each day listening to testimony on how her accused killer, a 53-yr old white man, was seeking to protect his stolen property & took her life. #TinaFontaine #ColtenBoushie https://t.co/GMMynMMAzw	190	@christibelcourt
RT @HollyMooreaptn OK, after seeing the banner under @CBCNews TV for the tenth time, it is officially driving me crazy. Neither #TinaFontaine nor #ColtenBoushie are on trial here. These are the #geraldstanley and #RAYMONDCORMIER trials. #wordsmatter #smartenup	190	@HollyMooreAPTN

RETWEET	OCCURRENCES	ORIGINAL AUTHOR
#OnlyinCanada are Indigenous victims on trial instead of the white people who murdered them. #TinaFontaine #ColtenBoushe	160	@RedIndianGirl
#ColtenBoushe #FrankPaul #BrainSinclair #PhoenixSinclair #DudleyGeorge #DonaldMarshallJr #TinaFontaine #CindyGladue #MMIWG #lethalracism	110	@Pam_Palmater
The arbiters of injustice cannot provide us with justice. #tinafontaine #coltenboushie	100	@christibelcourt
RT @NoLore I've seen a few journalists defend the coverage of #TinaFontaine #ColtenBoushie as "this is unfortunately how court reporting works." This defense is both true and proof of how systemic racism is woven through mainstream journalistic practice.	100	@NoLore (NoraLoreto)
RT @Pam_Palmater Love and jusice for #TinaFontaine #CindyGladue #HelenBettyOsborne #ColtenBoushe #FrankPaul #NeilStonechild #DudleyGeorge + 1000's more #racismkillswithimpunity #RISE	90	@Pam_Palmater
Total Occurrences	**2,540**	

you come from proud people, you are loved. Please remind the youth in your life of that. After the last few weeks, they'll need to hear it."[22]

Legacy media responded to these social media conversations by changing headlines and publishing a number of critical opinion articles, as did others on social media. #SettlerCollecter became a coincident hashtag so non-Indigenous people on Twitter could help deal with and respond to trolls (and well-meaning individuals) who sought to defend Stanley and the verdict, and harassed Indigenous people with intentionally (and unintentionally) racist statements.

Deeper Context and Settler-Colonialism

That this moment of colonial, racial, and gender reckoning is able to unseat journalism is significant given journalism's colonial history, and the fact that calls for change have been going on for a long time. In her article published in *Teen Vogue*, Manitoba provincial politician Nahanni Fontaine underlines the outcry over Tina Fontaine's tragic death and sets the conduct of media and the courts as occurring alongside long-time activism related to Missing and Murdered Indigenous Women and Girls (#MMIWG) in Canada.

> To understand the reaction to Tina's murder, one must situate it within the greater context of decades of blood, sweat, and tears rendered by MMIWG families and Indigenous women from coast to coast to coast. Most Canadians have begun to gain a sense of the issue of MMIWG in recent years, but that's only the latter part of a greater story of perseverance, courage, tenacity, forgiveness, determination, and unconditional love that families have shown for their missing and murdered loved ones, and by warrior Indigenous women who stood with families as voices and advocates, who have marched by the thousands, who wept, who attended feasts, memorials, funerals, ceremonies, countless presentations, and keynotes. . . . And so, when those first images of Tina first hit the news, in 2014, it's as if all those millions of seeds sown over the past 40 years suddenly sprouted—galvanized and converged in the being of little Tina. She became our collective daughter; our relative in which the issue of MMIWG could be intimately understood and nurtured.[23]

It's notable that Fontaine chose to write this commentary for *Teen Vogue*, a U.S. fashion magazine for teenage girls, which makes its own statement about where and what outlets are paying closest attention to issues of public interest throughout North America. The context for the #MMIWG movement involves more than 1,181 Indigenous women and girls in Canada who were identified as missing or murdered between 1980 and 2012 by the Royal Canadian Mounted Police. Of those, 1,107 were victims of homicide and 174 women and girls are still considered missing.[24] A 2019 national inquiry report on MMIWG concludes that the numbers are likely much higher with thousands of deaths and disappearances over the decades as many have gone unrecorded.[25] Indigenous women and girls are "far more likely than other Canadian women and girls to experience violence and to die as a result," with the rate "five times higher" for Indigenous women 25 to 44 years old than for non-Indigenous women in the same demographic.[26] Despite living under constant threat of colonial violence, it took decades of work from activists, individual journalists, and reports to result in a national inquiry on #MMIWG in Canada. Similar work is now being undertaken with the same hashtag by Indigenous journalists and activists in the United States, as Indigenous women there are 2.4 times more likely to be sexually assaulted than "any other ethnicity."[27] We will return to the contributions of Indigenous journalists in Chapter 6, but we raise it here in order to situate hashtag critiques as being the most visible short versions of critiques of both media and the actions of the state, whether in Canada or the United States.

Media representations of sexual violence involving Indigenous women and girls are a powerful example of our critique as these depictions are interconnected with colonialism, state structures, institutions and journalism's role in social ordering. For Hunt, the lack of safety of Indigenous women and girls co-occurs with representations of Indigenous women who trade or sell sex and the failure of Canadian law and its enforcers to take the victimization of Indigenous women seriously resulting in "legal violence that is fundamental to colonial power relations."[28] As a result, the context as it pertains to journalism contains multiple sites of contestation—for the narrative, for interpretation of events, for what context matters, and for the historical record. In the case of Tina Fontaine, her death and the trial for her murder occurred in Manitoba, which is part of a region in Canada where settler colonialism involved the systematic annihilation and removal of Indigenous peoples from their land referred to as a policy of "clearing the plains."[29] Her story then—which also includes resistance and multiple forms of persistent activism and resilience—is complicated in important ways often missed in journalism and news stories.

Journalism, as we have argued, has largely seen itself as both independent from the state and able to capture the stories of diverse publics through methods that involve fairness and balance, selection of facts and sources, source checking, verification, and eyewitness accounts all through the prism of news values. The widely used SPJ code of ethics states that part of the journalistic mission is to "give voice to the voiceless." A 2017 tweet from @VanishedWomen sums up this main ethical concern of journalism's relationship to historically marginalized sources and public(s) with respect to representations and their ability to share their stories. "There's no such thing as being a voice to the voiceless. Everyone has a voice, you just need to pass the mic."[30] But passing the mic, as Wente points out, means that "the story" might and likely will change, as well as who is authorized to tell it and the possibilities for content and community connection. Wente summarized it this way during a CBC *Unreserved* radio interview repurposed on CBC News online:

> We're very much in a battle for the story, for the context that this would have moving forward. And the context . . . becomes the basis of history, which becomes the basis for stories that have been told for generations, and then those stories ultimately drive cultural conditioning.[31]

This recent "battle for the story" involves public intellectuals, community members, and journalists who identify as Indigenous holding media to account for contemporary racist coverage that ignores the "well-documented history of Canadian newspapers' complicity with colonialism and state-sponsored violence against Indigenous people from pre-Confederation forward."[32] This collusion with the state has had material and harmful effects on Indigenous peoples as public discourse and journalism have gotten it wrong more often than not. Indigenous peoples are framed "as on the margins" while the brutality of settler colonialism is constructed as "natural and normal," narratives that are articulated and re-articulated affecting how fundamental issues such as Indigenous rights to land title, white supremacy, and the settler state are perceived and redressed.[33]

The notion of journalists as "speaking for" the public, and particularly for marginalized and historically under-represented groups, is a long-held norm among practitioners and the basis for foundational claims about what journalism could do—and what journalists should do. That journalists should speak for all citizens with a focus on the marginalized is considered part of their unelected role as intermediaries, watchdogs, and agents of a fourth estate in Western democracies. How they have understood speaking for people, however, is problematic. Their authority has rested on positivist approaches and claims to growing levels of professionalism concomitant with assumptions about methodological rigor that rest on 20th-century notions of science and objectivity and still-dominant notions of journalism authority despite decades of critique.

These claims have paradoxically underplayed and overplayed the journalist's role and power as proxies for democratic due process.[34] They also co-occur along with certain power relations with audiences and sources. Ericson, Baranek, and Chan, in their trilogy study of crime news and the criminal justice system in Toronto in the 1980s, argued that journalists have been fundamentally self-referential.[35] That is, journalists in their study did not develop their knowledge and understanding about the world through audience feedback, even though marketing surveys and ratings existed in parts of the journalism organization other than newsrooms. Instead, they found that journalists were primarily concerned with communications among "elite authorized knowers," in their case, sources within the criminal justice system.[36] In this way, journalists have largely made sense of their journalism from two kinds of data: elite sources and themselves. Combined with Zelizer's notion of interpretative communities, journalism can be understood as having been a relatively closed information system—journalists talking among themselves and a narrow range of sources.[37]

The tactics or rules of engagement with journalism sources have ranged from negotiation to conflict depending on the national and/or regional context and authority of the source.[38] Approaches to understanding journalism's relationship to its audiences have revolved around non-networked binary couplings—cause and effect, power and conflict, passive and active—all cemented through implicit paternalistic variations of "father knows best." The feminine and emotive are reserved for discussions about advertising and "sensational news content"—the pornography of news—what we watch but shouldn't because of its emotive and often sexualized nature. Wahl-Jorgensen's research on what she calls the "strategic ritual of emotionality" in journalism is relevant to the case we are making in this book about the still-dominant mode of journalism authority as rooted in the performance of white masculinity.[39] She compares the ritual of emotionality to objectivity, suggesting that it is as "embedded in, and central to, journalistic practice as is the strategic ritual of objectivity, though it is rarely explicitly acknowledged because it is at odds with journalistic self-understandings."[40]

Through this concept, Wahl-Jorgensen maps the process in which emotion becomes "a form of tacit knowledge, implicit in journalistic socialization processes and everyday work" yet one in which journalists do not "express their *own* emotions." Instead, they "rely on the outsourcing of emotional labor to non-journalists—the story protagonists and other sources, who are (a) authorized to express emotions in public, and (b) whose emotions journalists can authoritatively describe without implicating themselves" such that the perception of the objective nature of news processes are maintained.[41] Rarely is the masculine nature of news more clearly demonstrated than in the interpolation of the notion of a neutral method with how journalists manage emotion. These processes depend on performing a certain kind of white masculinity with the feminine as other such that the fourth estate is implicated in supporting the notion of a public sphere in which only certain identities can speak with authority while others are mined and extracted for their emotional charge and stories, trading in a form of notoriety and celebrity while reproducing a social ordering of social and political capital.

Liberal democratic understandings of the role of the press (like the fourth estate) and assumptions about journalists' proxy for the public and ability to speak are considered vital to civic engagement. Yet, the digitally fueled reckoning with gender, race, and colonialism suggests that what journalists thought they were doing in the 20th century is more uncertain, untested, patriarchal and open to contestation. Recent research gives credence to a more constrained role for journalists, which rests in a "democratic realist" approach and limited or "modest" ambitions yet still meaningful effects such as the provision of "accurate, accessible, relevant and timely independently produced information about public affairs."[42] Coupled with decades of critique about structural issues that include an historically male and white workforce in mainstream media in North America, what journalism should have done, could have done, and could be doing becomes more complicated and implicated. Indeed, despite important investigative journalism, a disjuncture between journalism's aspirations, ideals, and practices cement around their contributions to maintaining the patriarchal colonial status quo instead of actively working to transform systems— even its own.[43]

When Sources Resist/Rebel: #EllenPao

In her 2017 memoir, *Reset—My Fight for Inclusion and Lasting Change*, Ellen Pao talks about her reckoning with the Silicon Valley technology establishment after she decided to sue her employer, a prominent venture capital firm, for gender discrimination in 2015. She eventually lost after a five-week-long trial eliciting significant media attention in North America and globally. Pao would be considered an elite journalistic source in both her role as a prominent technology leader in addition to her position as a plaintiff fighting the establishment in a high-profile court case. Her story meets many of the traditional journalism news values: conflict, prominence, importance. That she opted to use social media to talk back during her discrimination case against Kleiner, Perkins, Caufield & Byers as opposed to solely operating as a mainstream media source is interesting for what it says about the power of technology as a way for sources to bypass media gatekeepers, as well as its ability to diagnose the limits of journalism to tell her story.

That's in part because Pao's story could be perceived as complicated. In many cases of institutional complaint about gender and racial discrimination reporting on "what happened" can be difficult to parse because it almost always includes insidious and implicit institutional structural biases, racism, and gender discrimination that reinforce existing power relations, sometimes conflicting legal, policy, regulatory, and human resource regimes in addition to individual personalities. Journalism, and news specifically, has tended to focus on the personal stories of sources as opposed to trying to make sense of what happened through larger systemic critiques, even as news forms have shifted to allow for more complicated storytelling.[44] For Pao, her personal motives were "not that complicated," according to a 2015 interview with Kara Swisher, a Silicon Valley entrepreneur and now an opinion writer with the *New York Times*.[45] She locates her pursuit of the lawsuit as emerging out of her origin story growing up in an Asian family in a small town in New Jersey, and her core belief in meritocracy, indicating that "when I saw that it wasn't actually the case I felt I had to speak up."

By talking back, Pao had significant impact through Tweets, conversations, and responses on social media. Over the course of her trial, there were more than 79,092 Tweets that used the main hashtag #EllenPao. Her trial initiated social media engagement with a spike in posts with the March 27 jury verdict—24,911 alone—on March 28. In her memoir, Pao references other markers as also relevant for understanding the impact of her social media engagement. She singles out that the hashtag #thankyouEllenPao "trended on Twitter" and that journalists referenced the "Pao effect" to describe the impact she had on eliciting more women to come forward about harassment and discrimination, exercising resistance and agency in their workplace.[46]

Pao personally tweeted 20 times between February 22, 2015 (the day before jury selection and two days before opening statements) and March 28, 2015, the day after the jury verdict was announced. Five of the tweets referenced inspirational quotes from prominent people—mostly women and men of color such as Toni Morrison, Kerri Washington, and Martin Luther King Jr.—about overcoming adversity, the importance of speaking out and empowerment. For example, she quoted Martin Luther King Jr.'s well-known quote, "Our lives begin to end the day we become silent about things that matter." A few other tweets were responses to conversations and well wishes, about her role at Reddit, where she had been hired as CEO. No tweets explicitly addressed issues from the trial although some reference gender challenges in the tech industry.

As a sophisticated media source, one could also consider Pao's inspirational quotes subtweets intended to subvert public discourse. For example, in the interview with Swisher, who founded Recode—and is well known for her commitment to issues of equity and inclusion in the technology sector—Pao is clearly aware of the issues of being a source during a high-profile trial.

> It was just so hard to really tell my story. And the courtroom isn't the best place to do it. I'm not able to talk about it outside the courtroom. So it's a very complex issue. People come to it with a lot of baggage. I think that a lot of people feel a super strong connection to me because we've had this same experience. They don't really know me but they feel a connection because we've had the same experience. Other people don't like me because of what I represent. This idea that the world is not a meritocracy and that there's unfairness [is] very uncomfortable for some people.[47]

Later in the interview, Swisher asks Pao about the most resonant areas for her, suggesting that "complexity is hard for people" even with the "same set of facts."[48] In response, Pao indicated that: "For a woman, it is hard. For minorities, it is hard because there are 1,500 things you have to do differently, and you have to thread that needle perfectly." In her memoir, one of the main lessons that Pao identifies in retrospect is that the culture she was working in was "*designed* to keep out people who aren't white men."[49] She goes on to say, "The status quo is bad for those of us who don't look like a 'white male nerd,' and it is unfair. It is also bad for business. Preserving the status quo is costing companies talent and keeping them from being competitive internationally."[50]

But it isn't only that journalism can't deal with complexity or that it has a hard time revealing and commenting on the structuring of society that systematically excludes. Rather journalism has had and continues to have a hard time dealing with contradictions that are not binary thinking and require multiple perspectives, in large part because it has not acknowledged its own perspective and dominant authority rooted in the performance of white masculinity as we discuss in Chapter 1. When there are multiple truths or contexts in which multiple sources offer contradictory representations, the narrative and accounting for "what really happened here" becomes that much more difficult to articulate in any kind of non-invested fashion. Where someone is speaking from (their situated knowledge) and who they are speaking to (their perceived audiences) becomes of utmost importance in understanding what kinds of truths are at stake, emerging, and in contradiction. That some facts can be "also true" is not likely to make for a pithy headline in most mainstream media.[51]

Pao became the source-as-media witness who talked back using multiple tactics of resistance. She was able to deconstruct many of the journalism norms in relations to stories in the process. In doing so, she is both expert and victim, showing her credibility, implicatedness, and accountability through exercising power at the "hard intersection of questions about race, class, gender, sex with the goal of making a difference."[52] Her situatedness is evident when Pao talks about her experience of the case and the public. In the introduction to the interview, Swisher asks Pao if she has any regrets. Pao responds "not at all" as there was a lot of public response. "I connected with *so* many people, and they felt a connection to the story that I told. And that was important to me, to give people this outlet to see: This is the worst thing that can happen to you, and you can come out of it, and it's fine."

Swisher later asked, "You lost, what is the symbol that you were hoping to have happened and what do you think you represent now?"

> I didn't plan on becoming a symbol. It was more, I wanted to just tell my story, share my experience and let people know what had happened to me and see what the outcome was. It didn't come out the way I wanted it to but it ended up that I became symbol for different things.[53]

Here, Pao recognizes the ways in which symbols developed due to media framing are both flexible and durable, but perhaps more nuanced and outside the control of media as well. Pao's definition of the symbol she embodied reflected her own relationship with those who paid attention to her case—and those with whom she chose to engage.

In the process of the interview, Swisher's questions also work to destabilize some of journalism's basic methods—in addition to common framings of victims and villains. While still asking the pointed journalistic questions, such as "are you likable," she also asks Pao to consider deeper questions of identity and personality such as, "What did you think happened to you as a person? You were sort of at the centre of it, are you the perfect victim? Or are you difficult, or are you problematic?" Swisher's sophisticated approach to interviewing which foregrounds the personal as relevant context and her own positionality supported meaning making of the case and Pao's story.

Some journalists indicated that years after the trial and verdict, they still had difficulty assessing moral responsibility in this case. One of the main journalists who covered the Pao trial said that she was conflicted about the coverage, the trial's result, and her perceived sense of inconsistency in Pao's memoir years later. In an article on BuzzFeed News headlined, "Ellen Pao's Story Is Messier Than Her Book Makes It Sound," Davey Alba tries to make sense of a case that she says she covered since the trial:

> Reading Pao's book brought back memories of my intense reporting experience covering her trial back in 2015, which journalists with whom I reported remember well. 'It's fascinating to me that the public's version is that Ellen Pao was robbed and should have won, but inside the trial room it really wasn't that clear,' said Shalene Gupta, who covered the trial for Fortune magazine. 'Sometimes I even go back and question the things I saw and heard, because I feel like the Ellen Pao story has become so powerful and taken [on] a life of its own.'[54]

For Pao, some journalists may never get it. In an interview for thecut.com, Pao references the role of gender and journalism, and the difficulties she had specifically with male journalists covering her story:

> 'Male reporters, for the most part, were skeptical of me and did not understand, had no empathy for my experiences,' she said. 'You could see it in the reporting.' On the other hand, 'I think a lot of the women reporters had had similar experiences, many of them had been harassed,' she said. Though some men related her experiences to those of their daughters, mothers, or female co-workers, Pao said that there was 'definitely not as much [support] from men as from women and more from people of color than from people who were white.'[55]

Hashtag #Ellenpao

We analyzed the networks activated by the top ten retweets for the hashtag #EllenPao over the course of her trial to assess the networks Pao was able to tap into as people retweet what resonates with them. We find that the confusion identified by journalists and from Pao herself in relation to her case is clear in the nature of the hashtag conversation. The number of retweets over an almost two-month period was low relative to the profile of the case and they did not cohere into a clear community of interest and/or counter-narrative. Two of the top-10 retweets emerged from mainstream media, journalist Ellen Huet who was at *Forbes* at the time ("If I've helped to level the playing field for women and minorities in venture capital, then the battle was worth it."), and @Newsweek (2.7% of 6,517 companies that received venture funding from 2011–2013 had women CEOs). These tweets are consistent with the event nature of the trial and the fact that most of the retweets occurred on March 27, 2015, and March 28, 2015, when the jury's verdict was announced.

Brené Brown, a prominent self-help writer and researcher, was the third most retweeted account in which she references her work on shame and gender in relation to the trial ("Speak up BUT don't talk too much." Advice from the shame playbook for women.) The rest of the accounts are individuals, spam/or now suspended accounts (five of the top 10 are from two accounts that are no longer active). We speculate that some of the inactive accounts included bots that took advantage of the spike of interest in the case. The most retweeted tweet occurred just before Pao's trial verdict was announced. The handle @hedgology describes himself in his Twitter bio as a financial analyst, trader, contrarian, blogger, entrepreneur, and gamer from New York. His tweet "Cries for sexism in three . . . #ellenpao" was retweeted 360 times and suggests a derision for the nature of the trial and Pao's allegations or at the very least a disagreement over the importance of the issues at stake. The last tweet of the 10 was from @hypatiadotca (Feeling sad & hopeless about the outcome of the #ellenpao trial? Go give @EqualRightsAdv money. This is what they do). The account is operated by Leigh Honeywell, a feminist tech entrepreneur, who has 24.7K followers as of 2019. This list indicates that Pao's trial via this hashtag did not generate a node of conversation around key issues that emerged in her case, such as discrimination in the workplace, or a community coming to her defense, at least in this admittedly limited online space. Instead there was a degree of noise in the form of spam accounts that emerged to fill the gaps.

Given the response to this hashtag, we turned to @ekp, which had a higher number of retweets, and appeared to be where publics were turning to in order to engage with Pao and her case. The top retweets also show a mix of technology and gender with the most prominent retweets from a Dubai-based tech marketing firm and Ellen Pao herself, some of which we reference earlier in this section. The complicated nature of the Twitter response and the number of problematic handles is reflective of Twitter's variegated landscape in public discourse, with hashtags not necessarily a default for robust conversation.

When Sources Create Communities: #notokay

Pao's story precedes the lead up to the election of Donald Trump where women's stories of sexual harassment and assault were also a central and contentious point of concern—both in terms of media coverage and the larger social and structural ramifications of women telling their stories. In case you lived in a media blackout zone during this time, a tape surfaced in early October 2016 (as Trump was running for president) of a conversation between *Access Hollywood* host Billy Bush (grandson and nephew to former U.S. Presidents G. H. and G. W. Bush, respectively) and Trump that occurred in 2005 on the set of a well-known soap opera, *Days of Our Lives.* Trump makes numerous "vulgar comments" about many women, including an actress whom the two later meet.[56]

Shortly after the tape surfaced in fall 2016, and shortly before Americans went to the polls, writer, screenwriter, and social media celebrity Kelly Oxford decided to tweet asking women to share their sexual assault stories after Trump's tape became public knowledge. She tweeted eleven times on October 7, 2016, with the last three about assault and #notokay. Her first tweet on the subject described her first experience of being sexually assaulted. It was: "Women: tweet me your first assaults. they aren't just stats. I'll go first: Old man on city bus grabs my 'pussy' and smiles at me, I'm 12." The tweet was retweeted 11,878 times, 13,722 people replied to this tweet, and it received 28 million total impressions. In a story that ran on NPR a few days later about the "torrent" of response to her tweet, Oxford said she received more than one million responses over one night.[57] On October 8, 2016, Oxford tweeted about the nature of the response: "Women have tweeted me sexual assault stories for 14 hours straight. Minimum 50 per minute. harrowing. do not ignore. #notokay" This tweet was retweeted 9,600 times.

In Table 2.2, we analyzed the networks activated by the top-10 retweets on #notokay over the first 10 days. We found that @KellyOxford was the most retweeted Twitter handle in six of the 10 tweets. Of the four remaining top retweets, two were from journalism organizations, *HuffPostCanada* and *TeenVogue.* The most retweeted tweet from #notokay was by Sareana Kimia, a youth activist and founder of Youth for National Change, who was in high school in fall 2016, according to her LinkedIn page. She had

TABLE 2.2 Top 10 Retweets for #notokay (October 7–17, 2016).

RETWEET	OCCURRENCES	ORIGINAL AUTHOR
RT @SareanaKimia 90% rapes go unreported Of those reported, only 30% go to trial Of those who faced trial, only 1/3 were jailed #WhyWomen DontReport #notokay https://t.co/UjNd18L0In	11000	SareanaKimia (Sareana Kimia)
women have tweeted me sexual assault stories for 14 hours straight Minimum 50 per minute. harrowing. do not ignore. #notokay	9,600	kellyoxford (kellyoxford)
I am currently receiving 2 sex assault stories per second. Anyone denying rape culture, please look at my timeline now. #notokay	3,400	kellyoxford (kelly oxford)
We are so proud of the survivors sharing their stories in light of #TrumpTapes. Rape culture is #NotOkay. http://t.co/ mPvwaFxs2v	2,800	TeenVogue (TeenVogue)
Calling sexual assault "locker room banter" or "a distraction" is textbook definition of rape culture in action. Women know this #NotOkay	2,700	AnnOlivarius (Ann Olivarius)
RT @ErinSchrode 3,000 sexual assault survivors tell Republicans to stop enabling Trump in full-page ad in WashPost today. #NotOkay https://t.co/VcGuT5xjkg https:t.co/ FraggKyeNxK	1,900	ErinSchrode (ErinSchrode)
I am in such horrendous shock and yet so proud of the women sharing their assaults. #notokay is trending in the United States. Not our shame anymore	1,600	Kellyoxford (kelly oxford)
If my @ feed were a ticker tape at the bottom of a news network, it would look like there was a war on women. #notokay #allofus	1,600	Kellyoxford (kelly oxford)

RETWEET	OCCURRENCES	ORIGINAL AUTHOR
Canadian writer's sexual assault story gets thousands of similar responses #notokay https://t.co/KOq0QKEDpq https://t.co/ilUirAXTaN	1,400	HuffPostCanada (HuffPost Canada)
3 hours ago I asked women to tweet me about their sexual assault & rape. 3 hours later, new women sharing—every second #notokay	1,200	Kellyoxford (kelly oxford)
Total Occurrences	**37,200**	

been an intern for the office of the Democratic Whip that summer for the first six months of 2016, as well as an election strategist for a U.S. prochoice group until November 2016. A prominent U.S. feminist lawyer, Ann Olivarius, also made the top-10 retweets. Her website indicates that her firm, in which she is a founding partner, "specializes in cases of race and gender discrimination."[58] The final handle referenced, @ErinSchrode, is a self described "activist, social entrepreneur and writer" and a "leading voice on sustainability, social impact and millennials" on her website.[59] Schrode's was the only overtly political tweet in the sample in the lead up to the election, despite evidence of possible political engagement from other Twitter profiles.

Oxford's motives for tweeting about her story of sexual abuse are unclear from reading Twitter. One has to go to legacy media to attempt to understand why. There Oxford's status would be considered anything from a source to a communications professional and social media celebrity. Before #notokay, she was best known for her fluency in social media, online community building, and humorous high-profile Twitter account.[60] Some mainstream media coverage of her ascent to social media star is highly gendered. In a 2013 *Globe and Mail* profile, Oxford is depicted as a stay-at-home Calgary mom who—incredulously—was talented enough to make it big in Los Angeles because of a successful Twitter account. The tone, both disbelieving and shockingly sexist, demeans Oxford's expertise and contributions in a number of gendered ways. In a 2017 interview with CBC about what led to #notokay, Oxford said her motives for tweeting were, "I was really really mad about Trump admitting to sexually assaulting women and I sent out the tweet asking women to share and sharing my first sexual assault. . . . I was shocked and saddened and excited you know that women were sharing and wanting to share. I felt a lot of emotions about it and still do to this day . . . I think over last year with the election, at least in Los Angeles, Los Angeles has become very active and its been really actually empowering for my kids to be able to go to protests and marches."[61]

Similar to critique of #MeToo in 2017, these accounts don't address race or the contributions of Black or Indigenous women to these movements.[62] Onwuachi-Willig explores a number of critical points in which Black women in particular were ignored for their participation before and after the 2017 resurgence of the #MeToo movement.[63] They include the contributions "that a woman of color played in founding the movement ten years earlier and in failing to recognize the unique forms of harassment and the heightened vulnerability to harassment that women of color frequently."[64] She begins her analysis with the story of Alyssa Milano's 2017 tweet, which similar to #notokay asked users to respond if they had been harassed or assaulted. She argues that while the goals of this movement are important, responses to Milano from women of color highlighted the fact that a white woman "yet again . . . was receiving credit for an idea originated by a woman of colour," and that Tarana Burke, who began #MeToo, had not received "the same level of support that white feminists like Milano received from the general public."[65]

In some ways, both Pao and Oxford defy easy categorization in digital journalism landscapes when they explicitly identify aspects of their positionality while engaging as sources and quasi-journalists trying to navigate and manage their own identities—often in spite of mainstream media framings. In journalism's historical hierarchies of seeing and knowing, they might be highly sought after as having a particular and diverse point of view and expertise: Pao as a racialized woman and Silicon Valley technology leader and Oxford as a gendered subject, whose race is not mentioned, and social media expert, succeeding in areas that journalism has struggled. They also might be considered less able to know than other experts and journalists because of their clear subject position. The varied framing of these cases thus highlights how the distinctions between who gets defined as a trustworthy source and/or journalist can collapse or amplify relative to testimony, experience, and positionality in this newer journalism landscape.

Credibility in this way has more than a passing relationship with expertise and epistemology. The term credibility has a specific history within journalism studies and is more likely to be operationalized in relation to the credibility of journalism outlets or various mediums.[66] In these examples, however credibility is about the ability to speak/intervene in public discourse, which is an ever-shifting terrain, goal, and form of social capital *both* for journalists and those active on social media. Choy's (2005) research on debates over environmental concerns in Hong Kong, specifically the use of international consultants in a local ecological dispute where their positions are counterintuitive, is relevant to this discussion. He questions anthropological analytic frameworks that have similarities to journalism methods in a transnational environmental because "to be credible," in this space, "expertise must bear universalizing and particularizing marks simultaneously,"[67] with both "produced through, rather than preceding political action."[68] For Choy, the process of identity formation and knowledge production are grounded in race, gender, power relations and form. As he suggests, if according to Haraway, witnesses in early science, "needed to be modest and civil," witnesses in his study needed to be social and positioned with identities produced through political action. This is similar to what we are seeing in social media journalism/activism and mobilizing various publics and counter-publics.[69] And in this process, these players become, as Choy articulates (drawing on Haraway): "a more modest, positioned knowledge—one more aware of its location relative to its object of knowledge and to other ways of knowing, and sensitive to the power dynamics at work between them."[70] The relationship between the universal and particular with respect to publics is an area of long tension within journalism and journalism studies in which the collective nouns—the audience and the public—remain largely undifferentiated despite the varied complex subjectivities and identities, and publics within.

Reductive, Instrumental Mythologies

Journalism's most recent efforts at transformation include one of its greatest unmet challenges and opportunities since the advent of the Internet—the quality of its relationship with the public(s) or the "people formerly known as the audience."[71] The phrase, coined by Jay Rosen in a 2006 blog post, forms the basis of his argument that digital technologies necessitate a sea change in the nature of the journalism–audience relationship—and that journalists need to take notice. For Rosen, the audience in the new media landscape becomes: "*the public* made realer, less fictional, more able, less predictable. You should welcome that, media people. But whether you do or not we want you to know we're here (italics in original)."[72] His blog post and articulation of *public or civic journalism* in his earlier book *What are Journalists For?* provided an important start in journalism studies, and he also could have gone further even at that time, as there has always been more than one public—and audiences have been responding, just not necessarily with a means or platform that accounts for the immense diversity of responses.[73]

For many scholars like Rosen, journalists, and publics, new platforms on the Internet offered an opportunity to rewrite journalism's closed system with its public(s) by supporting audience agency, and their ability to contribute, to collaborate with journalists, to affect information flows and the news agenda. Early beliefs during the nascent digital landscape claimed that improved audience engagement would result from the interactivity provided by new technologies, from user comments to choice of stories, to improved real time audience data. However, historic gaps in journalism's ability to connect with community, technological hope and hype, in addition to limited engagement among scholars and industry with the deeper questions of why and how the nature of the audience-journalism relationship evolved separate from its instrumental roles have deeply affected the nature of these conversations.[74]

Interactivity and the Internet became synonymous in a reconstitution of a journalism for the public to the extent that Deuze claimed there was an "(un)conscious consensus" about this trajectory and opportunity among journalists and researchers by the late 1990s.[75] Numerous studies extended the promise of interactivity to generate a new genre, participatory journalism, which was an opportunity to activate these aspirations and make audiences happier and more satisfied with news content.[76] Unfortunately the optimism of these studies could not make up for the ahistorical instrumentalism and practical necessity by which many in journalism see the audience. Nor could it counter the aggressive professional identity building of the newer interactive journalists who were trying to add value, skills, and knowledge while resisting sedimented institutional cultures that often undervalued their contributions.

Domingo presented one of the few cautionary approaches to the pervasive myth of interactivity in early 21st-century journalism.[77] Drawing from SST (social shaping of technology), he approached "interactivity as a concept that interplays with other material [staff size, resources] and social [professional culture, work organization] factors in the shaping of online news projects."[78] By reorienting the object of study through ethnographies of four online newsrooms in Spain in 2003, he found that instead of rampant engagement, journalism ideals and norms, largely immediacy, were inhibiting journalists' interest in and execution of interactive practices aside from journalists working solely online. The resistance was to such an extent that legacy media in his study found public forums a "problem they had to manage."[79] Only journalists working for the online portal saw interactivity as "an opportunity to enrich news with quality input from users," and even there they maintained a hierarchical distinction between user and journalistic news content.[80]

More recent promising approaches occurred when a number of scholars started to work with the concept "ambient journalism."[81] This was to account for the role that Twitter was playing in journalism in a "networked, always on communications" and immediate media environment.[82] Ambient journalism has been defined as:

> the collection, selection, and dissemination of news by both professional and non-professional para-journalists, where users undertake some of the institutional tasks commonly associated with the journalist . . . Users become part of the flow of news, reframing or reinterpreting a message through networked platforms that extend the dissemination of news through social interaction, introducing hybridity in news production and news values.[83]

Hermida references Hardey (2007) as articulating the main difference of digital media such as Twitter in that they are "inherently social so that users are central to both the content and form of all material and resources."[84] This in turn has displaced traditional news values (prominence, importance, timeliness, etc.) to include: "interactivity, participation, collaboration, and the distribution and dispersal of expertise and intelligence."[85] Papacharissi and de Fatima Oliveira examined Twitter coverage of Egypt in 2011 via #Egypt to explore how news values were mobilized. They found a "hybridity of old and newer news values, with emphasis on the drama of instantaneity, the crowdsourcing of elites, solidarity and ambience."[86] They also find a co-creation of news stories and events in the process in addition to a deviation from traditional logics by cohering "fact with opinion and objectivity with subjectivity."[87] These contributions are significant in understanding newer journalism norms and values promulgated through social media. Yet they fail to account for the fact that news values have long blended objectivity-subjectivity and affect in practice.[88] They also do not account for the power-knowledge-expertise turn that STS uses to address similar concerns in the public communication of science could be useful.[89]

Instead of exploring the roots of practice and epistemological underpinnings of the journalism-public relationship, journalism scholars and journalists have focused on largely instrumental assessments and aspirations, stopping far short of questioning the larger issues about power-knowledge. Boczkowski's study of early online newspapers found gate-keeping still a robust framework for journalism-user relations.[90] And what is gatekeeping if not a metaphor for managing peoples and keeping them largely outside? Ellis, Waterton, and Wynne take on similar issues in STS, using a barcode initiative (BOLI)—designed to encourage public, non-expert understanding of biodiversity classifications—as a site to critically examine science communications. They focus on how BOLI imagined its various publics, their relationship to the project, and to democracy. Drawing from STS and critical political theory, they identify important implicit assumptions in the public communication of science that include "distributed knowledge-agency, knowledge and responsibility, of global dimensions" such that the interaction between science and its publics have a lot to say about epistemology, in particular how publics are situated and called into being though their relationship to science.[91] They unpack this relationship by first showing how publics are "not only imagined or re-flected upon, but brought into being, or performed," while concurrently being erased of their diversity and the "politics of their intersection with science in part by a fundamental tension between the universal and spec-ificity required for reaching large publics."[92] To resist this reductive even-tuality they argue for the "active crafting of varying, diverse publics."[93] This is with the recognition that in this process the crafters move closer to Haraway's modest witness as both "finite and dirty, not transcendent and clean"[94] and "accountably so."[95]

Ellis and colleagues complicate and extend the concept of publics as having various subjectivities, personalities, and identities in effect creating the possibility for a number of different kinds of relationships. These in-clude: "publics explicitly invited to participate in dialogue" with scientific experts to "marginal, distrustful players who might be invited to partici-pate" to specific interest groups and finally "publics imagined to be waiting in the wings."[96] The latter has particular resonance for digital journalism studies as the literature often presents audiences as waiting to be engaged and/or interacted with, which is an underexplored concern in the interac-tivity myth identified by Domingo. Jasanoff also expands the possibilities for journalism when she explores the notion of civic epistemology and how publics have been situated with respect to science. She argues that cit-izens "are not seen as retaining independent stakes in steering science; nor are they thought to need an autonomous position from which to oversee the partnership of science with the state" post-election in determining their "needs and wants."[97] As a result, citizens have not been imagined as having an "active role in the production and use of scientific knowledge."[98]

Using technology then as a diagnostic, and drawing from STS scholars' thinking on science communication, journalism's lack of imagination—or perhaps because of its imagination (see Leonard for a discussion of journalism's "imagined" audience)—about its audience they lack a deeply engrained understanding of who is speaking, and who and what they are speaking for.[99] Integrating this critique with Haraway's understanding of the role of the modest witness in our conceptualizations of journalism methods from Chapter 1, we describe the deep gendered, colonial, and racial reckoning taking place under the guise of digital transformation and technological change. In this chapter, we are advancing arguments to show how the media's "trusted" relationship with its publics has been largely rooted in the received authority of a certain group—and how the authority of that group is being questioned, held to account, and unseated. Some journalism is indeed public service journalism; and some journalism is publicly funded to varying degrees depending on the national context. Yet, the metanarrative and aspirations that all journalists can speak to and for the public does not account for the historically and culturally situated power of who has been traditionally received as a journalism authority as journalists and/or sources. Nor do these metanarratives account for how this authority has been supported by journalism's often loose and sometimes paradoxically rigid methods, unrepresentative use of sources as proxies for the public and commercial contexts that have tended to privilege the status quo, instrumentalizing the audience—be it commercial or political—for the purposes of nation building and/or social ordering.

Conclusion

The three cases discussed in this chapter offer different tales of media failure and complexity. In the case involving Indigenous youth in particular, the narrative directly says to the media, you aren't doing a very good job—but we want you to. The participants we examine use the particularities of their experiences to shed light on universal suffering and structural concerns such as settler-colonialism, racism, and violence against women. They activate audiences not imagined as existing, as powerful, and as critical.[100]

Social media provides a terrain in which to posit more squarely what kind of experts journalists are and what kinds of knowledge they create, suggesting that a rethink and rearticulation of different identities and material relations are long overdue. Anthropologists have had to ask hard questions about what kind of experts they are because they were compelled in postcolonial contexts to address how anthropological experts were made, with what language, who was allowed to know and speak, and with what structured testimony. As this chapter shows, journalists, too, are being compelled by testimony from individuals such as Wente, Pao, and Oxford, who are producing a middle ground of journalism expertise with a deeper understanding of who can be a credible source and journalist—and can say things that a journalist can't or won't.

Journalism as well as journalists have been part of the entrenchment of colonial regimes through structures, practices, and news stories that do not account for systemic harm, colonialism, and their continued role in it that we discuss in Chapter 1. Hunt identifies tropes such as the "victim" as dangerous to Indigenous women and rooted in power relations such that the frame is "yet another silencing strategy" as it is "so familiar in justifications for colonialism and echoed in 'interventions' by dominant groups 'for their own good.'"[101] By reinforcing these tropes (see multiple studies of media representations of Indigenous women as victims), media coverage serves as an extension of the settler state—not a fourth estate—and is just one example of why the "battle for story" matters. The structural subordination of gendered, racialized, and Indigenous groups is deeply embedded in 20th-century journalism's aspirations, business models, and meta genre of holding power to account through speaking for and about the historically marginalized in ways that often maintain and reinforce existing power relations.[102]

In closing, this chapter argues that newer identities are emerging on social media through networked journalists grounded in relationships, history, and community as well as implicated in the results of the story and interested in transformation.[103] From Ellen Pao using Twitter to subtweet journalism coverage of her court case in order to articulate her point of view as alternative to being an elite media source to Indigenous activists and media professionals using Twitter as a platform for discourse and pushback, there is evidence of a growing middle ground to hold media in check.[104] Dahlgren's concern about the social cohesive role of journalism being under threat was for good reason, as multiple journalisms are emerging to resist the still-dominant epistemological framework and potentially to decolonize journalism.[105] It's clear from the sentiments expressed in much of the tweets that resonated with the social movements discussed in this chapter that media connect us, and it does matter who is speaking, who gets to be us, kin and other. Knowledge gets stabilized through the performance of the boundary policing of modest witnessing.[106] And journalists are no exception in this regard. But their role is changing and being subverted by many who choose to leverage new platforms such as Twitter.

We contend that technology—in this chapter, social media—is exposing the limits of journalism and journalists as transformative figures of systemic change. As Hunt argues, "Even raising the missing women into public discourse fails to trigger a change in the normalization of violence against Indigenous women, because Indigenous women and sex workers are categories of belonging predetermined by colonial power relations."[107] By boundary policing and categorizing who can speak, whose narratives matters and who is the audience, journalism has created an interpretive community with multiple exclusions.[108] In this process, journalists also can be seen (unwittingly perhaps) as supporting the settler state as conduits of Byrd's concept of "cacophony"—a method of empire that sustains the state through the creation of multiple competing voices and moral claims requiring the ability to be heard and discerned, distracting in the process "progressive and transformative activism from dismantling the ongoing conditions of colonialism."[109] The vertical interaction of colonizer and colonized is sustained through continual repetition of the defining event of settler colonialism.[110] In this chapter, voices such as Jesse Wente and the other mostly Indigenous social media actors from #ColtenBoushie and #TinaFontaine can be seen as decentering those narratives and the "horizontal histories of oppression into zero-sum struggles for hegemony" that "distract from the complicities of colonialism" and providing necessary "competing interpretations" and a transformative middle ground.[111]

CHAPTER 3 | "Speculative" Memoir Fragments
and Existential Dilemmas

Introduction

U.S. freelance journalist Carrie Ching pitched the idea for a first-person behind-the-scenes series on journalists' experiences in the field to Vice Media in 2013. Her pilot—which wasn't published with the rest of the series—was about a journalist who accidentally got "high on the job" and had a "paranoid breakdown" after eating a pot brownie while reporting on medical marijuana.[1] The format was animated graphic video with voices provided by journalists themselves. It was a perfect genre to explore and experiment with her professional interests in thorny questions of visual journalism and topics that ranged from "sensitive" to "brutal" and "dense" to show the "real subjects, real video, real photos."[2]

These interests emerged while Ching had worked with the Center for Investigative Reporting, a California-based nonprofit organization respected for its award-winning journalism. The approach was also intensely personal, as Vice Media, one of a handful of early global digital journalism success stories, was remaking journalism for millennials and branding itself as not "squeamish" about a "reporter front and centre telling their personal, subjective story."[3] The series, titled *Correspondent Confidential,* was eventually picked up and aired with six segments running 9 to 13 minutes each from a global lineup of journalists. The title draws cultural references from a 1958 crime movie and popular 1980s song about high school—not surprisingly given Vice Media's audience demographics—about contemporary moral dilemmas, such that there are ethical uncertainties and something potentially confidential to confess.

This chapter takes the 2013–2014 series of personal animated graphic videos as a starting point and diagnostic for a conversation about journalists' relationships with dominant ideals about the journalistic self; how they are dealing with the view from nowhere in a global journalism context that calls for increased location of identity and interests. These conversations have historically taken place at the dinner table, in bars, in newsrooms, and/or other insider professional contexts—and more commonly in the predigital era, such articulations came out in published memoirs released long after a journalist's career had been solidified (or when a career was near or at an end). Indeed, the ways in which journalists, in practice, synthesize ways around, through, and with professional norms and obligations have been largely internal discussions for internal audiences. Digital platforms, however, have afforded journalists the opportunity, space, and still precarious freedom (given labor challenges in the industry) to begin to co-articulate in near real time, however unevenly, previously internal debates, challenges, and negotiations with professional journalism's norms, ideals, and obligations.

These windows into understanding the persistence and/or evolution of such practices while they remain few are beginning to shift and open up such spaces though digital platforms such as *Correspondent Confidential* and social platforms such as Medium, Twitter, and blogs. A number of journalists have recently used these venues and arenas to share their experiences of leaving journalism jobs, commonly referred to as "quit-lit," and other personal accounts of internal to journalism struggles.[4] Yet even with digital sources, there are still few widely available and known sources for accounts from journalists that discuss how they navigate: (a) their own situated knowledge, (b) shared concerns with the subjects of their investigations, and (c) participation in or resistance to journalism as an apparatus for maintaining and/or idealizing particular social orders.

In this chapter, what we are calling *speculative memoir fragments* provide a novel site and terrain for understanding how journalists are trying to make sense of issues of subjectivity, implicatedness, and power in a global journalism landscape.[5] We find evidence of an emerging meta-genre as journalists publicly try and make sense of themselves and of what journalism is trying to do—and when it doesn't work—in a moment when journalism's dominant aspirations are being challenged and commercial models are failing with no road map in real time. The *Correspondent Confidential* series and these other digital conversations are unique in that they center the subjectivity of journalists from prominent organizations with sought-after professional accomplishments, in a variety of forms from graphic video to text. The six personal stories articulated in *Correspondent Confidential* would be considered a playlist of professional journalism achievement—coverage of war zones, to unsolved KKK murders in the southern United States, to drug cartels and post-earthquake Haiti.[6] All episodes describe work done by journalists for major media organizations that include the *Los Angeles Times, Al Jazeera*, Canadian Broadcasting Corporation, and other nonspecific American news networks. In keeping with the main themes of this book, these memoir fragments are an example of how technology can be a diagnostic and entry point to long-standing methodological tensions of truth and journalism's still-dominant authority in practice in a world increasingly tightly globalized in its consumption, wars, and inequalities.

We begin by examining what it is about the memoir genre that is compelling and relevant for journalists and how memoir has been discussed in journalism studies scholarship and within journalism. We next explore some of the themes journalists are struggling with through these memoir fragments, including: subjectivity, their humanity and implicatedness, and uncertainty and reputation in a hyper-visible digital journalism world that is increasingly freelance and precarious.[7] We find these speculative memoir fragments notable indications of how journalists are grappling with a kind of journalism that didn't work the way they thought it should or could—and unreliable for how they are still both speculative and fragmentary. We end by asking (and speculating about) why non-legacy media, social media, and/or free digital sites are the places and ways that we find journalists grappling and experimenting with epistemological concerns and developing/managing their personal reputations/brands during this digital reckoning.

Making Sense of Role Limitations

We situate our work alongside scholars such as Broersma, who has used memoir to explore journalism's role limitations with respect to its claims to represent truth and social reality objectively.[8] He found that truth telling via memoir about the ambiguity of journalistic epistemologies can rebut deeply held norms that news provides an unbiased account of the world, unfettered by the personal conditions of the journalist or economic context of the industry. Despite (and perhaps because of) these possibilities, the journalistic memoirist has been deeply "reviled by their colleagues" while "applauded by the public."[9]

Instead of revulsion, we find the emergence of a novel and rich meta genre of digital speculative memoir. We find this meta genre developing in spite of the risks of implicating oneself in a digital landscape where both front- and back-stage behaviors are potentially more visible—and more complicated to navigate. It is also in spite of the cautionary tale provided by what must be the profession's most compelling and frightening story of too much information and the author's own partial and problematic reflexivity: the classic 1989 *New Yorker* series of feature articles published together as *The Journalist and the Murderer.* Consistently named one of the top-100 nonfiction books of all time by the *Guardian* and others who keep such lists, Malcolm's book confronts journalism and journalists on page one with the opening salvo:

> Every journalist who is not too stupid or too full of himself to notice what is going on knows that what he does is morally indefensible. He is a kind of confidence man, preying on people's vanity, ignorance or loneliness, gaining their trust and betraying them without remorse.[10]

And it doesn't stop there. The entire book is a tour de force through journalism's dominant and dismayingly loose reporting methods as Malcolm scrutinizes the tactics and habits of her fellow long-form journalist Joe McGinniss. McGinniss stood trial in a U.S. civil court in the 1980s for breach of contract involving his conduct while writing bestselling true crime thriller *Fatal Vision,* about the accused and later convicted murderer Jeffrey MacDonald. McGinniss was on MacDonald's legal defense team, had a close friendship documented through letters at the time, and struck a deal that involved sharing profits with MacDonald. All three elements leave McGinniss open to professional and personal scrutiny, which Malcolm readily engages in. She opens up issues of journalism ethics that run the gamut of making a bland character for a work of journalism more "interesting" to the definition of truth and lies—and whether there can be multiple truths and what that might mean for both journalism and law.

McGinniss later settled out of court with MacDonald after the case ended in a mistrial because the jury voted five to one in MacDonald's favor and could not reach consensus. Malcolm's book reads like a record of why the jury should and did have reasonable doubts about the looseness of the journalistic methods that McGinniss employed, and the reader is thus left to wonder about the nature of journalism as a knowledge producing and truth-telling institution in society (i.e., whose truth emerges from journalism, what kind of truths are journalists after, and what kinds of methods do they use to seek truth?). The book is like an onion that slowly peels away the layers of journalistic practices, choices, ideals, and norms—even that of its author who offers her own reflections on journalists' practices (e.g., ideal, imagined, mythologized and practiced) even while she fails to disclose her own interests in the case—a signal of how difficult disclosing interests has been for journalists.

As a counterpoint to Malcolm, Sacco's 2013 compilation of his work in the graphic novel, *Journalism*, explains his own method and subjectivity with respect to confronting the view from nowhere and sets it within a broader framework of American journalism:

> I, for one, embrace the implications of subjective reporting and prefer to highlight them. Since it is difficult [though not impossible] to draw myself out of a story, I usually don't try. The effect, journalistically speaking, is liberating. Since I am a 'character' in my own work, I give myself journalistic permission to show my interactions with those I meet.[11]

Sacco argues that he can still "strive for accuracy" within a subjective approach using the example, "facts [a truck carrying prisoners came down the road] and subjectivity [how that scene is drawn] are not mutually exclusive."[12] He goes on to make the case for subjectivity and what he calls "personal exchanges which most mainstream newspaper reporters, alas, excise from their articles."[13] One of his best lines is that "the stories journalists tell around a dinner table . . . are often more interesting and revealing than what gets into their copy."[14] He closes with a statement on the impossibility of objectivity in journalism:

> Despite the impression they might try to give, journalists are not flies on the wall that are neither seen nor heard. In the field when reporting, a journalist's presence is almost always felt . . . This brings us to American journalism's Holy of Holies, 'objectivity.' To be clear, I have no trouble with the word itself, if it simply means approaching a story without any preconceived ideas at all. The problem is I don't think most journalists approach a story that has any importance that way. I certainly can't.[15]

In Sacco's framework, speculative memoir fragments might be seen as a story "journalists tell around a dinner table," and perhaps more centrally highlight the increasingly complicated roles that journalists have and their confrontations with still-dominant notions of objectivity. What is interesting about all of these confrontations we find in the next sections is that journalists are turning to this meta genre as both compelling personal content *and* a discussion of where and when journalism fails at what it says it is going to do and the confusion—in a context of North American commercial media market failure, risk of error and increasingly high global stakes.

Memoir and Life Stories

Journalists as writers and chroniclers have long had a penchant for various forms of life stories ranging from autobiography to literary journalism, "gonzo" journalism,[16] "confessional" journalism, and workplace memoirs and/or "war stories" of their professional life.[17] According to Spurr "most literary journalism is avowedly autobiographical."[18] Meanwhile, Coward explores an increase in what she calls "confessional" autobiographical journalism in the United Kingdom over the past 30 years.[19] She defines the genre from a practice perspective as "first-person real-life experiences . . . or regular columns by journalists detailing intimate details of their lives" such as dealing with cancer or the death of a parent.[20] These life storytellers tend to be focused on one major goal—to persuade readers "of their version of experience."[21] Motives for life stories tend to be about resolving parts of the self both internally and externally, in some respect, a coming to terms with larger, sometimes personal and cultural truths. These can include "justifying their own perceptions, upholding their reputations, disputing the accounts of others, settling scores, conveying cultural information, and inventing desirable futures among others."[22] Yet, this task is often a challenge, according to Smith and Watson, because "memory is a subjective form of evidence, not externally verifiable; rather, it is asserted on the subject's authority."[23]

That journalists are turning to a form of memoir is not surprising as journalistic work revolves around narration and the selection of facts, events, and details. That they are turning to an emergent and highly public meta genre suggests journalists see a need to work through normative issues that they can no longer ignore or address in the bar and/or on their own, among insiders.[24] A range of reasons relate to what memoir provides as a potential and provisional antidote to journalism's reckoning and existential dilemma and the need for a real-time digital check in and accounting. These include wider sociological and intellectual shifts consistent with research on a growing cultural "i-pistemology" such that the self is "the source and arbiter of all truth" with personal approaches increasingly informing public discourse in ways that are seen to contribute to social ordering depending on the nature of the account.[25] This form also circumvents charges of cultural relativism, which has been one of the ways that journalism has maintained power through supporting a distanced subject position that shows both sides, yet ultimately supports an implicit dominant approach to social ordering that we reckon with throughout the book.

Memoir in its range of forms then is an attempt to produce shared meaning in that it deals with different and more complicated understandings of truth as ultimately partial and rooted in multiple perspectives including the audience's. According to Fish, referenced in Smith and Watson, the pursuit of truth becomes both more ambiguous and potentially more accountable in life stories: "'Autobiographers cannot lie because anything they say, however mendacious, is the truth about themselves, whether they know it or not' . . . it is an intersubjective exchange between narrator and reader aimed at producing a shared understanding of the meaning of a life."[26] Attempts to produce a shared meaning of a life story or in this chapter's case, a life story fragment, inevitably involve persuasion about a certain version of the self and its authority. That journalists are turning to this form as a way to understand the professional self in real time suggests a number of shifts in that nature of doing journalism globally, the role/possibility of real time audience criticism and feedback concurrent with the decreasing power of the journalist's professional identity and uncertainty about its professional authority—represented by an impulse and ability to check that did not exist in modern journalism.[27]

Themes of ethical anxiety about whose truth and accountability are consistent threads over which journalists are trying to make their case. They emerge in the discussion of *The Journalist and the Murderer* in which the journalist is seen as a confidence man in a range of ethically comprised conditions reminiscent of trauma. Broersma also quotes one of his memoir subjects as concerned about his perspective and personal reputation as a truth teller:

'You can accuse me of incompetence, of being a shitty journalist or a shallow halfwit, but to say I would deliberately lie about stuff and manipulate information – nothing could be further from the truth. It can't co-exist with your role in journalism. All one is trying to do is tell the truth.'[28]

In this sense, the speculative memoir fragments that we analyze thematically in the next section provide journalists with an opportunity to make sense of the still-dominant journalism authority while negotiating their situated knowledges, devising ethical pathways through the maze of choices they are confronted with in the field where not only their story, but their reputations and lives and those of their colleagues may be at stake. These life story fragments become a means to access and assess journalist's navigation of subjectivity, distinct from previous forms of journalistic autobiography and memoir.[29]

Behind the Scenes of Global Journalism

Correspondent Confidential

In the series *Correspondent Confidential,* one of the six accounts involves Mimi Chakarova, a Bulgarian American filmmaker and journalist, who told the behind-the-scenes story of her award-winning documentary film, *The Price of Sex.* Chakarova's account is unique in the series in a number of ways. It's the only first-person journalism in the six where the journalist goes undercover: Chakarova poses as a prostitute in Turkey to examine the sex trade.[30] It is also one of two documentaries—while the other four are behind-the-scenes stories of traditional news events. In a *New York Times* review, Chakarova's documentary is described as: "a first-person,

IMAGE 1 "Image from 'I Posed as a Prostitute in a Turkish Brother,' an episode of VICE's Correspondent Confidential series featuring filmmaker Mimi Chakarova, directed and produced by Carrie Ching, and illustrated by Marina Luz."

unusually understated commentary about the sex slave industry that could just as easily be posted by an organization that combats human trafficking."[31]

Chakarova came to Vancouver, British Columbia in 2017 to explain her reporting approach during a talk sponsored by the Global Reporting Centre.[32] As a journalism professor at the University of California at Berkeley, she said she has to periodically apologize to her students for her previous commitment to and lauding of objectivity. She said she "used to talk about objectivity, but it's bullshit. Being a human being has to come first or you can't go into their houses [referring to the houses of her film's subjects]." For her, "being a human being" involved acknowledging her own subject position and emotions—in this case, "anger"—in that she identified with young women trafficked from villages similar to her family's village in Bulgaria. These young women, instead of having the opportunity to emigrate to the United States in early adolescence like herself, had few choices about how to deal with poverty and a lack of work options in a rapidly transforming economy previously based on agrarian village life and a Communist regime.

In her *Correspondent Confidential* account, Chakarova indicated that she could have been one of the women she interviewed, and instead of ignoring or avoiding the risk and dangers of telling this kind of story, she went back with her camera.

> I met with a friend of mine after one of the trips and he said to me, 'Do you think maybe you over identify with these women?' And it was a very brutal question because you know what, the answer is yeah I think I do. The origins are similar but this is not my story. I made a choice to go into these places, that was a choice that was not by force.[33]

Chakarova's behind-the-scenes story arguably anchored the series. Her critique of journalism's dominant authority and her engagement with her own implicatedness was well established and informed some of the motives for choice of genre—long-form first person documentary. Chakarova was part of the series because she had worked with the series producer, Ching in the past and had been teaching at UC Berkeley while Ching was a student there. They were the only two women journalists of the six. Ching recalls being particularly moved by Chakarova's account of her process during research for the *Correspondent Confidential* series: "For her to tell those stories that she had never told publicly, we turned out the lights in the interview room and sat in the dark so she could just unload. It was like a therapy session for a lot of them."[34] Ching decided to include her own story because she felt ethically bound to share her experiences after asking other journalists and former colleagues to do the same.

Four stories, including Ching's, emerged from news events—a fixture of modern journalism where journalists attempt to make sense of what happened during a singular event in highly formalized genres—from a war crime, to drug war, a meeting of American tourists and an earthquake.[35] All events focused on conflict, a defining news value, while two of the events ultimately suggested an alternative story to the one they had originally planned to cover. Two stories deal with the aftermath of or ongoing impact of civil war. The remaining stories were both documentaries focused on larger structural issues of violence against Black men in the southern United States and against women from formerly eastern bloc countries. While the trailer for *Correspondent Confidential* promises to "go behind the story," we don't know much about any of the journalists aside from elements of the news event and how they resolved methodological challenges—suggesting a universal journalist dealing with larger complex systems. The series is meant to record the dilemmas that aren't easily resolved and aren't in any codes of ethics. These are the stories that don't usually make it into reporting until a memoir might appear years later.

Specifically, besides Chakarova's documentary, the remaining five episodes recounted behind-the-scenes stories of the following:

- An American *Al Jazeera* reporter, Sebastian Walker tells of being in Puerto Rico when the major earthquake hit in Haiti and being one of the first and only journalists to make a harrowing journey into Port-au-Prince in the immediate aftermath.[36] He ended up staying for 18 months, and also through seeming happenstance, stumbled into what was likely the source of the cholera outbreak that has crippled Haiti's recovery.
- In Kosovo, American reporter Michael Montgomery tells of his searching for missing people who had been kidnapped and killed as part of an organ-trafficking scheme.[37] It takes many years for the reporter's observations to come to light and for confirmation of what he witnessed.
- In Colombia, an American reporter, T. Christian Miller looking to report on FARC stumbles into a rebel camp where he is kidnapped briefly and then released.[38]
- Carrie Ching describes being on assignment to interview U.S. war veterans about a political story in the episode, "A Bizarre Night in

Thailand."[39] What she slowly reveals is that some of the veterans living in this sex tourism hotspot were possibly engaged in pedophile-related activities.

- The last story is from an independent filmmaker, David Ridgen, who travels to the southern United States in search of justice for two young men who were allegedly murdered in race-related violence in the 1960s.[40] He recruits an investigative partner, one of the victim's brothers, who went on to have an extensive military career. Together, they reenact the likely murder scenario and confront the men who are suspected to have been involved with and/or perpetrated these crimes and are also long-standing members of the KKK. The story ends with one of the perpetrators convicted, and the other a key witness with immunity. The key witness then asks for forgiveness of the brother and the victim's families and invites the brother to attend his church as likely, the filmmaker suspects, the only African American to have ever entered this church.

We used qualitative textual and visual framing analysis[41] to examine the content and themes that emerged about the role of the journalist.[42] For example, how these journalists identified, emphasized, and omitted values, norms, and practices suggests categories of possibility and limitations or impossibility/implausibility for journalistic practice. That is, in their attempts to coherently tell their story, there is both an implied stance and non-stance. Overall, our analysis suggests an increasing subjectivity and situatedness of the journalist through the videos narrated by journalists and visualized through motion-animated graphic stills. The context shows a global journalism in transition from powerful modern change agent to curator.[43] It is at times random in that a few of the stories changed midstream, and interpretative in that journalists are sharing back-stage information from the field that includes mundane and cogent examples of a lack of resources. For example, Ching recounts one long bus ride and a taxi ride on the way to her assignment.

The main themes we find are: (1) the challenges of covering complicated global geopolitical systems, ongoing colonialisms, and journalists' locatedness in how they approach these concerns; (2) professional identity and uncertainty of what it's like to be a global journalist; and (3) personal implicatedness.

(1) "The people who suffer the most . . . are the locals who help them."

On colonialism and global journalists, the contingency of the role of journalist and his/her/their dependence on the presence, kindness, and credibility of those they work with is a key aspect of all of these stories. However, there is a wide spectrum of how connectedness and distance to sources and informants are articulated. Two of the stories involve what are termed "fixers," drivers/translators/assistants who know vital social and geographical aspects such that they can facilitate investigative reporting. In Haiti and Colombia, the fixers are in physical danger by working with these reporters. The reporter who is kidnapped in Colombia laments openly after his local "canoe pilot" is taken away:

> And then the commander turned around and he began shouting just a stream of Colombian swear words at the guy who had piloted the canoe. And that guy was just taken away. We thought he was gone, that he was gonna be killed. I felt terrible, because it's often the people who suffer the most, when some American journalists parachutes into some foreign country, are the locals who help them.[44]

We never find out what happened to the canoe pilot, but notation of his presence and subsequent absence sets a different tone and raises the stakes for collaboration. Fixers are not generally credited by news organizations, even though some are known journalists working in their country of origin and are often in danger should their journalistic collaboration be seen as a threat.[45] See Image 2, which shows the dangers faced by these local and international journalists in Colombia.

IMAGE 2 "Image from 'I Was Kidnapped by a Colombian Guerrilla Army,' an episode of VICE's Correspondent Confidential series featuring journalist T. Christian Miller, directed and produced by Carrie Ching, and illustrated by Arthur Jones."

Difference and distance are persistent as a theme, but it comes in many registers. Where in Colombia and Kosovo, it follows more traditional registers of empathy, Thailand provides a counterpoint, introducing sources who may be engaged in morally reprehensible behaviors. In the Thailand story, Ching refers to the woman who accompanies her as "a friend who is helping her out"—the animation clearly shows the friend doing the sound recording during what Ching describes as her first video story.[46] Race and gender are important factors in Ching's narration because she is both traveling through Thailand during a cultural celebration and visiting what she comes to realize is an ex-pat sex tourism hot spot with mostly sex trade workers and older white men. Ching thinks she could have blended in, as her ethnicity is "half-Chinese." But her blond friend "stuck out like a sore thumb," making them a "target" for the cultural hijinks (dumping water and white paste on them) that are part of the celebration.[47] The story's arc from seeming travelogue to serious and somewhat dangerous witnessing of the global sex trade while formally discussing U.S. politics on camera provides a disconcerting example of both the incoherence of the field and incomprehensibility of human behavior—what can't and won't be told but needs to be.

Difference also acts as a key factor in how vested and powerful the reporter is in his or her relationship with sources as informants and collaborators. The self-described white filmmaker, David Ridgen, who narrates his experience tracking down an unsolved KKK murder, works with the victim's African American brother as a collaborative team to instigate justice:

> We always had each other's back. Of course I was a white guy, and he was a black guy, and he was able to speak to Mississippi Blacks in a way that I could never do, and I could speak to people who were white in the community in a way that he felt he could never do—we would kind of use that to our advantage.[48]

For Ridgen, there was safety and lack of safety, access and opportunity, and direct justice in working with the brother of the victim.

In contrast, Mimi Chakarova must collaborate with the oppressors she is seeking to expose, briefly tilting journalist-source power relations when she is put in danger as an undercover investigative filmmaker, posing as a prostitute. Chakarova's investment in the story is clear as is her lack of distance from the victims she is impersonating. She follows up with a careful recognition and articulation of her privilege and goes on to narrate a moment with a source, who refuses her identification and empathy.

I made this terrible mistake in the middle of her story, I said in Russian, I know what you mean. Or I know how you feel. And she took that bottle and slammed it down on the table so hard I thought it would break. She said, 'Don't you ever fucking tell me you know what it feels like or you know what I mean, because you have no idea.' And she was absolutely right.[49]

This navigation between empathy/sympathy, distance/connection, and participant/observer has much more in common with ethnographic methods than a traditional journalistic stance. While professional codes of ethics support fair treatment of sources and minimizing of harm, Awad argues that journalists in practice prioritize the story and "truth" above all, often misrepresenting, manipulating, and mistreating sources.[50] We find journalists in *Correspondent Confidential* moving towards participant-observer approaches, attempting to locate themselves and their subjects through articulating difference in race, gender, privilege, access, and vernacular.[51] Yet, these power relations operate within global systems of oppression and colonialism.

We reference Spivak's concept of the subaltern more fully in Chapter 1. It is also relevant here because many of these journalists are grappling with both the "unrepresentability" of their sources and subjectivities. The ways in which the subaltern voice—which comes in many forms in a globalized media—is disappeared, silenced, or outside the forms and styles of journalism becomes palpable through graphic representations and the series as a whole. The journalist, while slightly more transparent and implicated, remains under-interrogated in terms of subject position and the politics and potential harms of representations.[52] Who gets to claim expertise and counter-expertise and to judge what kind of experts the journalists are is still up for grabs.[53]

"I was gonna drive around until I found the rebels"

As a corollary to the first theme, we found journalists struggling to situate their narratives within the larger historical, media, and geographical contexts, suggesting that the journalists are trying to make sense of their experiences using a focus on events first and foremost, a shallow integration of history and political economy, and their personal subjective and local knowledge in limited cases. In Colombia, Miller described his context as, "So my plan was I'd fly out to the trouble zone, I'd go to the nearest town to where the crash had occurred and I was just gonna drive around until I found the rebels."[54] This apparent haphazardness however is juxtaposed with a clearly articulated motive for the story on Colombia, which is presented as fact as opposed to a contextual and ultimately ideological rationale for doing the story: "Colombia was seen as this big drug hot spot and the United States had just decided to spend three billion dollars on what was called 'Plan Colombia.'"[55]

Two of the accounts mentioned local connections and personal narratives as ways of accessing information and/or sources as well as generating the motive for pursuing the story. For example, this re-inscription of the local and subjective occurred in the Chakarova story on sex trafficking as her motive for the story emerged from her personal history. Further, Chakarova identifies the gendered power relations of her role as a journalist in a dangerous situation undercover.

> In the middle of it, one of the men who knew I was a journalist, puts his hand on my leg and he looks at me. And there is nothing I can do about this because we're there in a basement. I have to play along. He is fully aware of the advantage that he's taking with me, and the situation that I'm in. Which is, he knows that he has the power to go to the owner to tell the truth.[56]

This account foregrounds the gendered violence women journalists face in the field, as well as the specific, local, historical nature of power relations.

(2) "I've fucked up, you know. This was stupid. This wasn't worth it."

On professional identity and uncertainty about the role of the journalist, journalists' describe themselves and/or the media they worked at, by nationality—all are Americans—as well as gender and race. They do not explicitly identify as foreign correspondents, although most of them would be considered in that professional category. The themes that emerged about how journalists describe themselves and their work show a continuum of frames from the professional journalist as change agent to the vested journalist in crisis and/or less powerfully in charge of her role and identity. For example, evidence of the modernist role of the journalist largely emerged from the stories in Haiti, Thailand, and the southern United States. In Haiti, the journalist described his role as both first and only witness and powerful agent:

> The first thing we did was to call the UN and tell them what we've seen and to ask them to comment on it. They wouldn't. We edited our footage in the car, made it into a short news report and just sent it off to our headquarters

and got the story out. It was the first time there had been any international coverage of a UN connection to cholera. If . . . we hadn't have been there and seen it, it might never have been known.[57]

This ability to effect change also emerged in the southern United States with the journalist's comment:

> We knew we were kicking the hornet's nest of a forty-three-year-old murder case that wasn't going to get the attention, and the truth wasn't going to come out, and the justice wasn't going to be found unless we kicked it often, and hard.[58]

Yet while some accounts situated journalists as change agents, others indicated an awareness of the contingency and uncertainty of journalistic roles and practices.

The accounts with the most significant uncertainty around the representations of the aims of the journalist emerged from Colombia and Kosovo. For example, T. Christian Miller indicated at one point that he "fucked up, you know. This was stupid. This wasn't worth it."[59] Indeed in a number of instances, he explicitly questions the power of the role of the journalist, framing it as "we're just journalists" and sharing the fact that he had "made up" his press credentials from the *Los Angeles Times*—"but it looked official."[60] The account from Kosovo, as well, is significant in that it undermines journalistic norms and methods of identifying a story. Michael Montgomery starts the story with an acknowledgment that he and his colleague intended to cover one issue, "an anatomy of a war crime," at "the scene of a terrible massacre by Serbian paramilitaries."[61] But instead, they found an organ trafficking ring, which he suggests is "where the story really started getting strange."[62] These accounts signal that the "parachute"[63] or "crisis"[64] journalist who is flown in at the last minute and has limited knowledge of the country they are reporting on remains an issue in global journalism. However, these journalists also appear to identify less with the importance of the professional label of "foreign correspondent," which suggests some reflection, anxiety, and concern about professional reputation and the impact of inexperience and lack of knowledge on the ground.

(3) "I realized that I didn't feel comfortable telling these people that I was a journalist"

While the tonal qualities and visual depictions of the episodes' narrations are layered, and become more complicated to analyze against the animated graphics, common to all the episodes is a confessional tone, although in varying degrees. Schultze's work on confessional accounts of ethnographic research suggests that a confessional genre potentially offers "a self-reflexive and self-revealing account of the research process.[65] It presents the ethnographer's role as a research instrument and exposes the ethnographer's actions, failings, motivations, and assumptions to public scrutiny and critique."[66] Overlapping the confessional, the tonal qualities of the narration range from disturbing and disturbed to despairing and cynical—and from vulnerable, fearful, and intimate to sensemaking and fact giving. For example, the narration tone of the stories from Thailand, Turkey, and Kosovo largely emerged as vulnerable, intimate, and disturbing. Montgomery described his feeling of vulnerability: "We were surrounded by villagers and people were asking questions, and I realized that I didn't feel comfortable telling these people that I was a journalist and what I was there for. I didn't feel safe."[67] Disturbed by the "scary" evidence that surfaced, he described the village as "a place where horrible things happened."[68] Whereas, Walker, adopted a less emotive and more fact-giving tone:

> We could see this horrible smelling liquid dripping from the base. Basically, across the path into the river. What we were seeing right there was the smoking gun. Eventually, one of the guys started talking to me a little bit and I was saying, 'What is this building? Can you tell me what this is? Is this a toilet?' He looked back at the building and looked back to me and just looked really guilty and eventually said, 'Yes, it's a toilet.' I remembered doing this very quick search on my phone for cholera outbreaks in Nepal.[69]

The tonal qualities of the narration suggest the journalists' grappling with the ways in which they are embedded in the stories they are reporting, and in some cases reveal a reflexivity regarding the performance of journalism. They also suggest a degree of needed interpretation not usually found in event-driven international news.[70] For example, Ching's interrogation of her own role as a journalist toward the end of her narrative is both moving and unexpected.

> It's just ridiculous. . . . We are in the centre of Thailand's sex tourism, child prostitution problem, and we are talking about John Kerry and his Purple Heart. It was insane. . . . We just wanted to get the hell out of there.

Drawing from Spurr, one of the few scholars of colonialism and nonfiction journalism, this example is suggestive of how Ching was "caught within the play of more powerful forces" in her event-centered reporting, yet trying to "claim . . . a space of interpretive authority" by nodding to the political ideology of U.S. international news.[71] Yet how is interpretative authority for journalists established in a complicated global geopolitics with ongoing and varied colonialisms, and a global digital media landscape in which a certain kind of public accountability is a tweet or comment away?

For Ching, the overall experience of sharing the behind-the-scenes story was "cathartic" and "very intimate at times" for herself and the other journalists, as well as "eye-opening" about "how the mechanisms of journalism work." She was particularly surprised by the public response:

> You should never read the comments on YouTube when you put out video, but I did. And people tore me apart. They were like, 'She's the worst journalist ever. How could she leave? She should have gone after those guys!' . . . I was actually in grad school at the time that I was doing that project. It was my first video story ever. I was doing it as a school project essentially, and I landed in the middle of this [alleged] basically child sex trafficking operation. And it was way over my head.[72]

IMAGE 3 "Image from 'A Bizarre Night in Thailand' an episode of VICE's Correspondent Confidential series featuring series producer Carrie Ching, directed and produced by Carrie Ching, and illustrated by Colleen Cox."

It's in this sense, Ching's stories and the others that are part of *Correspondent Confidential* are both speculative and memoir because they are using newer technologies to re-imagine how they made decisions in the field and what ramifications those decisions had ethically and personally in almost real time.

These accounts can be seen as transition from a modern journalism subject and testament to the cautionary, complicated, and implicated terrain of doing journalism today. The series reflects deep challenges and anxieties related to what journalism should and could do. It becomes increasingly apparent in each of the stories that objectivity and how it has been articulated is insufficient for journalists to report on complicated global journalism events, incomprehensible trauma, as well as its own colonial violence while trying to make sense of difference.[73] Here the meta genre suggests a divergence from modernist, colonizing subjectivities of journalists as truth tellers and objective witnesses to emerge with a stance closer to participant-implicated witness/observer and quasi-located decolonizing global storytellers.[74]

This divergence signals a significant shift in the performance of journalistic expertise and potentially the role audiences might—and are playing—as both fellow participants and engaged global citizens.[75] It reveals how closely the work of journalists has been tied to social ordering by not, for example, being able to talk about the potential criminal activities happening in the background during Ching's interview. There is also an "accidental" and generic quality to the nature of some of the engagement of journalists with the context as opposed to an explicit research driven orientation to specific times, places, and locations to the extent that in many cases the scene could be anywhere, ultimately leaving deeply complicated structural global power relations under accounted for. In *Correspondent Confidential*, the disregarded are largely the stories of journalism's limitations and things gone wrong, with the graphic illustrations a significant component functioning not just as illustrations or what in broadcast is termed, "b-roll," but to cover essential voiceovers for which no logical video exists. The animated stills and animations direct the viewer's attentions to how the journalist is making sense of his, her, or their role even as their career and understanding of journalism has progressed since this event.

Correspondent Confidential, in this sense, mixes genres and conventions related to memoir, graphic novel, and illustrations to produce a form of illustrated "speculative" memoir such that the role of journalist becomes one of participant, witness, observer, and sense maker navigating within and among the messy realities of the worlds it encounters—and what it must include and leave out in eventual narratives. In many ways, the graphic illustrations underscore both the precarious position of journalist as truth teller when truths are multiple, contingent, and/or hidden, and forms for telling them elude the grasp of the storyteller except in speculative hindsight. What *Correspondent Confidential* doesn't do, however, is explicitly question the positionality of the journalist as truth teller and narrator even while foregrounding the difficult decisions journalists must make in the field under duress, managing their own safety and that of their crew, which may or may not include fixers. Herein lies the gaps where analysis can be read into what's left out in a way that must be filled in by the viewer according to their own view of the topic and journalism—or filled in by hearing the journalists give a talk like the one we attended with Chakarova. Rao and Wasserman's postcolonial critique of journalism is one of the few scholarly articles to question the Western orientation of the ethics literature and its focus on universal norms over particular political, historical, and economic conditions.[76] This specificity is vital in global journalism where ideological influence on content has been identified as a concern.[77]

What becomes apparent in our analysis and in walking through each of the narratives in the *Correspondent Confidential* series is how central notions of journalism ethics—and what the right thing to do as a journalist—are difficult to navigate when locatedness and colonial contexts are considered. The mostly widely used code of ethics doesn't offer prescriptions of either how to locate oneself as a journalist or how that might implicate the telling and representations of a work of journalism. It's in this sense that *Correspondent Confidential* serves as a kind of intervention, revealing the messy decisions and ethical frameworks that do little to prepare journalists to make difficult decisions in the field.

Quit Lit and Other Media Fragments

Correspondent Confidential's articulations can be brought alongside other kinds of speculative memoir fragments of journalists, often from communities not well represented in newsrooms (e.g., Indigenous and South Asian in this case). These journalists are utilizing digital platforms from independent media to newer digital and social media to make sense of the limits of journalism—and its possibilities in near real time. Jenni Monet, a prominent independent Indigenous journalist whose work we discuss more in Chapter 6, wrote an article on *Literary Hub* about how she has taken the extra step of self-publishing an "Indigenous version" of her articles. She said she does this because she has found that:

> In a pursuit to expand the Indigenous narrative to wider audiences, I have seen what I consider to be relevant and worthy Indigenous perspective routinely gutted from the articles I write. Rarely do these omissions see the light of day by readers.[78]

She said that her "Indigenous version" offsets the pieces that have run in major mainstream publications where "editorial decisions are determined by those less familiar with Indigenous-minded points of view."[79] For Monet, a challenge is navigating a lack of editorial knowledge and finding ways to "cope with a culture of colonized newsrooms" who have "doubted and dismissed my Indigenous knowledge more times than I can count."[80] Monet's path provides an albeit innovative and courageous option given her reliance on varied news organizations to still publish her work.

Others, such as former *Globe and Mail* journalist Sunny Dhillon[81] chose to leave his reporter position at Canada's largest national newspaper, and write an essay, published on Medium and widely retweeted, liked, and commented on Twitter, titled "Journalism while brown and when to walk away."[82] In this example of journalism quit lit, he states, after describing a final difficult conversation with an editor: "What I brought to the newsroom did not matter. And it was at that moment that being a person of colour at a paper and in an industry that does not have enough of us—particularly at the top—felt more futile than ever before."[83] In both cases, Monet and Dhillon are suggesting that their situated knowledge—what they bring respectively as an Indigenous woman and a person of color are relevant to their work as journalists in ways that continue to go unrecognized by newsrooms that are predominantly white and managed by white men.

Scholar-journalists such as Minelle Mahtani are also contributing to developing this meta-narrative through original research and innovative genre experimentation that seeks to decolonize journalism and integrate scholarly critique. As the founding host of one of the country's first radio shows on issues of critical race on Vancouver-based Roundhouse Radio in 2015, Mahtani contributed to the development and practice of a critical journalism in Canada. Similar to the journalists we follow in this section, Mahtani sets out to

> explore my personal and professional ambivalence, through struggles and unsettling moments that have occurred over the past two years, as I created

and hosted a daily radio show entitled 'Sense of Place.' Through a series of vignettes, I focus on the concepts of risk, relation, revolution and repair to share with listeners what anticolonial approaches can do to engage and refuse ongoing forms of colonial violence.[84]

The fact that situated knowledge—and a view from somewhere—can be a form of journalistic expertise is often overlooked by scholars and practitioners. Instead, having knowledge or experience about a particular community or issue is often framed and discussed in terms of "bias," adhering (with or without saying so) to a norm of objectivity: an outside place of knowing that journalists must arrive at in order to produce facts, rationalizing what they do and their stories as requiring a "view from nowhere" to promote democratic participation and diverse audiences. TallBear, drawing on Harding and Haraway, makes it clear that objectivity cannot be conflated with neutrality. She goes on to suggest a programmatic approach for researchers that is highly applicable to journalists as well: "hypotheses, research questions, methods, and valued outputs, including historical accounts, sociological analyses, and textual interpretations must begin from the lives, experiences, and interpretations of marginalized subjects."[85] Additionally relevant, Jasanoff has suggested that expertise is not only about professionalization and attendant skills but also about "something acquired, and deployed, within particular historical, political, and cultural contexts." Given the rapid shifts in audiences, technologies and rising stakes for accurate diagnoses of multi-local problems, considering situated knowledge as a form of expertise in our view reflects the complex globalized systems that journalists are required to navigate.

Experimenting With Standpoint Journalism?

These speculative memoir fragments are appearing on newer global digital sites or social media and in experimental forms such as graphic video. These journalists are exploring experimental practices—innovating—in what Harding calls a "strong objectivity" where technologies, practices, subject positions, and "ways of inhabiting subject positions" must be made "relentlessly visible and open to critical intervention."[86] In news organizations like many institutions, experiments are not generally lauded until long after they've proved successful. Indeed, when journalists reach a certain point in their career, if they've taken risks and/or told what might be considered a "big" story, they are often asked to speak about how they came to or "got" a well-known story. All of these accounts showcase individual journalists experimenting with form and journalism's dominant authority in real time and often in earlier stages of their career.

These experimentations may be being aided by what Picard has called the "deinstitutionalization of news and the profession,"[87] which is destabilizing the historical relationships of journalists and media organizations to roles, norms, content, labor, advertisers, and audiences as well as geographic markets. Journalists are now able to supply content directly to the audience and/or through social media and blogging platforms (e.g., Medium), where we see journalists sharing their speculative memoir accounts. For Picard, some of these newer journalism companies/entities "practise the service mode of news provision" such that "journalists act as suppliers and partners in a business relationship that is very different from that of freelance journalists in the twentieth century."[88]

That Ching's *Correspondent Confidential* series appeared on Vice Media, while the others appear on smaller independent personal blogs or social media, is worth further consideration given the shifting political economy of North American journalism and the market failure of commercial media in a media system defined by commercial media.[89] Vice Media, which launched in Montreal and is now headquartered in New York City, has been considered one of the few wildly successful early stage global journalism organizations, known for its salacious journalism in a company that has been embroiled in its own gender reckoning after sexual harassment complaints surfaced against employees and senior staff.[90] A *New York Times* story suggests there are more than two dozen women who allege they have been harassed or have witnessed sexual misconduct due to a "top-down ethos of male entitlement at Vice."[91]

For Küng, a prominent media management scholar who has studied Vice Media and a number of other global journalism startups, "Vice Media is hard to define—even for itself (it describes itself as 'an ever-expanding nebula of immersive investigative journalism, uncomfortable sociological examination, uncouth activities, making fun of people')."[92] Küng goes on to further identify Vice Media's competitive advantage in a 2016 article that discussed one of her talks:

> Vice Media's core is its digital video offering—what it calls bad boy video. Lucy Kung believes that Vice skews male, BuzzFeed skews female. It has 60 video channels on Vice.com, lots of terrestrial channels including joint documentary services it works on with HBO. Vice content may be aimed at

millennials, but it is high quality all shot to work on multitude of platforms. Vice's trademark is its immersive journalism - the video journalist is very much part of the story.[93]

Küng identifies Vice Media's "true innovation" in "its ability to take traditional sources of competitive advantage from old media and shape them into an organization that can compete in the emerging digital world."[94] In addition, its journalism offers a unique journalist subject position in that it "shuns the 'middle aged talking to the middle aged' or 'young correspondents voicing words written by someone over 50' [interviewee] and instead relies on reports from young multicultural correspondents who find their own stories and tell them in their own words."[95]

Vice Media is not shy about talking about its appeal to global youth (13.5 million people viewed parts or all of its report on the Islamic State on YouTube[96]) and focus on sponsored content for its success.[97] To support its sponsored content model, the company's online empire—which has been described as "leaner and quicker" than mainstream media—spans multiple platforms: websites including Vice.com and Vice News; its YouTube channel; an in-house advertising agency called Virtue; and an ad network that distributes its branded content.[98] Advertisers can choose to go the more traditional ad route and buy banner displays or short ads that run before Vice's videos, or they can fund projects in exchange for editorial input and a credit as co-creator. This native advertising model is effective in part because according to Küng: " 'Generation Y is very cynical about ad messages . . . The Vice model is proper media content that happens to be made by a brand partner.' "[99] It is also not going away as a revenue model. Picard predicts that branded content, "often funded by corporations," will continue as a trend particularly for funding video documentaries, one of Vice's core contributions.[100]

What is clear is that Vice's innovations, coupled with its expressions of the durability of some forms of journalism such as video and tabloid journalism, could be considered a "norm entrepreneur"[101] in an environment in which legacy organizations are struggling. That Vice Media is the site of this critical experimental intervention is perhaps understandable both through what it is trying to intervene in with respect to historic journalism models in addition to its revenue model. In many ways, Vice represents what Chadwick describes as a hybrid media system where old and new media logics clash.[102] The ability of Vice to offer content across multiple platforms is also characteristic of the impact of digitalization on news organizations.[103] Certainly, this era of digital transmedia content—one in which journalists are part of the branding process and manage their own reputations publicly and privately in an increasingly precarious labor context, is worthy of much more in-depth research as Vice and others continue their ascendance.[104] In addition, as traditional boundaries associated with public and commercial goods are up for question, all of these factors combined with increasingly participatory audiences and newer journalism forms and technologies are affecting the kinds of interventions journalists are and are not able to make in their practices.[105]

Animated Graphic Video

In closing, *Correspondent Confidential* has much in common with Sacco's approach to his subject position and visual journalism. He writes himself into his graphic journalism, consistently asking questions about where the journalist is located: This is an example of a journalist actively experimenting in forms while pushing against the profession's dominant authority. For Hodapp, Sacco is inherently postcolonial because of the graphic novel form and that he chooses to focus on the disregarded—what Spivak (1988) has termed "the subaltern"—where the postcolonial condition remains "always on" in the background through the visual context.[106] In this sense, *Correspondent Confidential* has a lot in common visually with a graphic novel, a Ken Burns documentary, and early Flash animations. The graphic, animation style, and illustrator vary across all of the episodes, but in general, journalists recall what happened while reporting on a story or making a film while the camera pans over or zooms into graphic illustrations or animated elements move the graphic illustrations along. The movements act to emphasize dramatic moments in the narrative and provide an interesting (and at times comic) counterpoint.

In using graphic video, *Correspondent Confidential* is able to deconstruct a number of journalism norms and modernist orientations, experimenting with concerns that Carrie Ching identified in the introduction related to how to address difficult topics in a sincere manner. In this way, the use of cartoon-like graphic forms aids a move toward the conceptual and away from some of the ways that journalism has been understood within the profession and scholarship as a descriptive or performative genre. For example, in writing about the use of computer imaging and simulation in documentary filmmaking, Wolf has argued that there is a shift "from the *perceptual* to the *conceptual* . . . that underscores a willingness to exchange direct experience for the abstractions that open up wide vistas not directly available to the senses" (italics original).[107] What results in a simulation is more selective and abstract, severing both an indexical link to reality and freeing imagery from context as well as the burden of claiming to be evidence. Credibility thus lies not with the illustration but with "the discursive field around it"—in the subjunctive or what could have been.[108] The visual seeks to illustrate a narrative in which the real is incommunicable or unrepresentable in current forms, and crucially it brings the viewer into the conceptual field and the reconstructed memories of the journalist.

Graphic video takes the ambiguity a step farther by grouping the stories in a visual landscape that is dislocated in the present, reflecting postcolonial critique, as well as consumptive values that support a view from anywhere.[109] This is consistent with Mehta and Mukherji's argument in their 2015 book on comics and graphic writing, which suggests that postcolonial textualities "enter colonial discourse deconstructively," through "ambiguities and fissures," with "complex signifying resources . . . foregrounding colonial legacies and (re)inscripting missing or misrepresented identities in their precise contexts."[110] These ambiguities, missing identities, and colonial legacies—such as the role of the "fixer"— clearly emerge in the *Correspondent Confidential* accounts. Although their reinscription is still largely unintelligible in a system of journalism still coming to terms with multiple global histories of and ongoing colonialisms.

Finally, the graphic video form confronts journalism's instrumental relationship with its audiences, which we explore in Chapter 2 by including the audience in the storytelling in ways more consistent with memoir than journalism. Graphic novels and cartoons, according to McCloud, illustrate the "world within," and the ways in which words and pictures interact help readers to both identify with and participate in creating this world.[111] Graphic storytelling is thus not only a dance between the seen and unseen but also what the words can convey and what the images might suggest. Crucially, it collapses time and space so that the image and its movement support the speculation that we engage with throughout this chapter about what is happening or has already happened in the course of an act of journalism, engaging our perception of the importance of each element the story introduces. Thus, the form of these specific speculative memoir fragments as both video and graphic act as critique against the truth-telling capacity of the journalist while possibly signaling the capacity for larger truths that incorporate complex subjectivities.

Conclusion

These speculative memoir fragments and emergent meta-genre mark a turn toward vital conversations about the role of subjectivity, journalism practice, and its still-dominant authority. We find journalists engaging in a digital version of Sacco's dinner table conversation—real-time public facing conversations about epistemological concerns across a number of forms and outlets proliferating in a digital context. As Miller and Shepherd suggest, "Genres originate not only from changes in situation, context and culture but also . . . occasionally from the conscious effort of individuals to fill a previously unmet need."[112] The needs that emerged from these speculative memoir fragments are ways to make sense of the changing role and status of the journalist and journalism as a site of knowledge production in a complex global world. Here we find an acknowledgment of the contingency of both journalistic facts and methods, as well as a blurring of the modernist, institutionalized, and distanced journalist subject. In these behind-the-scenes accounts, truth still matters as do claims to truth, but the truth here is messy, plural and implicated, while the journalist is still a gatekeeper and privileged even while precariously placed as a newer freelance actor also reliant on personal brands.[113] For example, even the change agents in *Correspondent Confidential* are struggling with what it is to do journalism in this time but not fully making the connection that knowledge about colonial histories matters. *Correspondent Confidential* as such is confessional in approach but not just a confessional: in that it is at times both critical and defensive. It is also speculative in its attempts to understand how the journalist is coming to terms with their relation to truth, method, and epistemology more broadly in a global digital media landscape.[114]

Gender, race, and privilege remain largely unexamined in *Correspondent Confidential*, although these concerns are more thoroughly and deeply situated in some of the quit lit and other fragments. With respect to quit lit and social media, we find the emergence of situated knowledge as a form of expertise, with journalists of color referencing their labor in navigating a lack of editorial knowledge in newsrooms—and using that expertise to generate newer approaches. Representations of women in *Correspondent Confidential*, while empathetic in tone, still rest on sexualized imagery and gendered norms and practices in the Chakarova case in particular—although with some acknowledgment of the gendered violence faced by women journalists in the course of their roles.[115] In this sense, we see the journalists as subjects in transition signaling some elements of their understanding of their subjectivity and implicatedness as human participants in the world, while clinging to others that reify and reinforce the power of journalists to both tell truths and counter injustice. However, the moral dilemmas are still framed largely at the individual level without a complicated understanding of local, regional, and global impacts of systems of oppression and colonialism.[116]

Finally, this chapter suggests that we cannot understand this reckoning without considering the political economy of digital journalism organizations such as Vice Media and Medium, as well as the sedimentation of norms, which they are both embracing and pushing against. These journalistic actors could be considered part of the new deinstitutionalized players identified earlier by Picard. Part of the Vice brand is "Vice branded" outsider and alternative voices, while Medium is an open source platform where anyone can be a journalist and social media style accountability is embedded (e.g. likes, followers). Journalists are able to capitalize on their position and credibility as journalists with mainstream media outlets such as the *Los Angeles Times*. How these shifts are affecting role identity and power remains to be seen. Technology is also implicated in this context such that innovation has supported a proliferation of alternative international news sources.[117] And there has been the creation of an early career parachute foreign correspondent similar to transitions occurring on the crime beat in the United Kingdom, with earlier career journalists filling what would traditionally have been a more senior newsroom role.[118] The rich irony that branded content is constructed as both outside and inside traditional journalism—and that journalists themselves are engaged in personal branding—signals some of the tensions and precarity of the current political economy and labor context for journalists.

In closing, this meta genre suggests a diminishment of a modern journalistic authority.[119] This is not inconsistent with the wider social and economic contexts and indeed likely related to it.[120] Seeing behind form and structure obliterates parts of the journalistic front stage that is in fact already crumbling while pointing to areas of future possibility.[121] The next chapter continues this discussion in a markedly different context as we deconstruct the journalism crisis, bringing structure alongside issues of intersectionality and colonialism through the case study of a prominent Canadian legacy media organization: the *Toronto Star*.

CHAPTER 4 | Dominant Crisis Narratives and Changing Infrastructures

Introduction

Similar to earlier chapters, we approach technologies as a diagnostic tool for assessing what kind of inquiry structures journalism. We focus on the *Toronto Star*, a legacy journalism organization located in the heart of one of the world's most multicultural cities, with an international profile as a newsroom committed to award-winning social justice, investigative journalism, and improving public policy. Questions about race, gender, and colonialism are central to how the *Star* navigates its coverage and representations of Toronto—as well as its outreach to and representation of an increasingly national audience. Toronto is the fourth-largest city in North America and has a population that is extremely diverse with approximately 50% foreign-born, 50% white, over 50% women, and no predominant ethnic minority. Toronto is known for its many ethnic neighborhoods and enclaves. It has an active urban Indigenous community, with some now calling the city by its Indigenous name, Tkronto.[1]

The *Star* stands for trying to address issues of journalism's role in social ordering that we raise throughout this book through its long-form investigative reporting. However, it is also squarely ensconced in multiple industry crisis narratives, similar to other legacy newspaper and journalism newsrooms. Among journalism platforms, newspaper organizations are considered to be among the hardest hit with the causes identified as technological and economic, such as "outdated business models," declining advertising revenue, an "excessive profit motive," and "technological change."[2]

Technology is a key entry point for understanding the *Star*'s response to the crisis with one of the most dominant narratives exemplified by a quote from David Holland, former CEO of Torstar Corp., which owns the *Star*. In an interview on his retirement after more than 30 years at the organization, Holland responded this way:

'I can't claim that we've cracked the code of what the sustainable position is for great brands like the *Toronto Star*. As much as I'm very proud of my time in the industry today, it's been very hard to figure out how to develop a really sustainable position in the face of significant change,' he says. Holland admits that part of his motivation for retiring at this point is that . . . he feels his skill set no longer matches the reality of the business: 'I think someone who has more DNA about the digital ecosystem is the right person to lead.' He says that maintaining reader engagement is one of the major challenges the *Star* is currently confronting.[3]

Holland's comments are part of an article that attempts to account for a year in which the *Star* became "the story," making a number of headlines for the death of a *Star* journalist, as well as cultural, economic, and technological challenges.[4] The year 2016 began with the departure of publisher John Cruickshank, who had built what would be considered a distinguished journalism career, managing numerous media outlets including *The Globe and Mail*, the CBC, the *Vancouver Sun*, and the *Chicago Sun Times*. A few short months later in May, *Star* journalist Raveena Aulakh died, and the context of her passing became a critical moment for race, gender, and newsroom relations. Aulakh was one of the few women-of-color journalists at the *Star*, and part of a small minority of journalists of color in Canadian media in a white-dominated profession. This is despite more than two decades of diversity initiatives, in addition to increasing multiculturalism in Toronto and the country's other major cities.

In response to results of an internal culture review following Aulakh's death,[5] the *Star* launched a column by Shree Paradkar focused on "identity and discrimination."[6] In an interview, the *Star*'s then managing editor Irene Gentle (now its first woman editor-in- chief in the paper's 127-year history) linked the launch of the column to "broader changes at the *Star* and during an immensely sad time" referring to Aulakh's passing. Paradkar dedicated her first column to Aulakh, headlined, "Lack of Racial Diversity in Media Is a Form of Oppression," in which she outlined the broader challenges facing newspapers and the news industry in general:

Non-representation in journalism is a form of oppression. It happens when we—Canadians—invite or accept newcomers to our mutual benefit, but then allow only one dominant group—whites—to play gatekeeper to all the stories, generation after generation. . . . For an industry that demands transparency from public and private institutions, it offers surprisingly little when it comes to itself. When asked, media organizations have plainly refused to open up. As a result, there is no recent measure of staff diversity or how it is distributed through the ranks.[7]

In juxtaposing these two quotes from Holland and Paradkar, it's apparent how conversations about intersectionality, representation, and labor—and technology and crisis—both collide and are exclusive to each other in discussions about journalism by journalists. Holland's narrative of "significant change" does not refer to the gender, racial, and colonial reckoning with journalism that we find in this book; nor does it seem to explicitly reference the race and gender issues evident at his own paper. What is clear and not contested from an economic perspective is that as Holland suggests in an interview with the *Ryerson Review of Journalism*,[8] it was a much simpler business at the turn of the century for news executives. It was also a simpler business in the decades before and while he was building his career.[9] The business of news entailed selling and managing a single media product that "fits all" with relatively straightforward tech strategies.[10]

The news business now involves multiple niche offerings alongside more complex technologies. Since the 2000s, it has increasingly required a social layer of products, strategy, and resources. This growing complexity has forced media firms to "arbitrage" resources—2016 also included 57 layoffs at the *Star* mostly from the newsroom—while trying to ensure that all parts of the increasingly complex business "talk to each other" as compared to the clearer resource allocation context of the recent past.[11] This complexity extends to the nature of news and journalism itself with its increasingly diverse and often global audiences and multiple platforms for news delivery. Here, nuanced understandings of how STS scholars have tried to distinguish between technology as a revolutionary force and/or continuous presence become a relevant set of questions undergirding perspectives of how change happens in newsrooms and the open or closed nature of its systems and economic decline.[12] This relationship between technology's role and the nature of the system has significant impact on whose knowledge and whose meanings become articulated about and through journalism. For example, Callison's exploration of Indigenous publics and media coverage of climate change found that science can been seen as maintaining the existing social order such that "publics have been imagined and almost 'pre-constituted' by scientific projects and science communication endeavors without an attentiveness to wider commitments and diversities such that certain notions of race and gender are naturalized."[13] This chapter explores a similar set of concerns in relation to technologies and intersectionality, with an overarching goal of questioning "the politics that run through knowledge production at every stage"—in this case, dominant crisis narratives and their responses in a legacy journalism organization.[14]

Narrow Crisis Narratives

Given that newspapers like the *Star* have been seen as "in crisis" for nearly two decades as the Internet has offered audiences alternative digital platforms and news sources, this chapter takes a step back from the proclamations of a state of emergency to consider who and what is in crisis. In deconstructing the notion of crisis and the way it has been deployed in contemporary public discourse about journalism in Canada, it becomes clear that while there are significant challenges to the advertising model for commercial newspapers along with readership decline, the conversation has been narrowly circumscribed to the point that related and chronic representational issues aren't co-considered as either relevant or crises. Technology and economics, though audience-related and dependent in some senses, are somehow seen to be separate spheres for analyses unrelated to alienated and marginalized publics.

Technologies as a diagnostic helps explore changes that have been framed as a "crisis," and whether crisis is even a generative way of talking about and understanding what is happening in a domain as complex as journalism.[15] According to Zelizer, the term "crisis" as it has been deployed in journalism is both problematic and possibly even more wide ranging than the unitary temporal and geographic phenomenon that it has been characterized as:

Occupationally, the traditional view of what journalism should be— objective, detached, balanced—no longer holds. And technologically, the rise and entrenchment of digital media make most explicit what journalism has always tried to keep in its background—its problems with authoritative storytelling, separation from the public, reluctant response to calls for transparency, cozying up to officialdom. In this regard, the challenges facing journalism loom menacingly across all of its contours and have prompted doomsday-sayers everywhere to predict journalism's demise.[16]

The concerns then are both potentially broader and more specific than the term "crisis" can contain, describe, or imagine—or has largely been deployed to date. The title of Picard's Picard's 2014 journal article, "Twilight or New Dawn of Journalism?"[17] suggests a more nuanced and open-ended discussion of the contemporary economic context of journalism and notion of a unitary crisis narrative than more provocative titles such as McChesney and Pickard's edited book, *Will the Last Reporter Please Turn Out the Lights*. This chapter builds on some of these approaches and connects to what is set aside in analyses of technology and economics as articulations of both the source of and solution to the crisis.

The journalism crisis we are exploring has its own time, place, and narrative related to what journalism "should be" in Canada, which is defined by a largely commercial media system with a public service broadcaster, albeit a significantly underfunded one compared to its global peers.[18] The past few years have seen substantial cuts in the number of journalists at legacy media organizations across the country from buyouts, layoffs, and closures.[19] In response to these concerns, the federal government commissioned a 2017 report on the state of the media, entitled "Shattered Mirror: News, Democracy and Trust in the Digital Age," which has become a benchmark document in the construction of the crisis. The report mentions the word "crisis" 12 times, claiming at one point that "we are certainly witnessing a crisis for the traditional news industry." Specifically, the report found that "once indispensable agencies of information, the 20th-century news media are less and less prominent, except to provide grist for a public conversation they no longer control."[20] It goes on to caution:

Journalists, media executives, academics and policy analysts are all wrestling with what the waning status of traditional journalism truly portends. Are we merely passing through a turbulent transition to a more open and diverse future, or witnessing something that could inflict lasting damage on democracy? What interventions are warranted if the new information marketplace proves to be a poor guardian of the public good–if not, in fact, antithetical to it? Can we afford to wait and find out?[21]

The report was coordinated by Edward Greenspon, former editor in chief of *The Globe and Mail*, and former senior manager at the *Toronto Star*. Greenspon has been one of the main advocates for the country's ailing journalism organizations as both an analyst and advocate for the industry.[22] Similar to Holland, with whom we begin this chapter, his narratives largely frame the "crisis" as an economic, business model, and technological concern and arguably informed the government policy response.[23] That the crisis is also personal for Greenspon is apparent in the report's last paragraph:

> Two decades into its existential crisis, the news is in a state of distress and the social glue I encountered as a youngster is losing its capacity to bind. This report diagnoses the problem and offers up ideas as to what can be done. We at the Public Policy Forum hope our analysis and recommendations will stimulate a necessary debate and some carefully calibrated action to preserve a foundational social good.[24]

Another prominent figure in the movement to economically shore up journalism in Canada is Torstar Corp. Chair, John Honderich.[25] He is a member of one of the *Toronto Star*'s five controlling families who "took control of the *Star* after the death of owner and publisher Joseph E. Atkinson in 1948."[26] That journalism insiders from respected news organizations are sharing advice, analysis, and promoting a specific public policy course is in and of itself productive and relevant to understanding the state of the industry. However, their experiences and relations within media suggest a certain historical, normative, and medium slant that is also evident in the PPF report, which advocates for government subsidies for the journalism sector—subsidies that were announced in late 2018 in the amount of nearly $600 million. It makes 12 recommendations to nationally subsidize and further regulate a business model that it says has collapsed and now poses a threat to democracy in its waning ability to fulfill its role in society. The logic follows that journalism, even while it's an enterprise and must maintain its independence from the governments it seeks to hold accountable, also deserves and needs to be protected in the face of technological and economic challenges. Yet, this logic, according to political economists Compton and Dyer-Witheford, has resulted in contradictory and competing outcomes, with media firms merely replicating existing power relations while promoting the dominant "residual traditions of journalistic responsibility, serious reporting and investigative disclosure."[27]

Ken Whyte, founding editor of the *National Post*—one of Canada's two national newspapers—exposed the stakes and colonial power relations at play in less than 140 characters when he tweeted after the release of the PPF report on January 26, 2017: "But in the end, if they're going to spend another 100 million, at least this time it goes to my friends #ppf #cdnpoli."[28] He described the report as, "overall, reads like terrified response of high priests of Ptolemaic astronomy to the spread of the Copernican hypothesis #ppf #cdnpoli."[29] So while Whyte may not want to participate in the emotional tenor of a crisis narrative, he certainly considers himself able to understand the nature of the system and who stands to benefit from financial redress. Given his response, it's not insignificant to note that the *Post* is generally speaking on the right side of the political spectrum as opposed to the *Globe* and the *Star* that are considered center and left, respectively.

That Greenspon and Honderich, both white men located in central Canada, are also some of the prominent voices of the "crisis" and its transformation in Canada, raises questions about who and what are being left out given Roitman's conceptualization of how the framing of a "crisis" is ultimately teleological in its articulation and resolution—and therefore rooted in exclusions.[30] It is consistent with critique from postcolonial scholars on how it is important it is to understand the development of media technologies in relationship to larger social systems, organizations, and cultures. Specifically, in the case of the journalism crisis in Canada, the relationship of these structures to imagined futures when the public is funding those aspirations.[31] And here, there are multiple considerations according to Felt, which include:

> Who has a voice to make legitimate knowledge claims, who defines what matters, or who participates in imagining and shaping the future? . . . Asking these 'who questions' points to concerns not only about actors and identities but also about exclusion, oppression, inequality, and social justice. It means proactively looking for resistance to conventional knowledge orders, for dissident voices, for neglected knowledge and experiences, and for alternative conceptualizations of progress and futures.[32]

When it comes to journalism, such questions and observations are not mere sidebars but reveal the deeper challenges in understanding the state of the industry and its proposed solutions. In this case, the dominant narrative of a journalism crisis rooted in the decline and market failure in commercial media in Canada caused in large part by technological change, and its corollary that there should be an independent profitable journalism industry dedicated to democratic engagement, points to its inevitable resolution: funding for transformation of the existing industry with the main focus on newspapers.[33]

Perhaps it should not be unanticipated then that the government started to support local journalism in the 2018 federal budget with $50 million in funding —$10 million a year over five years—to fund "one or more independent non-governmental organizations that will support local journalism in underserved communities."[34] That same day, the CBC's flagship morning radio program, *The Current*, had Greenspon and David Beers, founder of *theTyee.ca*, one of the early award-winning digital media startups in Canada (and an adjunct professor at the University of British Columbia School of Journalism where we also teach) as guests. Beers and his Vancouver-based journalism organization, *theTyee.ca*, are singled out as a cautionary tale in the 2017 PPF report as evidence of the economic underperformance of digital startups in Canada, *without* the relevant context that literature on media startups globally suggests "there is not a single working business model . . . but this does not mean these startups are not making it work as business."[35] Thus, the funding, its coverage and support for the "crisis" is disappointing, not for its support of quality journalism, but for the narrow range of voices able to make legitimate knowledge claims about what is quality journalism, the "crisis," and its resolution, in what has been and continues to be a medium to highly concentrated industry in Canada.

The conversation on *The Current* might have sounded different had it included Erin Millar, founder of *the Discourse*, and Linda Solomon Wood, founder of the *National Observer*—two of the few women who own and operate journalism organizations in Canada.[36] The conversation would have been quite different again if Indigenous journalism organizations, such as Aboriginal People's Television Network (APTN) or *Media Indigena*, a new crowdfunded digital podcast, had been included.[37] Or if the discussion had included one of Canada's approximately 300 ethnic print journalism organizations and numerous broadcast media—both growing journalism sectors.[38]

Taking into account Zelizer and Roitman's approaches to understanding crisis as discursive constructs that rest "on particular temporalities and geographies at the core of its imaginary," the framing of the PPF report and the crisis narrative in Canadian journalism more broadly is open to interrogation about its own articulation of "discursive cues set in place long ago to a now outdated and spatially narrow notion," and "understanding of institutional disarray and of what was required to control it."[39] In other words, PPF follows a well-trodden path of defending certain media in distinctive terms and language. Such articulations chart a path that sets up exclusion zones reflective of both geography and other fault lines in Canadian society.

These geographies and temporalities reflected in the PPF report would position Toronto as a main site of journalism power for English-language commercial legacy media that emerged alongside settler-colonialism.[40] By contrast, APTN, the first national Indigenous broadcaster in the world, has distinguished itself in many ways in terms of its multiple and decolonizing contributions and innovations in content and infrastructure.[41] These include its award-winning investigative journalism on issues such as housing, water, Idle No More, and MMIWG, which it helped put on the news agenda. APTN launched in Winnipeg in 1999 during the early Internet era, and is now among the few—but growing number of—charitable journalism organizations in Canada. It is also serving audiences more often than not marginalized by legacy media. A submission by APTN to the Standing Committee on Canadian Heritage in 2009 on its 10-year anniversary about government funding bias for journalism organizations identifies how power is assigned to audiences according to region:

> The audience in Iqaluit is not the same as the audience in the Greater Toronto Area—and the potential return from these audiences is, obviously, not comparable. It is a real question for us whether smaller audiences, in Iqaluit, Thomson or even Regina and Winnipeg, for example, will be given the same kind of weight as an audience in Toronto when funding decisions are made.[42]

That audiences are valued differently has been one of commercial journalism's developments over the previous century with higher income, professional, and educated audiences largely rating as more valuable than others.

Another exclusion is the growing number of digital journalism startups, which range from nonprofit to commercial/nonprofit hybrids and university initiatives that have launched since the end of the last century and early 21st century across Canada.[43] These newer digital players have been constructed as lacking the resources, expertise, and time "to get to the bottom of the story or to get onto serious investigative journalism, which to me is key," journalism ideals that are not linked to data on shared definitions of what is quality journalism, who is doing it, and evidence of its consistent articulation.[44] According to Winseck, similar arguments have been effective in securing government support in the past as Canadian Radio-Television and Telecommunications (CRTC) decisions have favored established "media providers on the dubious grounds that they possess the deep pockets and inclination to invest in . . . high quality journalism."[45]

If the list of newer players included APTN, one could see what has been circumscribed as a period of crisis during the past two decades as a nascent, vital, decolonizing, growing, and challenging economic space in the history of journalism in Canada. Here digital born organizations as well as CBC, could be seen as strategic investments given that, according to Winseck, Internet news has the lowest concentration and is arguably the most competitive and future-focused journalism space in Canada compared to more highly concentrated domains, such as newspapers (moderate) and broadcast journalism, which have greater systematic barriers to entry.[46] The losses are substantial in having a few industry insiders speak for the "crisis" and the future of journalism.[47] Given that numerous and sometimes contested understandings of what journalism can and should do—and indeed multiple journalisms as we argue in this book are already being practiced in North America—it's clear that the country's English- language newspaper journalism elite represents one set of approaches to both media in Canada and their crisis. Broader analysis reveals that there are competing framings of the nature of the cause of the problems confronting journalism and its possible solutions-and that ways of defining quality journalism are changing in this digital reckoning.[48] There are a number of other approaches rooted in competing conceptualizations of what is journalism and journalism authority that we explore in the next section.

Chronic Inequities and Erasure

In the last chapter, we argue for situated knowledge as a form of expertise, particularly for journalists who are addressing issues related to gender, race, and colonialism. Given the demographics of Toronto, and the lack of diversity in the *Star* newsroom as well as its commitment to social justice and public policy, situated knowledge provides a starting point for examining chronic problems related to journalism epistemology, representations and inequities. However, an examination of chronic problems can't happen separate from discussions of crisis and its exclusionary articulations. Desmond Cole, a prominent Black journalist who made national headlines when he left his regular columnist role at the *Star* in early 2017 after he was criticized for doing activism, not journalism, is an example of where these concerns intersect. Cole left the *Star* after his coverage of a Toronto Police Services board meeting in which he protested the police practice of gathering information based on race.[49] In a column by the *Star*'s public editor, the paper claimed that his actions and stance were counter to newsroom policy according to its *Journalistic Standards Manual* that states: "It is not appropriate for *Star* journalists to play the roles of both actor and critic."[50] The *Star* responded to Cole's actions by citing the "rules," a reference to journalism's heavily critiqued dominant authority on stance.

In a blog post about his departure, Cole described a meeting with the *Star*'s editorial page editor about how his journalism, which can be constituted as having a view from somewhere, contravened the organization's norms:

> This week I met with Andrew Phillips, the Toronto Star's editorial page editor, who has essentially served as my boss at the newspaper. Phillips called me in regarding my political disruption of the April 20 meeting of the Toronto Police Services Board. Phillips said this action had violated the Star's rules on journalism and activism. He didn't discipline me or cite any consequence for my actions—Phillips said he just wanted me to know what the Star's rules are. I have no formal employment with the Star. I've never signed any contract or agreement, and no one ever directed me to any of the policies Phillips cited. However, I knew my police protest was activism, and I could have guessed the Star wouldn't appreciate it. At no time during this week's meeting did Phillips try to tell me how I must conduct myself in the future. He did say he hopes I will continue my bi-monthly column. I appreciate the offer but I'm not going to accept it. If I must choose between a newspaper column and the actions I must take to liberate myself and my community, I choose activism in the service of Black liberation.[51]

That this was the organization's response after it hired Cole in the role of columnist, a role defined by point of view and expertise, says more about journalism and its challenges with integrating structural concerns than it does about his journalism. This is where who is speaking, what it tells us about journalism methods, and the profession's imagined future, is revealing. As author of "one of only three columns written by a Black journalist at any major daily print publication" in Canada according to Domise, Cole had been writing about issues related to race for a decade.[52]

In a 2015 interview with *J-Source*, he talked about his journey into full-time journalism.

> I didn't take a conventional path. I was blogging and writing my own things from time to time. And I had written about racial profiling and started publishing things in other places. More than five years ago now, some folks at Torontoist, including David Topping and Hamutal Dotan, approached me and said, 'We'd really like you to write for us.' I was really shy and didn't think a whole lot of my writing. I usually wrote when I got angry—it was just kind of venting. So when they said . . . to come and write for them, I didn't really take them up on it. Then I wrote a piece on how police were being introduced to our schools—something I thought was a terrible idea. Torontoist asked if they could reprint this. I was surprised, and then I thought maybe I should start doing this seriously.[53]

In the interview, Cole also discussed his anti-racist approach to journalism. He said that he is "intentional about bringing these issues to my work . . . that in my particular case has something to do with my experiences being a Black person growing up in Canada." He then added but "our media doesn't like to talk about racism."

Of Toronto's metropolitan audience, 8.9% of its population is Black, the third-largest visible minority group after South Asian and Chinese, which accounts for almost 50% of the city combined.[54] Yet, the lack of diversity in newsrooms is such a problem that Shree Paradkar called out Canadian media, including the *Star,* for their "antediluvian" approach to race in a 2016 column:

> The major newsrooms in this country—the *Toronto Star* included—are unnaturally white. Journalism is a field so antediluvian it is patting itself on its back for opening up to women—white women. I invite any media organization that wants to challenge that assertion to share its racial diversity data.[55]

This has been a perennial question for journalism organizations. Researchers started to explore issues of race and journalism in Canadian newsrooms in the 1980s, largely using qualitative interviews with journalists to examine diversity in newsrooms.[56] One of the early studies by Pritchard and Sauvageau (1998) found that 97% of newsrooms were white.[57] Miller associated lack of diversity with a decline in media quality in his late 20th-century book *Yesterday's News: Why Canada's Newspapers Are Failing Us*. While there have been attempts to improve diversity over the past

20 years from the CBC and journalism organizations more generally, racial groups remain under-represented, and organizations are increasingly criticized for that lack of representations by journalists of color, which we discuss in the previous chapter,[58] compared to their proportion of the general population.[59]

What happens when the newsroom's white hegemony is called out, and how is it taken up? What happens when journalists are no longer able to understand themselves and their roles from solely talking among themselves? And, further, what happens when that shared history and hegemony include historic harms? Finally, what happens when some of journalism's main norms and practices of "speaking for" the public are disrupted as rooted in a paternalist and power-laden view from nowhere, and that public becomes multiple publics who increasingly matter to journalism's future?

These questions underlay some of the core under-addressed challenges facing journalists today as journalists have used their understanding of prominent past events and shared notions of history to construct their professional identity and sense of community.[60] Zelizer describes how journalists judge and generate "meaning about journalism."[61] They do this through an internal/intra "shared discourse and interpretations of key public events."[62] For example, the Newseum in Washington, DC (which is scheduled to close at the end of 2019) is a museum devoted to the history of U.S. journalism. The museum narrates the civil rights era as a triumph for journalism and journalists who shed light on protests, police brutality, and injustice without any suggestions about the persistent whiteness in journalism then and now. Zelizer suggests that in a professional understanding of journalism, it is "journalists' ability to decide what is news" that "has constituted the expertise that distinguishes them from non-reporters" with that expertise deployed largely on behalf of the audience, and indeed, paradoxically often in lieu of explicit audience agency.[63] It is in this way that journalism becomes a surrogate for the public, acting on behalf of a generalized public and/or ideal: in this case, democracy. Professionalism and the ability to decide on behalf of and to speak for and to the audience also required a need to claim an authoritative stance, which emerged through the deployment of objectivity as a method for truth telling.[64] Journalists in this view became "objective neutral balanced chroniclers" in order to "offset the dangers inherent in the subjectivity of reporting":[65]

> journalists' authority is assumed to derive from their presence at events, from the ideology of eyewitness authenticity. In producing metaphors like

'eyewitnessing,' 'watchdogs' 'being there' practices of discovery or 'being on the spot,' reporters establish markers that not only set up their presence but also uphold its ideological importance.[66]

It is not surprising then that objectivity remains a dominant stance despite the critique, as it underpins so much of how North American journalists see themselves, their role, and why they matter for audiences. It is also not surprising given that accountability in this system has largely been understood in relationship to sourcing; as an insider's responsibility in the form of editors, ombuds, and/or reader editors; and as part of the overall "interpretive community" function of journalists. This accountability that is internal to journalism is confounded and supported by journalism's underacknowledged history of exclusion and the digital reckoning that we explored in Chapter 2. It is also reinforced by the distance and focus on elite power relations consistent with critique about the nature of professional journalism organizations and power. Prominent media economics scholar Picard is one of the key voices supplying commentary on journalism's power relations alongside an economic analysis. In his assessment of the changing relationship with audiences necessary in a context of digitalization, Picard identifies relational distance less in epistemology and more in the nature of journalism's closed professional community.

> News organizations and journalists will need to interact with audiences in new ways that are outside their comfort zones. This is problematic because journalism has traditionally had highly paternalistic role definitions, seeing its functions as educating the rabble, guiding thought and opinion, protecting social order, and comforting the people. These definitions combine with professional values promoting wariness of social alliances and distrust of sources of information to make most journalists stand separate from the society and people they cover.[67]

Cole's articulation of his contributions to *Star* journalism is relevant in thinking through these historic relationships and their implications for whose voices have been and continue to be excluded from defining the journalism crisis and its solutions:

> I doubt any freelance columnist in the recent [or even not so recent] history of the Star has consistently generated more interest and readership, and consequently more revenue, than I have. . . . I believe I have been good for business during a time when our industry is desperate for new voices

and new readers. Although I was recently warned about my actions, the Star's leadership has previously warned me about its limited appetite for my very political and unapologetically Black voice. In April of 2016, John Honderich, the chair of Torstar Corp., who was also serving as the Star's acting publisher at that time, asked to meet with me. Honderich suggested I was writing about race too often, and advised me to diversify my topics. The next day I published a piece in support of Yusra Khogali, a Black Lives Matter Toronto co-founder who was the subject of a racist, Islamophobic campaign to distract from her activism. It was the most popular piece I wrote all year—my editor contacted me to congratulate me on its reach.[68]

Reading Cole's experience illustrates that it is not merely a matter of hiring more bodies or enacting affirmative action-style policies. Rather, as Ahmed's research on equity in higher education and institutions broadly outlines, diversity strategies and approaches in and of themselves do not and will not address systemic exclusions in journalism.[69] It is here that we are trying to make our intervention in the ways that journalism and the industry's construction of innovation and technology have largely excluded ways of knowing that destabilized hegemonic power relations in the field and/or institution of journalism. Or as Kreiss pointed out in a 2019 tweet in relation to fake news (which is relevant to conversations about technology and journalism), "It's a hell of a lot easier talking about fake news than identity and race."[70] Alongside these exclusions, technology as we discuss in other chapters, is useful as a diagnostic of shifting power relations more than as it is commonly framed—solely as the magic bullet that has irrevocably changed journalism and might be its savior.

Data Journalism as Diagnostic

"Changing Infrastructures"

With an eye to technologies, proclamations of "crisis" and its exclusions, we turn now to examine data journalism—an emergent technology dependent category of journalism. We are interested in how a legacy media company widely respected for its commitment to quality journalism is incorporating technology as a response to digitalization, crisis, and an extension of its focus on investigative, computer-assisted reporting.[71] We define data journalism with the widest possible remit: as a subfield of journalism with a range of practices and processes that are still developing, including a unique set of forms, professional roles, and identities.[72] We include the caveat that a specific definition is difficult to identify "as it would require normalising tensions between the competing ontological features displayed by a variety of journalistic methodologies that deal with data."[73] It's in this sense that data journalism and data journalists provide a diagnostic for understanding journalism's dominant method and approaches in a time of change and articulations of crisis and relations with technology given that data practices are proliferating and becoming an "integral part of many newsrooms."[74] And the practices are also starting to align processes of production with consumption.[75] These shifting geographies and temporalities suggest a newly explicit link to publics and knowledge about the audience-journalist relationship—"the who" journalists have long been claiming to speak for. In a sense, data journalism begins to open up the sutures that have long been maintained in legacy media.

The *Star* is nearly as old as Canada itself. The first edition published in the fall of 1892, about 25 years after Confederation in 1867. The history the *Star* tells about itself sounds, ironically, like one we might hear now about the launch of an online news source: a group of people disgruntled in their roles at mainstream news organizations, launching their own news outlet.

> Born on November 3, 1892, The *Evening Star* had been created almost overnight by 21 printers and four teenage apprentices who were locked out during a labour dispute at the afternoon News. Their aim was to publish a serious journal—and possibly to teach the News a lesson. Little did they realize that their bright new four-page sheet would grow into Canada's largest daily newspaper, The *Toronto Star*. Those printers may have lacked capital and business experience. But they were inspired by the hope that a paper reflecting the concerns of working people like themselves could catch on in an already overcrowded field.[76]

The *Star* tells its own history as one of a dream that eventually became a business, complete with a merger with other newspaper chains and the eventual launch in the early 1990s of a $400 million printing press. In 2016, the newsroom was a quiet cavernous open concept room, with numerous seemingly unoccupied desks located in an office tower in the heart of downtown Toronto—evidence of both the decreasing number of journalists since the beginning of the century and the paper's historic site as an important hub of metropolitan news. Senior newsroom managers occupied the offices with windows on one side of the newsroom, with a few conference rooms, with news meetings of about 20 editors—a balance of almost exclusively white men and women—held in the center of the newsroom a few times daily. A screen that showed images being considered for the *Star*'s journalism products was located at one end of the table—and one of the few visual nods to technology in the newsroom aside from computers. In contrast to the space and openness of the newsroom, there was a clear, yet implicit hierarchy, with seats reserved for individual editors.. One editor quipped after a meeting in 2016: "Sometimes someone changes places and it freaks everyone out."

According to Deuze, newsroom geographies are leaner, a sign of industry decline as well as pressures to converge multiple organizational functions.

> Today's newsroom looks quite different than those of the mid-to late twentieth century—as they are largely empty [because of mass lay-offs and outsourcing practices], as well as gradually transforming into integrated operations where content, sales, marketing and a host of other functions [including circulation management, design, multimedia operations, and IT services] are supposed to converge.[77]

The *Star* specifically has seen a harrowing 64% decline in the number of its journalists in the early 21st century from 475 people in 2004 to 170 in 2016.[78] Data journalists are an emergent professional identity in this changing landscape as both a newer category and one that acts across traditionally separate organizational functions. In 2016, the *Star* had decentralized pockets of data expertise, which included a small data visualization team (three people), people experienced with data associated with the Star.com, investigative journalists, as well as individuals in disparate areas of the news organization from audience and product development to advertising, circulation, and business geomatics. Three years later, there is a significantly increased interest internally on data, with a *Walrus* article quoting secondhand the paper's new publisher—whose leadership background includes data-driven marketing and analytics—as "we can't be a department store anymore," the newspaper needs to "learn what readers want" through an increased focus on data.[79] As of 2019, the *Star* now has a formal data desk of three reporters and two manager/editors, and others (up to 10) in data-related and investigative roles throughout the newsroom, plus four digital designers and a database specialist on retainer outside of the newsroom (who is not in the union).[80] These figures are consistent with numbers in global newsrooms that have the biggest commitment to data expertise according to a 2017 survey of data journalism that included 206 participants from 43 countries.[81] A study of Canadian data journalists found these individuals increasingly mobile, extending beyond historic geographies and rigid boundaries relative to their physical location in newsrooms.[82]

Today these data journalists and analysts do an increasing range of work across various floors and departments. They are focused in four main areas: investigative, methods support, presentation/visual journalism, and audience analytics/audience relations. On the business side there is also research and product development, which uses some of the data analysts, and is not considered data journalism. Some of these roles elicited confusion in 2016, with Matthew Cole, a data analyst with a wider remit that crosses some of the business functions at the *Star*, indicating there was uncertainty about where to put his desk:

> I was the odd duck out and I needed a desk and they knew it didn't matter where I sat so they gave me the choice of the back of finance . . . or Torstar legal. I'm like, 'I'll take the lawyers.'

As of 2019, Cole has had ten different desks on a number of floors. A few journalists also indicated there was some historic negotiation about professional identity, union membership, and pay rates (in this case lower) related to attempts to bring a new category of digital journalists, which included some data journalists, into the newsroom.[83]

These tensions are relevant to the growing ways that data is being used at the *Star* between the newsroom and some of the organization's traditional business functions such as user analytics and experiences—areas normally kept quite distant in modern understandings of what is journalism. One interview subject described the growing interrelationship between these areas:

> The way my team operates with the newsroom is that we report on user behaviour in terms of top content that's read on the site, top videos that are viewed and answering any questions they may have if they're trying to add or modify content. We support the sales team when it comes to helping them with pitches to sell advertisement on our site, what the traffic is to a particular page, etc. We also support the product team when they're thinking of doing any changes to our products. They'll ask for data on how our users are using a particular component and whether we can experiment with the components. Lastly, we support our engineering tech team by monitoring

the data for any odd spikes or dips in traffic and advising them so that they can go and take a further look.[84]

From an organizational perspective, these cross-domain roles related to audiences are also tied to resources with data analytics considered important factors in deciding how to allocate resources. Here the movement of data practices between and beyond the newsroom suggests that the "the production-consumption divide [which] is still an important dynamic in many media and information contexts" is breaking down.[85] The turn to include data about audiences and the public within the newsroom is thus both a significant transformation within journalism organizations and circumscribed challenge to professional identity.[86] Zelizer's contribution to understanding the journalist-audience relationship then is relevant to assessing the degree of innovation and adaptation in this space, given the instrumental role that audiences have performed for legacy journalism organizations, such that they were rendered invisible to the news process yet highly important for coalescing and cementing the appearance of epistemological coherence through professional ideology and groupthink.[87]

Accountability: When Objectivity and Balance Are Not Good Enough

Interview subjects experienced this expansion of the role of data journalists and its challenges in complicated ways. They identified their skills as highly sought after, contested, misunderstood, and at times undervalued, which is consistent with literature on the emerging journalist technologist in which newsrooms revert to traditional practice.[88] One interview subject said that he was in high demand for support for news content that involved quantitative data and visual data. Another indicated that the newsroom in 2016 was still in the "integration phase" for data journalism and analytics, describing the results as "interesting" and expansive for journalism content as well as growing "all over the place" for analytics and user experience more generally.[89] Other subjects shared experiences of interest and demand in addition to resistance and misunderstanding about their roles in the organization both in story generation and in the business-oriented functions. That journalists are struggling to make sense of the complexity of data journalism's addition to what is journalism is not surprising given its wide range of activities, motives, scope, and methodological complexities.

The proliferation of data journalists, analytics, data practices, and expertise is evidence that the *Star*—similar to other studies in technology adaptation—is incrementally adapting in the digital journalism landscape. This continual adaptation is often missed in internal narratives such as Holland's story of change that we began this chapter with, as well as industry critiques of the *Star* that indicate it is struggling to shift with the times.[90] The continuity view of technological adoption is relevant as the *Star* is also building on decades of "groundbreaking stories" in computer-assisted journalism. For example, according to Bozckowski and Lievrouw, "the continuity view rejects the revolutionary rhetoric and asserts that the social consequences of technological change tend to be more gradual and incremental because they are necessarily situated within the context of established technologies, practices, and institutions."[91] Of the range of activities, it was clear in the interviews that using data and statistical experts in the course of a major investigation was of high value, as well as a clearly understood and systematic methodological contribution to quality journalism at the *Star*.

Its value became less clear when data was integrated into more traditional news stories. Consistent with literature from journalism studies, which has examined the rising number of journalist/technologists and their integration into newsrooms, it has been difficult for the technologists to contribute to existing norms and practices. Heravi's study indicates that data journalists see their role as adding "accountability" within journalism, which is relevant to the main area that data journalists found some contestation—methods, specifically assessing the validity of data, how to describe it and interpreting results.[92] One early career data journalist found his attempts to integrate data journalism into the newsroom challenging when he was working on a complex story about a ranking project in Toronto.

> I was trying to fight against just making a 'this is the best' and 'this is the worst' and I was trying to get rid of a top ten list and rather say it's sort of an open debate and this is what the data shows us . . . Trying to make it not just black and white this is the best this is the worst, it was more open to interpretation. I've written an entire methodology section so people can go through it and say you know I agree with this, I don't agree with this and they can make their own ideas.[93]

In this case trying to unpack the demand for facts over interpretation, evidence and accountability were part of the challenge for a data journalist working in a legacy newsroom. Anticipating disagreement over method meant that methods for interpretation needed to be made legible—something that isn't commonly done in legacy journalism where implicit socialization is usually the mode through which news values and styles of interpretation are learned and adopted.[94]

Data journalism thus requires an articulation of methodological values as they are imbricated in methods for identifying, understanding, and interpreting data and in the production and narration of facts for public consumption. As Felt indicates, there are "regimes of valuation which foreground some values," and in journalism it has been the notion that facts are separate from interpretation, and either/or binary thinking is prioritized in a newsroom context as is the face value of source expertise over validating the quality of the information.[95] This rejection of the role of interpretation and importance of assessing the validity of information along a continuum complicates the way that journalists deal with content, particularly in a context of emergent data journalism where there can be both methodological demands and sense making that require a deeper engagement with the nature of the evidence. This data journalist talked about how challenging it can be for data journalists to share charts and datasets in a context where interpretation, in this case, often statistical, can be required:

> There's a lack of communication in coordination and in the events where some folks have gone on and we've basically given them what is a stripped-down version of a bar graph or something that we've created, basically just . . . the raw numbers. A number of times the execution has been misleading . . . and [they have] not realized the correlations and interpretations that they're making. They lack the expertise on their side.[96]

Another example of the need for interpretation emerged from a data journalist recounting working on a story that emerged from a freedom of information request for transit offences in Toronto on all bus routes. He recalled a colleague identifying the potential of data to help a story and asking: "How can we make this interesting or what is this telling us?"[97] He said they worked together, and in the process he suggested a bar chart, a map to make it "more interesting on the web," in addition to a conversation about which numerical information was important.[98] This data analyst added, "I think my role in the story was just as important" as the more narrative aspects of the story. These disputes tend to be talked about and understood as technology clashes in journalism studies as well as within news discourse. Zelizer makes a contribution to reframing these discussions, however, as potentially more about how "neglected knowledges" are taken up in journalism by using her framework of "interpretative communities" to unpack the hidden "elaborate mechanisms" by which journalists construct their reality. She singles out journalists' relationship with narratives and how they have "ascribed to themselves the power of interpretation" without fully understanding how that power operates.[99] In trying to make sense of that power without a full understanding—and to be fair, as Borges-Rey suggests, there are indeed deep ontological questions with respect to data and journalism methods specifically—journalists often resort to ideal typical values.

At the *Star*, an underlying sense-making tool for a number of the journalists interviewed involved the Atkinson principles as part of its commitments and history of high-impact journalism investigations. The *Star* has used data journalism and computer-assisted reported to execute on these principles with numerous award-winning contributions that have had significant impact on public policy. These investigations have taken on a range of issues, many including race and criminal justice.[100] They have also required financial commitment on behalf of the *Star* which has spent tens of thousands of dollars on Freedom of Information requests to access public data.[101]

These principles emerge from publisher Joseph Atkinson, who was employed by and editor of the newspaper in the late 19th and early 20th centuries. According to the *Star*'s website, "He was particularly concerned about injustice, be it social, economic, political, legal or racial"[102] with his central principles identified as: "a strong, united and independent Canada, social justice, individual and civil liberties, community and civic engagement, the rights of working people, the necessary role of government."[103]

Referencing the Atkinson principles could be considered reflective of the organization's historic normative commitment to a certain kind of "progressive" journalism that "should contribute to the advancement of society through pursuit of social, economic, and political reforms."[104] A number of interview subjects mentioned the principles as a way to situate their journalism decision making about what's important. However, while the Atkinson principles espouse a distinct approach to journalism and social justice, they also promote nation building of a particular kind—one that has been dangerous to and incommensurate with Indigenous peoples, their self-governance, and sovereignty.[105] According to Simpson, these silences and "process of elimination . . . marks the settler-colonial project" and the colonial violence implicated in a "united" Canada.[106] Vimalassery, Hu Pegues, and Goldstein extend the analysis to the concept of a deliberate "colonial unknowing" and disavowal, which is not primarily a matter of a forgotten or hidden past, at least to the extent that forgetting might be viewed as a passive relation or a concealed past might suspend culpability. Instead this ignorance—this act of ignoring—is aggressively made and reproduced, actively invested and effectively distributed in ways that conform the social relations and economics of the here and now.[107]

It is also consistent with the history of systemic representational concerns and stereotyping of Indigenous peoples in Canadian print journalism.[108] Indeed, this colonial critique, as other chapters in this book argue, is still relatively nascent despite its necessary and transformative potential by calling into question whose social order is being upheld by and for journalism.

Closed Systems

The focus internally on the need for digital DNA and revolution may signify less about the *Star*'s ability to adapt technologically, as these capacities are evident in interviews that indicate growth in data journalism practices across and beyond the newsroom consistent with studies of other global journalism organizations. It may signify more about the nature of the organization as Canada's largest English-language metropolitan daily newspaper with the only explicit and historic commitment to uphold a set of long-standing principles. A story written by Sean Craig in 2016 in the *Financial Post* indicated, "The *Star* has been called the best investigative newspaper in Canada."[109] Such accolades are relevant to considering observations about change more broadly by Küng, a prominent media management scholar, that "the more successful the organization has been, the stronger the culture, the tighter the management, and the higher the hurdles to change are likely to be."[110]

Herein lies the multiple challenges that this chapter records of managing and advancing traditional notions of "success" via awards, technological advances and integration, and differentiation in mission thanks to long-standing social justice commitments and powerful, expensive investigative journalism. This is even as efforts at advancing diversity in the newsroom reveal much deeper and more difficult challenges to journalistic practices and solutions for the crisis confronting (as defined by) news organizations. This disjuncture was also reflected in a thematic analysis of our interviews when it came to gender specifically. Aside from the disparate and complex ways that these journalist technologists were greeted in the newsroom, there was evidence of "durable infrastructures" with respect to masculinity and whiteness that emerged most often in conversations about talent and professional identity in the newsroom.[111] For example, one interview subject suggested,

> I certainly credit the *Star* as well as the people that we've hired in recent years who are working knee deep in data for bringing me along on that journey and doing at least that initial cleansing of the data, which is really important and passing it along to the editors in the way that we can then say, 'Oh my God that's the story, it's right there. . . . I find that to be tremendously exciting and the guys who, and I always say guys only 'cause they are three guys, guys who are doing it are so proactive at uncovering these things that you know I would never have come across or heard about unless I was using the sources and strings that they're using in order to uncover what can be our next investigation.[112]

In 2016, a newsroom manager suggested that it was a struggle "to find people who were not men," and when they were able to find someone they were often lured away, describing women with journalism, data design, and development skills as "a triple threat."[113]

> The complexity is the lack of recognition by institutional media of . . . the way that tech roles or aspects of technology and journalism or reporting should be recognized media roles . . . So I can't say to you that there aren't people and women in particular out there doing the things that I think are valuable, we just don't have positions for them here.[114]

Three years later, four of the five members of the data desk are women, while two women were data analysts and team leaders on the business side of the organization in 2016. Jim Rankin, an award-winning investigative journalist with 25 years of experience and chair of the *Star*'s bargaining unit, indicated that these demographics have been changing with more women on the data desk and in data leadership roles than in the past. Data expertise in the wider newsroom has historically skewed more male, he pointed out. At the same time, the newsroom has remained largely white with no internal data on diversity.[115] According to Rankin, the organization has been unable to diversify because of buyouts and layoffs, despite a clear commitment by management and the union to inclusion:

> It's something that has been on the radar for a long time with the union. And there's an effort to bring in diversity training, again subject to budgets. . . .

But it's a real challenge . . . and at a time when you want to be reflective of the community that you're writing about and serving, and the challenges that we have with a business model that's in trouble.

Here Felt's critique of STS as more focused on knowledge claims than infrastructure could be applied to journalism and journalism studies—and their focus on content and representations over internal systems.[116] These systems include power regimes that standardize and classify who can speak and who can be heard—or hired—within journalism's dominant authority, and whose futures matter, depending on their intersectional locations. It is also reflective of literature from feminist media studies, which has found a predominantly gendered cast to this work in the newsroom and how it is practiced, and is consistent with previous research on gender and news that finds women's work undervalued in relation to the male norm.[117] At the *Star*, despite efforts to diversify, we find evidence of "inequality regimes."[118] These regimes include "interrelated practices, processes, action and meanings that result in and maintain class, gender and race inequalities."[119] In these regimes, white men and white women specifically have benefited, consistent with the literature that white women tend to benefit from a focus on equity and inclusion.

Conclusion

In this chapter, we explored how the *Toronto Star*, one of Canada's most prominent and storied journalism organizations, is attempting to stem the newspaper financial crisis, innovate, and keep up technologically while addressing the reckoning we explore throughout the book. We find a number of competing threads. Members of Canada's journalism elite—including two journalism leaders affiliated with the *Star*—successfully advocated for government financial support. Journalists of color at the *Star*—including Shree Paradkar, Desmond Cole, and Tanya Talaga, the *Star*'s first Indigenous columnist—are recasting and/or resisting journalism authority and the persistent whiteness of newsroom power relations.[120] We also find data journalism activities and processes being integrated in and beyond the newsroom, bridging the production/consumption divide, and incrementally adapting in many ways while talking about journalism methods in more robust ways.[121]

We find this digital reckoning opening up the sutures and making visible persistent erasures such that a narrow range of voices and people have been able to speak for journalism in Canada. We find systemic inequities built into normative approaches such that multiple journalisms are hard to imagine within the current context. At the same time, we find evidence of changing infrastructures, yet with limited explicit engagement with the problematic role that news stories have played in social ordering versus the real contributions of longer form journalism that more closely resembles systematic research methodologically. Finally, we find a lack of attention to internal accountability about the role of interpretation in journalism given that objectivity and balance are not good enough.

That the Canadian government committed to subsidize journalism is a result of this context and the historiography we are writing against in this book, which includes a dominant crisis narrative, who it is deployed by, and the historic contributions of newspapers such as the *Toronto Star,* which have been committed to an interventionist stance and award-winning journalism. In the words of *the Discourse* co-founder Erin Millar: "The policy seems purpose-built to help only one kind of media: newspapers."[122] Yet, while this may seem like a win for journalism in service of democracy, and it accounts for the workhorse role that newspapers have played and continue to play, it neglects the chronic representational and epistemological concerns we engage with throughout this book and what the reckoning portends for a certain kind of journalism.

As Picard warns in his 2016 written submission to a Canadian Heritage House of Commons Standing Committee on the state of local media:

> Subsidies supporting news provision can serve useful purposes, but should not be merely a means funding declining legacy media. For the past half century, many Western nations have used forms of subsidisation to support news provision, particularly in the daily newspaper industry. General subsidies to daily newspapers have failed to halt newspaper mortality or the reduction in local news capacity, but there is evidence that they can be useful for more specific and short-term objectives. If subsidies are selected as a response, care should be taken to ensure that subsidies are used to support company transformation, specific journalistic functions, or start-up and young enterprises, not merely to put money into declining media businesses that decreasingly serve Canadian audiences.[123]

We find audiences are still commodities instantiated in a capitalist mission and not active, diverse publics. This policy decision then is remarkable for the fact that contrary to claims of a journalism that uniquely acts in the public good it, too, doubles down on business as usual—with white masculinity a core stabilizing force—as opposed to multiplicity of perspectives and approaches or a strong business case as the rationale. Here we argue that the *Star,* similar to other journalism organizations, has not taken gender and race seriously enough, which is part of the reason they are in crisis.

We find less concern about how a journalism for the public good accounts for its own protectionist tendencies, internal structural inequities and changing global audiences, exposing exclusions of peoples, relations, and "alternative conceptualizations" of the future.[124] Tworek's history of news in Germany in the early 20th century is salient as it explores how "news is a form of power," with the goal—control over competition for communications dominance during this historic period—including multiple actors and perspectives, which ultimately "did not happen in full view of readers."[125] An important question for her research was "why certain groups became interested in news at a particular moment and how they tried to influence it" including some of the forces that we explore in this chapter, which involve the technological, economic, and political.[126] In the next chapter, we turn to a new startup venture in journalism where questions related to crisis and repair, technology, gender, indigeneity, and colonialism are equally challenging but configured differently.

CHAPTER 5 | Startup Life

Introduction

The first day we entered the boardroom of *the Discourse*, a rare women-founded North American journalism startup, the white board posed one major question in red lettering: "*How can journalism support reconciliation?*"[1] That question signaled most profoundly that we had both entered a different space for journalism, and a differentiated conception of what journalism could, should, and might do. The still evolving concept of reconciliation refers to the process Canada has been undergoing to understand its history and ongoing relations with Indigenous people. The Truth and Reconciliation Commission (TRC) spent five years traveling across Canada listening to stories of survivors of Indian residential schools and in December 2015 released 94 "calls to action" of which three pertain to journalism and the media. Residential schools were tools of genocide, assimilation, and oppression operated by churches and the federal government beginning in the late 1800s, and the decades of trauma, death, and severe abuses they inflicted on many generations of Indigenous people reverberate today. The TRC was the result of a court decision on a class action suit brought by residential school survivors, and the hearings were covered at various times by local and national media throughout Canada.[2]

Reconciliation has also become a slippery, fraught, powerful—even magical—word and concept in Canadian discourse, tossed around by politicians, communities, journalists, educators, and many other seeking to address (or instrumentalize for their own means) the deep rifts and wounds related to colonial histories and entrenched structures and institutions.[3] That it arrived at the beginning of our fieldwork at a journalism startup in 2016 was both surprising and not. Our research question going into this startup had much to do with the "should"—the larger questions this book addresses related to what structures journalism as a tool for inquiry, how journalists are practicing journalism in a digital era, and when and where journalists' professional identity, norms, values—and gender, race, and colonialism matter. Specifically, we wanted to know what happens when a journalism startup is both mostly female and has been identified as a digital and data journalism innovator.[4] *the Discourse* is one of the few women-led journalism startups in North America that has been exploring newer approaches to journalism. These include data-driven storytelling, collaboration with communities, a focus on local as well as various commercial economic models that range from foundation funding to investment capital and most recently, audience funding models.[5]

We became interested in this startup because instead of focusing on journalism as an inherent good, *the Discourse* has been trying to experiment with a number of approaches to what journalism is and how technology might undergird its vision in an innovation context. Its experimentations with practice and social transformation within journalism help illustrate how journalists are grappling with the digital reckoning—and the limitations and possibilities of journalism—that are central themes in this book. This newsletter excerpt from Erin Millar, CEO and founder, about its commitments to publics from 2018 illustrates why:

> When I woke up yesterday to the news of the Ontario election and Anthony Bourdain's death, I was overwhelmed with sadness. The world looked so divided in that moment, so polarized, so lonely for many. I reflected on the choice journalists make when they decide how to tell stories. In a model that rewards clickbait, media often feeds off our worst sentiments fueling polarization, division and alienation. The recent political polarization in Ontario is one reason several weeks ago [the startup] sent a team to listen deeply in the Greater Toronto area . . . asking what really matters to the public in four communities underserved by local media.[6]

Given the challenges with legacy media organizations that the previous chapter records, this chapter addresses how journalists repair, reform, and rethink their practices and storytelling when technology, data, gender, and colonialism are up for debate and re-consideration without the kinds of structural constraints that beset legacy media organizations.

We are drawing both on work produced by the startup until the summer of 2019 and on 2016–2017 ethnographic fieldwork and interviews.[7] During our fieldwork, *the Discourse* was undertaking two major reporting projects. The choice of project was related to both funding availability and identification of niche topics for which the organization's digital and data skills would be well suited. Thus, having a sense of which topics were considered timely and underserved by potential funders, such as reconciliation, was paramount for the organization. As an ethnographic site, the startup is situated within social and economic networks with multiple audiences and modes of intervention and practice. Since the time of our fieldwork, the startup had an ambitious arc, becoming a destination news source, providing in-depth coverage and collaboration for specific topics and locales. In 2018 and 2019, it experienced contraction and retrenchment when funding fell short.

The chapter is organized into four sections that reflect the themes that emerged from our fieldwork: repair, ownership, innovation, and decolonizing journalism. We begin by bringing these findings into conversation with scholarship related to startups, gender, data technology, and settler-colonialism. Journalism studies scholarship has only begun to bring studies on innovation and startups into conversation with similarly emergent themes of repair and reform.[8] Alongside this, we suggest that STS frameworks for thinking about repair are necessary to explain how this commercial startup is not just innovating for the sake of saving journalism but to improve journalism as a tool for intervention and responsibility: in the words of one employee, to "move the needle" on what kinds of work journalism is able to do.[9] We see these kinds of commitments playing out particularly in fieldwork related to these three aspects: ownership and structuring, professional identity and innovations related to collaboration, and deliberate focus of the startup on reconciliation as a public good in a settler-colonial society and media in Canada. We complicate the emerging focus in journalism studies on repair and reform as largely a function of the nonprofit and philanthropic journalism sector—and internal to journalism change.[10] We suggest that in Canada at least, a country with an historically less agile corporate governance context and significantly less robust philanthropic sector for journalism compared to the United States, we find evidence of a wider "systems approach" to repair in commercial media, as well as a focus on "safeguarding capabilities" in ways that extend beyond merely saving extant forms and dominant approaches to journalism.

Journalism Startups in Context

Like our previous chapter on the *Toronto Star*, this startup exists within an increasingly tumultuous Canadian journalism landscape. After a report on the state of the media in 2017, the Canadian government engaged in consultations and discussions with media owners and journalists about supporting journalism, eventually allocating $600 million to the industry.[11] In various op-eds and the startup's newsletter over this period, Millar had a markedly different response compared to the legacy players detailed in Chapter 4. She spoke up about how funding "*could* catalyze growth and long-term sustainability for the industry," with a strong emphasis on "could." She pointed out that "if it is not implemented in a way that incentivizes innovation and long-term sustainability, it will simply prop up a dying model." Innovation, from her perspective, includes addressing the lack of diversity in newsrooms, greater accountability to the diverse public news organizations claim to serve, and the need to "support local journalism in underserved communities." She further stated:

> So far, the conversation about the future of media in Canada has almost entirely focused on what is broken—the number of newspaper closures and journalism jobs lost. Meantime, dozens of outlets have opened during this challenging period, including some with models that are already working.

While the latter point might seem self-serving given it includes an undisguised reference to her own organization, her response to the announcement had few similarly outspoken peers. With the notable vocal exception of another innovator, *Canadaland*'s Jesse Brown, many commentators from media expressed relief and/or focused on how the challenges confronting journalism were mostly economic and competitive neglecting any mention of persistent critiques or reckoning we deal with in this book.

The implicit, highly differentiated move that Millar makes toward improving journalism—not just revenue models for journalism—is something we witnessed in our fieldwork as well. When we sent her a draft of the article we published as a prelude to this chapter, she acknowledged our critiques of journalists "owning" a story and our suggestion of the claim to collaboration by the startup as uneven at best (and other critiques we discuss later in this chapter) and concluded her much longer e-mail response by saying:

> After having experimented with how to challenge that 'the journalist owns the story' idea through on-the-ground reporting, we're now in the process of prototyping a technology product to enable us to scale a co-creation with community approach to journalism. 'Collaboration in a journalism

sense does not mean co-authorship,' you write [quoting from Young and Callison, 2017]. But why can't it?

Anyways, I share all this because I think you're right to point out that we haven't broken down that wall yet. But I wouldn't underestimate our commitment to doing so. We may be hesitant to label ourselves as innovators but we are stubbornly committed to our mission, which will, in turn, require a lot of innovation.[12]

The openness to critique, innovation in method and technology, the "why can't it?" attitude, the "stubborn commitment" to mission-orientation all reflect approaches of *the Discourse* and underscore how the opening question about reconciliation might centrally emerge in such a startup. Her response also suggests that journalism has and can play a role in larger shifts in society—that it can be done with a "mission." Instead of proffering journalism as an inherent good, she and (by extension) the organization appear to be opening up the "internalist" epistemology of journalism to experiment with "epistemological pluralism" (i.e., how they do journalism, what that journalism is, and how technology might undergird their vision).[13] Building on research in journalism studies and STS, our analysis understands the work of this startup as a form of repair and an effort at reform, which despite growth globally isn't always the rationale or the goal when new journalism startups get started—nor is it often a measure of success.

We turn first to the growing body of scholarship that has sought to understand and track the emergence of journalism startups globally in order to situate *the Discourse* in broader observations and analyses—and to differentiate their approaches that enroll technology, economics, and persistent critiques. Global studies on innovation and startups have focused on a variety of research questions and methods, including assessments of startup success, comparative analyses, the prevalence of digital startups, individual case studies and a discourse analysis of startup vision statements.[14] The literature has tended to orient around what Wagemans and colleagues describe as "exponential growth" in the space, what factors contribute to a successful startup, and how these startups have to differentiate themselves from legacy journalism organizations in order to be successful.[15] They have found generally that despite explicit attempts to distinguish themselves from the past, traditional journalism norms and practices tend to be reinforced. In their study of 10 journalism startup manifestos, Carlson and Usher suggest that "these startups draw on technological superiority as a way to differentiate their offerings from traditional news. . . . Yet they did not advocate disrupting journalism's core tenets or rebuilding the epistemic grounds on which news rests."[16]

Studies also identify innovation in areas such as organizational structure, promotional material/vision statements, and marketing. Bruno and Nielsen found that market differentiation, such as identifying "niches poorly served by the incumbent industry" in addition to high-quality output and cost-effective structures, lead to the "most successful startups" in a European context.[17] Wagemans and colleagues found that *Mediapart*, a French investigative journalism startup, was distinct in its organizational structure, which included less hierarchy, marketing innovation, and close relationships with the public.[18] Gender and intersectionality are underdeveloped areas in all of these studies, despite early research that indicates the emerging domain of the journalist/technologist is male dominated.[19] Wagemans and colleagues' references to Mediapart's senior team indicated that it was largely male, with one woman, and all originated from legacy newspapers.[20] Powers and Zambrano studied the social profiles of startup founders in two cities, Seattle and Toulouse, France.[21] They neglected to include gender, despite finding that "social and symbolic capitals are the crucial resources for startup formation" with journalism experience being a key variable.[22] In addition, these studies, like many in journalism scholarship, erase or ignore race and colonialism—factors that have driven the launch of alternative media sources and startups. For example, there are a number of Indigenous journalism startups in North America and successful nonprofits such as APTN, which is a registered charity. Other examples of Black, LatinX, South Asian, and other-focused media sources often grouped under the problematic umbrella term, "ethnic media," abound in both the United States and Canada. Given these gaps, it seems reasonable to wonder how intersectionality is relevant to a journalism startup context, as well as how studies of other professional technology fields indicate that gender, race, colonialism, and technology interact.

One of the largest global studies of 17 commercial and nonprofit startups—which vary in definition and organizational structure depending on the national tax context for philanthropic organizations—found that while the main motivations to launch filled a gap in the competitive landscape, the four most prominent involved larger concerns unrelated to the perceived crisis in journalism, including culture, society, technology, and the economy.[23] Deuze suggests that these startups are often seen as saviors "better able to embrace and pioneer innovation" than traditional journalism organizations.[24] This theme of "saving journalism" as we point out in the previous chapter relates closely to conceiving of journalism as being in "crisis." In the Canadian context where *the Discourse* operates, it seems that the "saving" is currently coming from government support and tax benefits—and is closely linked to how the crisis in journalism has been circumscribed and by whom.[25]

Comparatively, as the following sections will elaborate, the kind of repair and reform the startup we study is intent upon is much broader than "for the good of the field" itself—though it is that as well, and funding is obviously one of the main determinants of success. The opening up of journalism practices means that the startup actively works to extend and experiment with economic models, partner with non-journalists, collaborate with communities, hire non-white journalists, and privilege underserved, feminist, and diverse perspectives. In Canada from an economic perspective that has meant trying to work within a limited corporate governance context with only three choices for journalism companies to incorporate—for-profit, nonprofit, or a registered charity. Part of the government funding package referenced earlier may extend the ways for journalism organizations to access charitable tax status.

This startup—similar to others experimenting in this space in Canada— is inherently trying to move in the direction of what Julia Cagé in *Saving the Media* advocates as the optimal economic context to save journalism— hybrid nonprofit and commercial governance and funding models.[26] Cagé, whose research has focused on the United States and Europe, not Canada, envisions an antidote to how "the traditional media are under siege, with their backs to the wall. News is borrowed, relayed, and duplicated without compensation, even though it is costly to produce."[27] She proposes a structure that is in between a foundation and corporation in order to benefit from "the crossroads where state and market, public sector and private sector, intersect."[28]

The uneven successes and challenges in the nonprofit governance context alone are highlighted in a number of recent U.S. studies that draw from field theory.[29] A 2017 study by Ferrucci interviewed 19 journalists at digital native journalism nonprofits in the United States and found they are largely funded through a traditional range of sources for that sector: "a combination of donations from the public, grants, and corporate sponsorships, and by hosting various classes, live events, and workshops for the community."[30] Meanwhile Benson examined the relationship between board membership and U.S. foundations with nonprofit journalism organizations to test the limits of these funding models for journalism. He found they risked a form of "media capture" related to the short-term and "impact"-focused nature of grant funding. For Benson, true reform requires "increased funding and greater autonomy."[31] Others have found nonprofit startups showing examples of success that include shifting historic cultural and economic capital approaches to journalism, to sharing and collaboration from competition. For Graves and Konieczna, these efforts reflect a newer approach to what journalism should and could do—and how—that is about protecting "the autonomy and integrity of the field as a whole."[32]

Journalism Startups as Repair

This emergent scholarly focus on the relationship between the business of journalism in journalism studies is vital to understanding how the energy to contribute to repair in journalism is commensurate with ongoing financial demands of an organization. The statistics are not encouraging—with the majority of startups shuttering because of lack of funding.[33] This startup reached five years of longevity—but not without its own sustainability concerns. In their study of three U.S. journalism startups, Naldi and Picard indicate that "despite their advantages, most startup enterprises have poor business plans, have limited access to capital, rely on mixed sources of funding, and will—ultimately—fail."[34] They suggest that agility and flexibility are required, particularly in a startup's first three years of operation because of these challenges. This startup has faced similar concerns.

Millar wrote an article in late 2018 talking about how the organization is challenged by Canada's distinct journalism funding, governance, and regulatory context.[35] Her openness about the organization's struggles is a departure for the sector. In another newsletter in 2018, she talks about how the startup missed its funding target in its first equity crowdfunding campaign, which launched in October 2017, indicating that the organization made 60% of the $500,000 it set out to raise from the community. Her willingness to be transparent is a signal of a commitment to wider change as well as a recognition of the newer kinds of questions and precarious contexts that journalists are faced with—how to survive economically and create sustainable funding models that balance growth and available resources. She talks about the specific impact of these challenges on her organization in both the internal newsletter and other public venues:

> Our funding was cut significantly with little notice. Layoffs were necessary. With fewer resources than expected, we had to ask ourselves some difficult questions: how could we continue growing . . . and have a real impact with

less bandwidth? The words of Jessica Lessin, founder of The Information, offered guidance: new media outlets flourish when they focus on what they are 10 times better at than others. Yes, we could produce award-winning investigative journalism, but were we 10 times better than the CBC or the Globe and Mail at that? Sacred cows were slaughtered.[36]

She goes on to identify how the startup went on to interview members, potential readers and research which stories "had a measureable impact" in order to assess next steps:

... a theme emerged: the best stories were those that were firmly rooted in distinct places, produced by journalists who nurtured real relationships with their community. Our most successful stories were the product of listening deeply to diverse people excluded from media and political dialogue.

She outlined how this engagement contained a surprise with respect to why their journalism mattered and what journalism could and should do in their context:

By analyzing analytics data, surveying our members and interviewing people we *wished* were our members, a picture emerged—and it surprised us. The Discourse had been organized around beats, deep coverage of a specific topic. So we assumed the majority of our members supported us because they cared about a specific issue we reported on, be it child welfare, sustainable development goals, reconciliation. We were wrong. Instead, they valued our process and wanted to see it applied to a wide variety of topics. They wanted in-depth, nuanced journalism, the kind of stories produced by slowing down to listen to people other media are not listening to. They valued how we served the public, instead of advertisers or interest groups. But, most importantly, they wanted media that helped them deepen their connection to their community, to get out of their bubbles and experience the diversity of their cities.[37]

The tools and end result are both novel, open, and still within the parameters of producing journalism: hence, we see this startup as on a spectrum of multiple journalisms and with a commitment to making this thing we know as journalism and its relations to/with society better. Innovation in funding goes hand in hand with these efforts at reform.

STS scholar Jackson's definition of repair is a useful extension of field repair in journalism studies in order to incorporate the work of hybrid organizations operating in a commercial middle ground.[38] Jackson describes his approach instead "as an exercise in broken world thinking" that involves (a) appreciation of limits and fragility, and awareness that the world is always in the "process of fixing and reinvention" and (b) "deep wonder and appreciation for the ongoing activities by which stability (such as it is) is maintained." Jackson is writing about many forms of technology and infrastructure, but his elegant argumentation about repair presents a quite differently configured framework within which to consider both legacy journalism as older and in crisis and startups intent on providing repair:

> Repair is about space and function—the extension or safeguarding of capabilities in danger of decay. But it is also an inescapably timely phenomenon, bridging past and future in distinctive and sometimes surprising ways. Repair inherits an old and layered world, making history but not in the circumstances of its choosing. It accounts for the durability of the old, but also the appearance of the new (a different way of approaching the problem of innovation, as will be discussed: behind and prior to the origin stands the fix). Above all, repair occupies and constitutes an *aftermath*, growing at the margins, breakpoints, and interstices of complex sociotechnical systems as they creak, flex, and bend their way through time.[39]

Repair in Jackson's sense is both about the present and past—and imagining a future in which unpredictable and sometimes intentional bricolage of old and new result, where aftermath and innovation reside together. The quote from Millar regarding new government funding reflects this deeper commitment to repair—the "could" of saving journalism rests not just on financial models or even on technological fixes, but in "safeguarding capabilities."

In many of its newsletters to supporters, like the one following the government funding announcement, the startup is likely to explain its own difference by employing critiques of journalism around issues like who collects data, what kinds of contexts are missing, and how journalism is only at the beginning of providing better coverage of, for example, Indigenous people. Such articulations speak to the process of reinvention and commitment to repair underway not for the betterment of journalism as usual but for the work that journalism could do as a tool to support a better society. As Millar also told us in the previously referenced e-mail and in response to an earlier version of this chapter, she and fellow startup employees had a "profound feeling of responsibility" to change the way they practiced as journalists. An example she offered is this:

> We are working on new ways of doing journalism that are attempting to produce co-owned stories or 'a negotiated series of events.' That work looks like a lot of things. For example, our child welfare investigation involves kids currently in foster care as 'fixers' who help us navigate the system. They provide feedback throughout production process and produce their own content.[40]

In this sense, repair presents a kind of reordering of power relations and conscription of professional language to address persistent critique even as limitations and histories of the practice of journalism are recognized.

Origins and "Ownership in Our Journalism"

Like many startups in journalism startup literature, *the Discourse* articulates an explicit, evolving "manifesto" or mission that situates the organization within the gaps in the journalism ecosystems of Canada. In 2016 interviews, the startup publicly claimed it was formed to contribute to public service journalism that analyzes difficult subjects such as education and transit, and long-term aspirational societal goods such as reconciliation and ethical energy production—with data stories as a priority.

> Our team of 10 employees, plus freelancers and collaborators, produce in-depth journalism about complex issues, the sort of journalism that is difficult to jam into the daily news cycle because it takes time, resources and analysis. We prioritize data journalism that not only visualizes existing data, but presents new data or analysis . . . We spend weeks on investigative reporting to get the nuanced story, not just the news story . . . *We immerse ourselves in communities for as long we need to build trust,* even if it takes months before we produce any content.[41]

The focus on both data and time spent reflects the repair orientation. Data also addresses a number of gaps in the startup landscape both in Canada and globally. Data journalism, as we pointed out in the previous chapter, has largely been the product of legacy media organizations in Canada with only a few organizations identified as having the capacity to produce quality data journalism in a sustained manner in French- and English-language media organizations.[42]

A second differentiation involves the startup's gendered ownership, leadership and initial staff complement—a rarity in any journalism land-scape to both have women owning and leading a journalism startup and practicing data journalism.[43] *the Discourse* is one of approximately 70 digital born organizations to have launched in Canada since the turn of the century in a space that is challenging to say the least.[44] This number is also likely low as the industry and those who report on it are unlikely to acknowledge transnational, Indigenous, and alternative media.[45]

Since our initial interviews and meetings this startup moved offices and briefly expanded to a national focus in 2018, increasing the number of its employees and changing its business model to diversify revenue from a mix of philanthropic foundations, reports, workshops, consultations, and partnerships with other media with the launch of a crowdsourced mem-bership funding drive for investors.[46] It later refined its focus to local jour-nalism in a few communities across the country. However, 2018 ended with a significant retrenchment, which the CEO described in the newsletter and we reference earlier in the chapter. This retrenchment deepened in the summer of 2019 as Millar indicated that the organization did not meet its most recent funding targets in what it had called its "do-or-die moment" to solicit monthly supporters. In her May 2019 pitch, Millar identified the tremendous difficulties of funding a journalism organization:

> The Discourse is not yet sustainable. We don't have a big corporation or a super-rich person behind us. We survived our first five years by bootstrapping and with startup funding. A year and a half ago, our community members pooled together funds and became owners in our company through an equity crowdfunding campaign. Value-aligned partners and investors also pitched in—including SheEO, CFC Media Lab, Vancouver Foundation, McConnell Foundation, Marigold Capital, Waterloo Global Science Initiative and our family members. . . . These people made a bet on us, affording us the runway to build The Discourse from the ground up. But that funding will run out soon. And to be truly accountable to you, we need to be funded by you.[47]

These developments are consistent with studies of journalism startups as according to Schaffer, most startups focus on editorial strategy for the first few years as they identify success as about "community and public service" and less about investment.[48] The nimbleness of the startup and its focus on repair is reflected in its origin story as well. The startup began with three white women who had worked in legacy and startup journalism organizations in Canada, and/or the nonprofit sector, deciding to collaborate in order to create in-depth journalism. They created a journalism model that prioritizes the role of community, expertise, and data in story idea generation and articulation, as well as impact. One of the founders recalled that the group, of which Millar is the only one still at the startup, wanted "to have ownership in our journalism and . . . be able to shape and have more control over our journalism" which included "access [to] money to do the kind of ambitious projects that we wanted to do" which was challenging "as freelancers doing piecemeal projects."[49]

They initially considered organizing as a nonprofit and solicited funds from friends and family to launch, opting in the end to create a for-profit company and experiment with different revenue models that included philanthropic funding and media partnerships. They quickly succeeded in differentiating themselves. A 2017 report on the state of the media in Canada references the startup as among the most prominent and "attractive digital organizations" in the country only three years after its founding.[50] Yet, their origin story and approach to organizing work underplays some of their contributions, in addition to motivations that appear to have emerged out of alienation from news organizations and journalism practices.

Interviews with two of the three founders suggest that these women understood their alienation as a function of the precarity and limits of the journalism landscape, which has seen the three major media unions in Canada indicating a significant decline in the number of journalism positions over the past few decades.[51] There was a general hesitance to locate themselves as specifically gendered and/or racialized professionals seeking to innovate in technology and method.[52] Gender emerged only as an afterthought both in our interviews and in their telling of how the company emerged.

> It's only now that we're two years in and we haven't gotten a man to stick around here that we start to kind of go, 'Hmm I wonder what this means?' But at first it was just an organic beginning of something and it was just a small group of people and it could just be . . . a coincidence, right?[53]

This hesitance translated into an initial uncertainty about the power and contribution of the startup's intervention in digital journalism. For example, one senior member of the group resisted defining the startup as a technology company or firmly claiming the innovation space. "I kind of hate the word innovation but I use it all the time because it's actually what we're doing I think and trying old tricks with new technology."[54] This is despite recognition by other media, funders, and respected North American journalism publications, as well as the ability to acquire capital, space, and qualify for and win awards—all of which are independent measures of success.

These women experienced a conjoined challenge in clearly claiming the professional identity of the journalism innovator along with an origin story of shared gender alienation—and its underlying motivation to exercise more control over their journalism. International studies into the status of women in media note that there is a persistent glass ceiling for women in media in general and in Canada, particularly in commercial media, and certainly the alienation these women articulated reflects the lack of maneuverability and power experienced by women within mainstream organizations.[55] Studies of women in news in Canada have tended to focus on white women journalists' experience, which is evident by the exclusion and erasure of minority women's experiences in the relative absence of intersectional and decolonizing approaches to gender and newsrooms aside from research by Mahtani in the early 2000s.[56] The startup did not initially address diversity among women, as there was a lack of minority women in the early stages of the startup.[57]

The story and norms they were able to mobilize identified motives such as an increasing precarity of the profession in Canada, in addition to a commitment to methodological innovation that included locating themselves more closely within communities, using a language of collaboration and focusing on data journalism. That they were able to mobilize their frustration with journalism's inability to tackle meaningful issues and offer both solutions and data to make decisions suggests a choice on how they understood their ability to exercise agency, articulate difference, and seek possibilities for contribution in the startup space.

In a study of women's broadcast ownership in the United States, Byerly makes one of the few attempts to examine how women become broadcast industry owners and the impact of economics, gender politics, and policy on participation rates.[58] Her research, which included interviews with 40 women owners and experts, found that the majority of women became owners through inheritance, with a number of factors undermining women's ownership efforts in general. These included: consolidation in the U.S. media market, a "hostile, exclusionary regulatory environment," difficulty accessing financing and a "masculine environment in which women are unwelcome and systematically squeezed out."[59] Byerly concludes that the "marketplace has undermined women's most minimal efforts to own stations and it has overwhelmingly favoured men's" and that despite these challenges women still hold strong community values.[60]

Counter to Byerly and in a marked turn from our interviews in 2016, this startup claimed a more gendered identity as it evolved. They raised money from venture funds aimed at women entrepreneurs and explicitly located their approaches to journalism. For example, the subject line for a 2018 newsletter read "Let's be Feminist in public."

Who Gets to Claim Innovation?

One of the largest challenges for these journalists has been how to identify themselves in this professional domain. Are they innovators? Is it a technology company? Are they data journalists? They are not alone in this. Identity crises vis-à-vis technology and innovation in journalism are playing out in news organizations globally, in journalism scholarship and education.

How these tensions and identities emerged in our interviews and participant observation reflected gendered experiences, opportunities, and framing. We asked our interview subjects about the role of data journalism and again discovered an initial hesitation to claim this professional identity. One of the journalists, when asked if she considered herself a data journalist, told us a story about how she got into the j-startup. She began by doing pro bono work for the startup when she heard about its data ambitions on a regional transit project. She said, "You guys are going to screw it up. . . you can't just decide you're data journalists one day right? And they're like 'well what are you going to do about it?' So, I said: 'Well, I'll help you out'."[61] She went on to say, "Although every now and again, I go to a conference and . . . I introduce myself as a data journalist. This all just kind of happened to me by accident."[62] This individual has an academic background in mathematics and science similar to other high demand journalist-technologists integrating into mainstream journalism newsrooms and claiming that identity. Yet, she frames herself as an "exception to the norm" similar to the women engineers studied by Faulkner.[63] Faulkner found that women had a harder time belonging as engineers because their interests were not seen as gender authentic, compared to men—and that paradoxically this made them both more visible and invisible.

This individual was also described by Millar as someone who is "leading our data journalism" with the caveat that "there's no senior data journalist here, which I think is part of the reason that she's so good just because she's coming from a completely different way of thinking about it."[64] This equivocation around the ability to claim senior data journalism expertise while attempting to differentiate her approach from the mainstream is somewhat at odds with the hybridity and fluidity of this space in newsrooms, in that this individual's background make her a highly sought-after professional in legacy journalism newsrooms.

Gender is one axis that informs articulations of professional and organizational identity and data highlights methodological shifts. However, the startup also in varying ways makes a conscious effort to question and shift models for measuring success. They recognize communities as both a source for story ideas and a source for collaboration. One of our main findings relates to the startup's "method and model" and how it measures success—which is through "engagement" and discursive change. For example, the startup has articulated an explicit chart that involves first identifying "community demand" in part to determine the "subject/domain challenge" and then producing an "analysis of current dialogue" of the issues from within journalism as well as the relevant research. Instead of funneling this data through traditional journalism news values, the method's key orienting focus is to fill a "gap in public discourse" and to connect with communities.

As one journalist said in an interview, "We're a mission-driven organization, so we aren't just going to do any project, we do a landscape analysis and see where there's holes in our beats and try to push those."[65] Millar put it more strongly when she said, "Journalism values to me are just like a functional tool, they're not like some universal law."[66] Their approach to story and idea generation is grounded less in the editor's intuition[67] and/or long held internal-to-journalism news values such as conflict and unusualness and more in an approach one might take to an academic literature review. The journalists start by examining important gaps in journalism as well as reading about academic studies in order to develop a research question that will inform many works of journalism on a single project.

When the startup tackled regional transportation, it created a data journalism series focused on the "systemic story" of a region facing a transportation crunch with limited public transit.[68] There was a distinct lack of reporting and data available to the public on this issue despite a city-wide referendum looming. The startup partnered with 13 local media outlets that were traditional competitors—a significant accomplishment and an important contribution, as scholars have pointed out that competition has been a masculinist proxy for norm-setting in journalism.[69] Indeed, as a journalist on this story, one interviewee said, "Maybe that's not sexy, but we're trying to figure out how to make it compelling."[70] The Moving Forward series was a finalist in an international journalism awards competition, and one reason the startup was recognized with a national journalism innovation award for its "collaborative approaches" and data journalism rerouting journalistic methods through multiple epistemologies, community and complexity.[71] The series mobilized data from a number of areas including the costs/revenue of transportation in Metro Vancouver and travel patterns. It used the data to generate an interactive "Cost of Commute calculator" to consider social costs such as climate change and other full cost accounting approaches in advance of the referendum. As a result, the startup was able to intervene in journalism norms and innovate in methods and outcome.

When it comes to gender, technology, and journalism, most studies haven't been able to shed light on the concerns we encountered at the startup. Appelgren and Nygren provide some insight in their study of data journalism in Sweden finding that expertise was a defining factor in journalists' participation in data journalism, with men tending to describe themselves as more experienced than women.[72] An article by Royal on journalist programmers at the *New York Times* examined the number of women participating at *New York Times* interactive and found a lack of women with the skills or inclination to be programmers.[73] It further identified a concern given the increasing number of women attending journalism schools compared to men, questioning how this disjuncture can be mitigated and translate into technology oriented journalism career opportunities for women students upon graduation. Royal locates the lack of participation of women programmers at the *New York Times* interactive within what Faulkner identifies as concerns about "women in technology" as opposed to the more nuanced questions that can emerge from approaches that explore how gender and technology are coproduced.[74]

The notion that gender, technology, and power relations are co-produced is a fundamental addition that feminist and postcolonial STS makes to feminist media studies. Similar to the generative and novel conceptual orientations that STS approaches have recently spawned in journalism and media studies more generally, the incorporation of feminist and postcolonial STS represents nascent possibilities to a journalism studies literature that is still in motion.[75] Indeed current approaches in feminist and postcolonial STS that characterize technology as "both a source and consequence of gender relations," with that relationship "not immutably fixed," are important contributions in a journalism context because of the integral role that technology is likely to continue to perform within the profession.[76]

This approach is necessary in that it attempts to address critical gaps in understanding how gender and technology are co-produced in journalism and postcolonial contexts. For example, while it is clear from feminist STS that masculinism translates into every technology and system, journalism studies and its relationship to technology remains underdeveloped, despite evidence of gendered norms, hiring practices, labeling and structural bias in the emergent domain of the journalist technologist, and data and computational journalism more specifically.[77]

This approach also supports a deeper understanding of the "often complex and contradictory gendering that takes place at the level of technical knowledge and practice—both symbolically and in terms of gender differences in styles of work."[78] For example, Faulkner's contribution to engineering culture has relevance for journalists in that she identifies taken-for-granted subtle gaps and gender dynamics within engineering culture that create women as the "exception to the norm."[79] These include what she terms the "weight of history": cultural perceptions of "masculinity" linked to "technology"; and the persistence of gender norms that construct the "man engineer as the norm and the woman engineer as the invisible non-sequitur."[80]

Feminist STS stresses the importance of investigating the distinct (but related) connections between symbolism, structure, and identity in gender-technology relationships, with the understanding that if gender and technology are understood as socially shaped then it follows that they may also be reshaped.[81] According to Turkle and Papert, who studied computer culture, some of this reshaping can occur at the epistemological level by "accepting the validity of multiple ways of knowing and thinking."[82] They contrast two approaches or styles of "organizing work" and object relationships—a "closeness to objects" which results in a "bias against the abstract formulas that maintain reason at a distance" and a "distanced relationship" which "supports an analytic, rule- and plan-oriented style."[83] They further suggest that the latter constitute an "epistemological elite."[84]

One could translate this closeness to objects as a way of understanding this startup's multiple and varied attempts from the beginning to open up its relationship to audiences through both community-oriented and defined journalism, as well as funding models that are rooted in membership as an accountability check on the journalism. In this sense they tackle the shifting production-consumption divide differently than the legacy media organization. In the previous chapter, there is a turning to data analytics and increased organizational coherence around audiences in order to ask different kinds of questions about the audience: with different visions of who the audience is and its potential relationship to journalism. Rao and Wasserman's argument that a postcolonial critique in media ethics should be "concerned with social change and the disruption of patterns of power, not merely with the incorporation of different points of view in order to reach consensus" is then both relevant in internal-to-journalism as well as external-to-journalism visions of its limits and possibilities.[85] They warn that seeking truth, the main goal of journalism—as well as other concepts such as harm, empowerment, and dignity—are "culturally mediated and constructed."[86]

This approach questions colonial assumptions about the newer and celebrated role of digital technology in journalism—not to deny its contributions—but to recognize the inherent structural messiness that underpins it and to deploy it more as a diagnostic of how the case studies we explore throughout the book are both reinforcing and upending across multiple domains of power. Thus, in this startup we situate journalists as adding to the archive and sedimentation of journalism about audiences, funding models, and Indigenous people in Canada and as such, as contributors to Indigenous-settler relations with Canadian institutions that include media.[87] In this section, we explore how the startup seeks to repair and reform in this arena as well.

How Can Journalism Support Decolonization?

While starting from academic critique, journalism gaps, and questions like "how can journalism support reconciliation?" are innovative, they also produce distinct challenges on a topic like reconciliation, which is a contested process and calls into question Canada's settler-colonial structures, history, and media. Scholars like Coulthard see reconciliation as a political dodge, part of ongoing colonial structures, conditions, and systemic oppression of Indigenous peoples.[88] It is a way for settler Canadians and their government to attempt to rhetorically redress relations with Indigenous peoples without recognizing their dislocations and first honoring treaty obligations regarding land title, and addressing other forms of continuing injustices, such as high youth suicide rates, Missing and Murdered Indigenous Women and Girls (MMIWG), and lack of clean drinking water in Indigenous communities. As such, the challenges for journalism as a system of knowledge, which has been found in practice to largely operate in service of the structural status quo with some prominent and important exceptions, include: (1) dealing with Canada's colonial history and relations with Indigenous people; (2) journalistic methods and Canadian media's history of persistent stereotypes and racism; and (3) accessing stable revenue sources that support journalism startups who like this one seek to do things differently, particularly on Indigenous issues and with Indigenous communities.[89]

Since the time of our initial study, and in part because of work like the reconciliation project, the startup has grown in prominence. To focus on these kinds of issues and to access funding, it has interrupted business as usual. As part of its reconciliation focus, it launched Toward Reconciliation, "a sustained body of journalism about how governments, institutions, communities and individuals are responding to the challenges of reconciliation."[90] The project goes on to say, "Our reporting aims to track the journey to change, to hold Canadians to their pledges and share stories about successes along the way."[91] Examples of stories include a partnership with the Canadian Broadcasting Corp.'s Indigenous journalism unit on reconciliation in small towns in Canada and a story on housing in First Nations communities.

The website also offers ideas for media reporting on Indigenous issues that address sourcing, use of experts, accountability, diversity within Indigenous communities, and avoiding clichés and stereotypes. In other words, major efforts are required in order to seed collaboration and interrupt the structures, tools, and colonial history of journalism. Compared to the well-known dominance of event-driven news, this sustained thematic approach is a generalized departure from traditional news norms and values. What became clear in our discussions is that older notions of what journalism has been and what stance should define a journalist sit uncomfortably alongside newer technologically enabled impulses to collaborate. In talking about the challenges of collaboration, the founder of this journalism outlet suggested:

> The other piece is competing interests and agendas. We try really hard to . . . be a little bit separate from that. Of course, like any organization, we have our own interests and agendas, but we're trying very carefully to create a neutral, safe space for organizations to be collaborative. There needs to be space for them to serve their audience, while also contributing to the spirit of the project.[92]

In this approach to the practice of journalism lies an important area for examination. As we argued in Chapter 1, there are no professional resources for articulating frameworks of and for collaboration. Journalistic identities and methods continue to be entwined in notions of distance and objectivity. Historians of journalism have noted that early notions of objectivity have roots in North American journalism in a turn to science in the 1920s when journalism was looking for legitimation and a lift out of the tabloid-style approach.[93] We add that it's also when the newsroom excluded all people of color and the violence and dispossession associated with settler-colonialism was well established and supported by media of their time.[94] Journalists then and now are also unlikely to admit to having "their own interests and agendas." The feminist critique in science studies has not penetrated much of the thinking about objectivity or agendas and structures, however latent, within journalism scholarship or the profession.[95] There has been some pushback on objectivity in the industry. As we note in several places in the book, the Society for Professional Journalists removed objectivity from its code of ethics in 1996, but distance is still a valued elemental foundation and a stand-in for objectivity in professional discourse. These are the kinds of issues we also see the startup working to address and confront—and without industry, professional, academic resources, or well-trodden paths to follow.

In confronting these issues, more questions emerge. Recognition of community and communities also implicitly must consider the communality of facts—the ways in which issues and concerns have meaning and are articulated by groups and by potential collaborators.[96] Where does such an acknowledgment leave journalists seeking to contribute to and innovate within mainstream media? Or to put it more succinctly, who are you if you are not professional, distanced/impartial—if you are collaborative and in conversation with a specific community or set of communities?

The picture becomes more complicated when race and colonialism become central aspects for consideration as they did with the reconciliation project. For example, when we attended the first meeting on the reconciliation project, which was well attended by almost all women freelancers and employees, there was one early-career Indigenous journalist. The group was quick to quote important critical literature and adopt a stance laden with good intentions; yet the palpable lack of Indigenous voices in the room perpetuates what has long been the case—Canadian legacy media is still predominantly white.[97] And up until the late 20th century, it was mostly male.[98] Canadian journalism has often been critiqued for its misrepresentation of Indigenous peoples, and Indigenous people continue to be woefully underrepresented in newsrooms across the country. Research by Kirkness and Barnhardt on North American universities and Indigenous peoples has found that organizations need to be able to prioritize institutional change by establishing "a vision of working *with*" Indigenous people as opposed to focusing on the success or failure of individuals.[99] They recommend a decolonizing approach that focuses on the "Four Rs of respect, relevance, responsibility and reciprocity."

When we sent our initial article about the startup with the above critique to Millar, she responded with an acknowledgment of it as well as a narrative of how they addressed it:

> On the reconciliation issue, I think you're right to point out that at the point in time you observed we were struggling to connect with Indigenous journalists and storytellers. In fact, we were repeatedly discouraged from focusing on the reconciliation project by Indigenous and non-Indigenous people who challenged us on our intentions. We were also at the beginning of an ongoing learning journey to understand what reconciliation means to us as individuals and professionals. However, we stuck with it out of stubbornness and a profound feeling that we (as non Indigenous journalists) had a responsibility to take these issues on. Since then I think we've come a long way in earning the respect of Indigenous journalists, sources and others, and challenging the norms that you write about.[100]

Since the initial meeting, the startup has sought to redress inequity and exclusion in the newsroom. It employed several journalists of color including Wawmeesh Hamilton, a member of Hupačasath Nation who often speaks publicly about what it means to practice journalism in Indigenous communities and about Indigenous people. For a time, the startup offered a specific and separate newsletter on Indigenous topics, usually authored by Hamilton. The newsletter subscription page suggests that the startup's uniqueness has not only been in quality of coverage but in focus, such as undercovered urban Indigenous communities in Vancouver.

The newsletter described its 2018 participation in a community-led urban meeting meant to address issues that Indigenous communities tend to have with harmful media representations. Millar shared her experience at the meeting as being "struck by just how much the conversation between media and Indigenous leaders has changed for the better." She quoted Hamilton as speaking at the event and saying: "Media is hiring Indigenous journalists. They are asking introspective questions about their newsrooms and stories. But we're still at the beginning stages of the change. We're at the kindergarten stage, but make no mistake: School has started and there's no going back."[101] This perhaps reflects the challenge of reconciliation as a kind of continuum or pathway that once embarked on rarely finds those who've begun it shunted back into business-as-usual modes. Indeed, the CEO suggested that their embrace of reconciliation has been much more than a mere topic: "These days, we think of reconciliation not so much as a distinct project we're working on but as a lens through which we look at all our work, and a mind like Wawmeesh to help us challenge our own assumptions is invaluable."[102]

Our previous article was also strongly critical and suspect of the startup's claims to collaboration. We suggested that journalistic voice and identity was still rooted in masculine news norms, practices, and colonialism at the startup, and that journalists "own" "a story." In other words, as much as a journalist spends time in the community and even discusses approach and result, it is still a journalist's version of events—not a negotiated version of events. We referred to the persistence of "loose methods," in order to describe how journalists wrestle with objectivity and fairness and balance and distance their own and others' "interests and agendas" in order to justify their role and right to describe and circumscribe a story—its importance and its need to be told—and to decide who speaks and explains events and/or societal objectives like reconciliation with limited ways to validate their approaches aside from the subjective.

We didn't at the time of our fieldwork see conceptual shifts occurring that might take into account Indigenous storytelling, or differentiated communal meaning making of a still-evolving concept like reconciliation.[103] We stated that it left us wondering *not* what journalism could do to support reconciliation but rather how journalism can deal with reconciliation without journalists locating themselves in social structures and colonial histories or addressing the role of journalism in social ordering. It also raises questions about journalism's use of storytelling as an abstraction and clichéd method dislocated from linguistic and cultural roots and not grounded in evidentials and approaches to story grounded in systemic knowledges and epistemologies. In part, the startup has begun to answer these concerns with content related to Indigenous issues, developing new collaboration tools, hiring an Indigenous reporter and freelancers, and developing a different lens for their reporting and relations with Indigenous communities. Along the way, we would argue differently now that *the Discourse* had tried to locate itself among the uncomfortable histories of Canadian media, with a "lens" informed by their work on and around reconciliation.

Conclusion

the Discourse, similar to other startups globally, is mission driven with a clearly articulated statement of editorial values and process that attempts to address gaps in the Canadian journalism landscape. Unlike other studies of startups, however, they did not largely draw on technological superiority in order to distinguish their product from others within the journalism startup context.[104] Instead they explicitly focused on innovating through method and impact on public discourse. The startup utilized gendered approaches to method successfully in part by opening up traditional epistemological areas of journalism to experimentation through collaboration and an approach that draws from academic research methods. While gender can be understood as a conceptual ground for this innovation, feminist critique was not used as a rationale or motivation for innovation. Paradoxically, this gap may have initially limited the startup's ability to make professional identity claims in the journalism technology space and to foreground its real advances in leadership in journalism more broadly given evidence about the importance of gender inclusivity in journalism organizations and the historic challenges of women in ownership.[105]

The looseness in journalism's methods allowed for easy proclamations of innovation and the persistence of unexamined power relations vis-à-vis the media's well-documented complicity with colonialism. Part of the challenge involves an inability to recognize and articulate a journalist as located in social relations and history.[106] The lack of resources within the profession for journalists to locate themselves leaves journalists like those in this startup working hard to address how journalism might support reconciliation—and with high stakes, particularly because they are committed to collaboration and communal relations. Yet unlike many legacy organizations, this startup with limited resources has made attempts at addressing issues arising from the TRC recommendations despite entrenched and ongoing colonial media structures. In doing so, they address as a matter of course persistent critiques and chronic crises in representation as well as acknowledge past harms and prior journalisms. We suggest that gender and colonialism matter in expected and unexpected ways as catalyst for change and re-articulation of important questions of epistemology, method, and moral stance in journalism, while paradoxically silencing questions of identity and contribution relevant to startups, gender, and data journalism. Here, strong objectivity, as feminist media studies scholars have been arguing in support of since the late 1990s, presents an alternative framework to the view from nowhere that we critique throughout the book.

Studying this startup over a period of several years as it has moved through various iterations in funding models, approaches to journalism, moves to collaboration, evolving emphases on technologies, gender, and reconciliation reflect its deep commitment to repair and efforts at reform. We've utilized Jackson's notion of repair in order to extend journalism studies approaches that have focused only on repair to the field. Instead, we see this startup contending with entrenched practices and opening up epistemic commitments in journalism, while trying to survive economically. Millar described the organization's 2019 financial context and next steps this way:

> The reality is that we didn't meet our goal. That means, at least in the short-term, we can't do everything we planned. And so we've been struggling through some tough decisions about focusing our resources to make the biggest impact toward our ultimate goal: developing a replicable business model for in-depth local journalism. . . . The bottom line: The Discourse is taking this chance during the summer to slow down, listen, learn and readjust, by focusing on a single community.[107]

Given the amount of expertise required to run a startup and work toward repair of journalism, it's troubling that the Canadian government media bailout referenced in Chapter 4 doesn't make more of an effort to focus on and fund digital journalism organizations like *the Discourse*. Jackson defines "repair" as these kinds of "subtle acts of care by which order and meaning in complex sociotechnical systems are maintained and transformed, human value is preserved and extended, and the complicated work of fitting to the varied circumstances of organizations, systems, and lives is accomplished."[108] Being feminist in public, adopting a lens of reconciliation, developing tools for and an ethos of collaboration—these are simultaneously subtle and enormous shifts in articulations of professional journalism that contribute to a repair consistent with some of the most egregious persistent critiques of journalism in relation to gender and colonialism. In the next chapter we discuss the role of Indigenous journalists in North America and what further transformation of the dominant approach to journalism might look like.

CHAPTER 6 | Indigenous Journalisms

Introduction

In late 2018 and early 2019, several articles emerged in U.S. and Canadian publications by Indigenous journalists about the rise of Indigenous journalism.[1] In contrast to the long history of misrepresentations they labor against, Indigenous journalists are producing distinctive coverage and challenging media systems and organizations that reflect deeply colonial priorities.[2] Reflecting the hopefulness in many of these articles, Salish Kootenai journalist Tailyr Irvine, in an interview with Cree journalist Roseanna Deerchild (host of CBC Radio's *Unreserved*) called this period "a golden age of native journalism." She attributes this golden age not just to powerful voices in media but to Indigenous people being seen as audiences and as part of diverse publics.[3] Indigenous journalists are actively using social media to engage with Indigenous culture while working to improve coverage and representation despite being underrepresented in most mainstream media and many regional outlets across the continent.[4]

This final chapter draws from interviews with Indigenous journalists and Indigenous scholarship to address questions that have lingered throughout this book: What would it look like if journalism took into account gender, race, and colonialism? How might journalism be practiced if journalists considered their own situated knowledges and standpoints as a starting point and/or as expertise—or lack of expertise?[5] How might journalism consider its role in reifying and upholding a particular social order, *and* its potential to shine light on persistent inequities and injustices?[6] What kind of a tool is journalism for Indigenous journalists given both the emergence of new technologies for self-representation and the long history of mis- or non-representation by mainstream media that we briefly articulate in Chapter 1?

In addressing these questions, this chapter moves beyond the repair and reform described in the previous chapter toward transformation of social ordering and histories that include the imposition of settler-colonialism as structure for both media and society. Drawing on ethnographic and paraethnographic methods, we suggest that Indigenous journalists are actively shifting and transforming expectations, framing, and modes of representations of Indigenous people.[7] Specifically, we find that Indigenous journalists are likely to: (1) define their approach to reporting as countering erasure and framing Indigenous presence as persistent, with Indigenous people in an abiding relationship with lands, waters, non-humans, and each other; (2) describe their reporting as emphasizing resilience and re-surgence in ways that set their stories and sources as navigating structures/institutions of settler colonialism; and (3) explain their doing of journalism and methods as being accountable within a framework of relations with land and peoples, locating themselves and their stories within histor-ical structures and relations and drawing on Indigenous knowledges and expertise.

These are key distinctions because instead of solely relying on jour-nalism norms as the dominant authority, which we critique throughout this book, a relational framework emerges closer to TallBear's adaptation of feminist standpoint theories.[8] Indigenous journalists are keenly aware of prior journalisms and the counter-narratives and counter-histories that have informed Indigenous peoples' experiences with media as an enforcer of social orders, and in particular as tenderers of and for settler coloni-alism.[9] Herein lies a differently configured notion of crisis defined by chronic mis-, under-, and non-representation and harm by media that have set a gauntlet for Indigenous journalists to correct, address, and contend with/against even as they must also experiment with and transform profes-sional norms and practices.

Indigenous Journalists in Newsrooms

The prominent journalists we've spoken with work at a range of journalism organizations across genres and mediums. Many started their careers at legacy media organizations, and almost all have transitioned to Indigenous-owned and managed media and/or are experimenting and innovating with journalism genres as freelancers and/or with startups, podcasts, blogs, and nonprofits.[10] All are active on social media, and many have covered major social movements like Standing Rock in 2017 in the United States, and

Idle No More in 2012–2013 in Canada. Both movements saw the borders between states mutate and become fuzzy as Indigenous people from all over North America and globally participated. As we make final edits to this chapter, the Kānaka Maoli-led defense of Mauna Kea is underway after several years of legal interventions to stop the building of the Thirty Meter Telescope. Much of what this chapter suggests and questions is relevant in that context as well in terms of Indigenous journalists' coverage, and pushback via Twitter against mainstream media coverage by Kānaka Maoli with widespread support from Indigenous people that crosses multiple nation-state borders in North America and throughout the Pacific rim.[11]

In part, our approach to this chapter reflects the perspectives and articulations of Indigenous journalists who are likely to pay attention to and share challenges across borders.[12] For example, social movements in Canada and events related to the trials for the deaths of Colten Boushie and Tina Fontaine, Missing and Murdered Indigenous Women and Girls (#MMIWG) and the Truth and Reconciliation Commission (TRC), which we've described in Chapters 2 and 5, have relevance and resonance in American contexts. We've also monitored Twitter through the movements surrounding #JusticeforTina, #JusticeforColten, #MMIWG, and #NoDAPL as Chapter 2 in part has shown. Indigenous journalists working in the United States that we interviewed were well aware of social actions in Canada, and vice versa, particularly in the case of #MMIWG.[13]

Technology has enabled the Indigenous journalists we interviewed to intervene in news agendas, share stories, engage with audiences, encourage a transformation of perspective that allows audiences to see various colonial histories and Indigenous perspectives. Yet, the role of technology, while recognized by Indigenous journalists as necessary, is not reified as "the future of journalism," unlike much of mainstream journalism and academic discourse on the "perceived" crisis in journalism discussed in Chapter 4. Here, our use of the digital as diagnostic reveals how technology supports an extension of the resistance, persistence, and organizing already ongoing in Indigenous communities: Indigenous journalists have been using new digital platforms to a great extent because the Indigenous communities they cover and are part of have a prominent social media presence.[14] All of the journalists we interviewed offered observations and insight into how they considered the distinctiveness of their approaches to deeply historicized colonial narratives, keeping in mind that many of the stories they report on would otherwise not be covered or not be covered well by mainstream journalists.

The United States and Canada are different media contexts, and our intention in bringing them together is to reflect the standpoint of Indigenous journalists. Media representations of Indigenous people in both contexts reflect different and similar settler colonial histories, media systems, and impacts on Indigenous journalists and journalism. Stereotypes like the "deficit model," over-emphasis of conflict between two parties—instead of multiple parties and perspectives, missing the complexity and historical context, and ignoring fly-over or rural communities are common critiques of media. What makes this particularly problematic when covering Indigenous issues and movements—whether in the United States or Canada—is both the long history of media getting it wrong about Indigenous people and issues and the implications this has for land, shared histories, and new technologies. The United States and Canada, and the regions within them, reflect different approaches, institutional contexts, and histories when it comes to diverse Indigenous peoples. Yet, the persistence of erasure in mainstream media coverage—except in regional media across the north in Alaska, Yukon, Northwest Territories, and Nunavut—is palpable.

In Canada, the past five years have seen a surge of mainstream reporting on Indigenous issues in Canadian media as a result of both the Truth and Reconciliation Commission and the Indigenous-led Idle No More movement. Anishnaabe author and *Toronto Star* columnist Tanya Talaga, who has worked as a journalist for over 20 years described it in stark terms: "Before Idle No More and the TRC, thoughtful, fair, non-racist reporting on Indigenous issues was hard to find." Talaga is not alone in this candid observation. Many of the mid-career Indigenous journalists we talked to describe the shifts in media as epic and transformative in terms of Canadian editorial interest in their story ideas. They see this change as due mainly to the perception of broad public interest and the deeming of Indigenous issues as important and newsworthy.

Indigenous journalists working in the United States describe a differently configured landscape in which erasure of Indigenous presence and concerns is common. Cherokee writer and podcaster Rebecca Nagle, argued in a widely circulated *Teen Vogue* article that erasure is a form of racism that is both structural and has dire consequences for public support:

Invisibility is the modern form of racism against Native people. We are taught that racism occurs when a group of people is seen as different, as other. We are not taught that racism occurs when a group of people is not seen at all. Yet the research shows that the lack of exposure to realistic, contemporary, and humanizing portrayals of Native people creates a deep and stubborn unconscious bias in the non-Native mind. Rooted in this unconscious bias is the idea that Native people are not real or even human.[15]

Indigenous journalists in the United States are actively resisting this by publishing across a range of publications and platforms. The Native American Journalists Association (NAJA) has created a number of reporting guides to help mainstream media. *Indian Country Today* has gone as far as to create its own style guide, distinct from mainstream media.[16] Yet, mainstream media are unlikely to cover issues like Standing Rock or Mauna Kea until movements are well underway and/or reaching dramatic peaks. Mainstream journalists generally do not pay attention to the serious legal and jurisdictional issues that continue in the months and years that follow a movement or protest. Instead, U.S. media attention is often spasmodic and light, with little knowledge of the complexities of land rights, settler-colonial histories, and ongoing relations between Indigenous people and their lands. Jenni Monet is an independent Laguna Pueblo journalist focused on Indigenous rights who publishes in both mainstream and Indigenous media and began her career in local U.S. television. She was arrested at Standing Rock, which we discuss later in the chapter. In looking back at her career in varied platforms (television, radio, print, online), Monet said:

> When I look back at that, I look at all the women who are able to cover hard news, and very rarely was it women of color out in the field covering the investigation . . . I would say that the majority of them were white men who were doing that kind of coverage.

The solution for many in the United States, like Monet (even with experience in mainstream media) has been to work on a freelance basis and/ or to start their own sources online through blogs that offer Indigenous narratives and data.

But the challenge in the United States is not only in newsroom representation. Monet points out that even statistical data reports exclude Indigenous people.

> If you know anything about Indian Country, it is often called 'Asterisk Nation.' Because all of the datasets that are available, at least at the federal and state level, when it comes down to Native Americans and Alaska Natives, they typically have asterisks by them because the data is so poor, or

incomplete, or nonexistent. And so, the asterisks are always the sidebar note of how there needs to be more information collected.

In Canada, Indigenous people are more likely to be included in statistical data reporting, and to be covered by media, but more coverage doesn't mean good or appropriate coverage. Most mainstream coverage has reflected a deficit model where Indigenous people are represented as lesser than the mainstream public, degenerate, in conflict, and/or unable to manage their own affairs. The one stark difference has been from APTN, launched in 1999, and among the first to consistently cover issues like housing, water, Idle No More, and MMIWG, increasingly winning awards for their investigative reporting.

Another stark exception in Canadian media has been the success of Talaga's recent books, *All Our Relations* and *Seven Fallen Feathers*. *All Our Relations* is part of a well-known national series of lectures called the Massey Lectures that are published in book form and broadcast/podcast via CBC Radio. Talaga is notably one of a few Indigenous journalists working for a national mainstream print publication in Canada or the United States. She began writing a regular column for the *Toronto Star* in early 2019 as we note in Chapter 4. Talaga is careful to situate her own journalistic practices within an Indigenous framework of both accountability and storytelling. She said explicitly in our interview with her: "I don't want to be a story taker. I don't want to take stories and not give back. I got into journalism to make the world a better place. I want to help people."

Talaga's experience in writing her recent and much-lauded first book, *Seven Fallen Feathers*, reflects this challenge of who journalism is for and who benefits when she relates how she was sent from a major center to cover Indigenous stories—often for the benefit of audiences in major centers.[17] She describes in the book, and in several public talks we've heard her give, being sent to Thunder Bay, a larger hub city in northern Ontario to find out about Indigenous responses to the election in Ontario. She headed first to the Nishnawbe Aski Nation (NAN) offices, which are located in Thunder Bay, but serve 49 communities in northern Ontario including Talaga's community. Talaga began by asking questions related to the story she was sent to cover by the *Toronto Star*. Instead of answering her questions, the NAN chief at the time told her to look into the deaths of seven youth who were attending high school in Thunder Bay. Another journalist might have batted it away, but Talaga chose to listen and eventually wrote a deeply contextualized book that reflects the complex lives of the seven youth (the *Seven Fallen Feathers*), who come from a few of the

49 communities hundreds of miles away from Thunder Bay where they are sent to high school.

Talaga begins her book by telling the story of Nanabijou, which situates Thunder Bay as a place deeply known and in relation with the Anishnaabe people. It's from this vantage point that the story of colonialism and racism specific to Thunder Bay gets told—of treaties, residential schools and reserves, colonial settlement and ongoing everyday violence, and communities and individuals who continue to resist, survive, and celebrate their survival. These elements are relatable to Indigenous communities and regions across Canada. Talaga points out that "there are historical inequities that I think a reporter with an Indigenous background is far more attuned and aware to" because schools and universities have only recently begun to address Indigenous histories and perspectives. In Talaga's book, it becomes clear that understanding Canada's settler-colonialism is essential to understanding the stories of these youth and their families.[18]

Settler-Colonialism and Journalism

With few exceptions, journalism scholars have not tended to look closely at media coverage of Indigenous people until recently. Anderson and Robertson's history of Canadian newspaper coverage of Indigenous people provides a seminal text for understanding the media's long history of complicity with colonialism, as well as a profoundly disturbing set of malleable and durable stereotypes that have been used to represent Indigenous peoples as lesser and "other." They argue that Gramsci's idea of hegemonic ordering helps to understand how and what rationale lay (and continues to lie) behind the "othering" process that unfolds in pages of newspapers, and they suggest that the colonial mindset persists with threads found in the earliest coverage, pre-Confederation. The othering in turn has helped to "promote a nation" such that the "imagined community" of Canada in Benedict Anderson comes into being with Indigenous people always on the margins and the brutality of settler colonialism, natural and normal.[19] Even as strides have been made to better represent Indigenous issues and peoples, this perspective remains enshrined at every level of journalism in Canada.

For the past two decades, Indigenous studies scholars have been writing and thinking with the concept of settler-colonialism as a way to understand the profound decimation, disruption, and transformation that has occurred during the past several hundred years across North America—and its ongoing impacts. Tuck and Yang summarize it this way:

Within settler colonialism, the most important concern is land/water/air/subterranean earth [land, for shorthand, in this article.] Land is what is most valuable, contested, required. This is both because the settlers make Indigenous land their new home and source of capital, and also because the disruption of Indigenous relationships to land represents a profound epistemic, ontological, cosmological violence. This violence is not temporally contained in the arrival of the settler but is reasserted each day of occupation.[20]

In this lies the challenge, as Anderson and Robertson show, precisely because mainstream media have, in historic and current instances, helped to support and legitimize many aspects of settler-colonialism.[21] Some journalistic norms and practices might change with (a) Indigenous journalists, (b) new Indigenous news sources, and (c) Native Twitter and Facebook disrupting the usual lack of attention to Indigenous stories and concerns and deep structural biases. Yet, the ways in which Indigenous articulations and relations are erased, ignored, and/or overwhelmed can still be seen so clearly in mainstream media coverage.

A case in point is the coverage in early 2019 of an incident that occurred on the steps of the Lincoln Memorial in Washington, DC, where Omaha elder Nathan Phillips sang the Raymond Yellow Thunder song in the midst of a tense situation involving white students from Covington Catholic High School and the Hebrew Israelites. Phillips was stopped while walking into the crowd in a widely seen photograph showing Phillips opposite one of the students. Multiple crowdsourced videos showed a complex situation that didn't fit easy narratives for covering race, youth, protests, or Indigenous people. As Ahtone, writing an op-ed in *The Washington Post* pointed out:

> If history tells us anything, it is that the journalism industry has no desire to be equitable or be accountable. But refusing to acknowledge a tomahawk chop as racist isn't the first time journalists have failed to address racism as seen by people of color.[22]

Ahtone wasn't the only Indigenous journalist to speak out in the mainstream press, and he cites differing approaches in specific articles by Nagle published by *Think Progress* and by Tsq'escen and Lil'Wat journalist Julian Brave Noisecat in *The Guardian*.[23] Similar to themes we explore throughout this book, Ahtone is critical about the structures of journalism and the makeup of the newsroom and the impact this has:

Of course, when called out, legacy outlets promise that they will get it right, one day. That, someday, their newsrooms will be diverse. That in the very near future, they will be competent when reporting on matters of race and racism.

Journalists, as we've argued throughout the book, are witnesses and storytellers who deal in and with meaning through decisions about what captures the attention of their audiences and publics, the research and framing of that content, choice of experts, and the inclusion of relevant context and history. The story involving Nathan Phillips is not a stand-alone, individual encounter with media shortcomings. Events that range from the several-years long legal and physical defense of Mauna Kea on the island of Hawai'i to the defense of unceded non-treatied Indigenous lands from a planned pipeline in Wet'suwet'en territories or the persistent calls for justice over the deaths of Indigenous youth in Thunder Bay – all of these events reflect the ways in which cultural frameworks and a myriad of deep historical contexts get passed over. Colonial structuring and the prerogatives of media institutions persist, with few exceptions, amplifying and cementing dominant interpretative frameworks.[24] As Cree-Métis-Saulteaux editor and writer Lindsay Nixon put it recently in an article on the ethics of writing about trauma:

> Indigenous writing forces Canadian literary communities to confront the question of whose truth is witnessed as authoritative truth, and whose truths are not considered truth at all, because they negate a naturalized colonial and capitalist order in Canada (and Canadian publishing).[25]

The histories of journalism in Canada and the United States are distinct and similar in that they have both long-excluded minority perspectives, prized objectivity, and have similar largely commercial media systems, which are in decline as Chapter 4 elaborates. Except in rare instances such as the much-celebrated civil rights era in the United States, journalists and news organizations in both countries have often consistently acted to support the objectives of the state and the status quo of social ordering. As Rhodes points out in relation to the history of American media: "A racist society also requires a racist media to disseminate these values and beliefs to a mass audience."[26] Read alongside histories of objectivity and the profession detailed in Chapter 1, scholars have demonstrated the ways in which neither emergent nor current professionalism are a defense from widespread, deeply entrenched cultural views and stereotypes. And alongside Zelizer's concept of interpretive communities, scholars and many of the journalists we spoke to show exactly how powerfully debilitating "group think" among editors and throughout the newsroom is when journalists perceive themselves as somehow able to act independently from cultural norms and check their subjectivities at the door.[27]

Drawing from Haraway, the question that emerges, underlying both the experience and history of practicing journalism, is: How do the "social and literary technologies" of witnessing in journalism arrive at the "earth shaking authority to ground the social order objectively?"[28] As we argued in Chapter 1, this kind of question has been asked of science but less so of journalism despite the kind of social ordering that Anderson and Robertson's text demonstrates and despite what journalists themselves have continually articulated. Echoing Carey's lament in the 1970s, Anderson and Robertson suggest that journalism's history is understudied; and we would add, as we've suggested in previous chapters, that it's equally under-theorized.[29]

Colonialism in Canada and the United States reflects a deep history of dispossession and Indigenous resilience, where Indigenous people must navigate systemic injustices and discrimination while also arguing for basic needs like clean water, education, and food security—and a well-documented history of, in Canada's case, newspapers' complicity with state-sponsored violence against Indigenous people from pre-Confederation forward. Wolfe's observation that "when invasion is recognized as a structure, not an event, its history does not stop" has special relevance for journalism then as both a set of practices that rely on observations and as creators of records of note that impact both current and future alterities.[30] Too often under settler colonialism, the "fourth estate" has served as the rationalizing propaganda wing of the other three estates. Here we want to turn to and center Indigenous studies scholars who have identified the underlying logics, grammars, hypocrisies, and contradictions of the state but also the profound refusals, resistance, and counternarratives that parallel moves by the state.[31]

Specifically, we follow Simpson's scholarship and her elaboration of the concept and framework of refusal in asking about the "means through which Indigenous people have been known and sometimes are still known."[32] Simpson questions the role of anthropology as it has "imagined itself to be a voice, and in some disciplinary iterations, *the voice* of the colonized"—a statement that has enormous resonance with journalism where the most widely used code of ethics instructs journalists to "give voice to the voiceless." We suggest that like Simpson's critique of anthropologists, journalists have "accorded with the imperatives of Empire" and created an archive (the sedimentation we refer to previously) that Indigenous people must counter, contend with, and refuse. Indeed, there is deeper resonance, too, in Simpson's point that early anthropological accounts were both "sometimes very popular" and "were required for governance, but also so that those in the metropole might know themselves in a way that fit with the global processes underway."[33] "Othering" in this sense facilitated and facilitates colonization; ongoing settler-colonialism defined by dispossession of land, bodies, and governance; and the ordering and ranking of knowledge, historical narratives, and social lives. Simpson argues:

> Voice goes hand in hand with sovereignty . . . Within Indigenous contexts, when the people we speak of speak for themselves, their sovereignty interrupts anthropological portraits of timelessness, procedure, and function that dominate representations of their past, and sometimes, their present.[34]

This same articulation was clear in speaking with Indigenous journalists who have sought out new venues, freelance interventions, and established their own sources and outlets.[35]

Historically, mainstream journalism has not been, as Anderson and Robertson point out, a supporter of sovereignty or self-determination and arguably has often contributed to an erasure of Indigenous voices.[36] Contemporary journalism may in many cases offer more Indigenous voices, but the underlying challenges persist in terms of negotiation with editors, forms, and styles for journalism and objectivity. What Haraway has called "the god-trick" or "the view from nowhere" has been further developed by TallBear, who suggests that considering one's own knowledge as situated and "actively [incorporating] knowledges from multiple locations" is not merely a "multicultural gesture," but rather "a call . . . to inquire from within the needs and priorities articulated in marginal spaces."[37] It's in this sense that the view from somewhere, of inquiring "from within" marginal space, also includes an accountability component. As TallBear in collaboration with Subramaniam, Foster, Harding, and Roy argue "colonial practices of 'just observing' and 'just reporting what was seen' were often framed as having no consequences at all for what was subsequently done by others (such as militaries and corporations) with those observations and reports of them."[38] Objectivity and distance in these cases often reinforced dominance and had dire consequences for those voices who were, to quote the novelist Arundhati Roy, "deliberately silenced, or preferably unheard."[39]

Herein lies the challenge for journalists in both assuming a stance, objective or otherwise, and in their use of experts as well as the forms and styles of journalism that very well can and do privilege some views, perspectives, contexts, and cultural frameworks over others. TallBear relatedly situates the challenge as a struggle over meanings that influence the structures of the state, law, and policy even as persistent colonial practices in newer scientific projects become apparent. Her charge to scholars and Indigenous people is relevant to journalism in many respects as well.

The fight for indigenous peoples—and for communities more broadly who are regularly subject to the scientific gaze – is to debate *which* meanings and *whose* meanings inform law and policy. That is where we should be working. To make sure that science, and the state, are more democratic, that our stories are heard as clearly as those of anthropologists and geneticists when the state acts to influence our lives. Or rather, that our stories should be heard more loudly than theirs when we have more at stake.[40]

Acknowledging settler-colonialism reorganizes perception and demands a different set of commitments from journalism and journalists in terms of narrating a shared history, prioritizing structural concerns, and articulating injustice. As TallBear points out, this includes assigning and prioritizing meanings, relations, stories, histories, and their impacts. Indigenous and non-Indigenous scholars based in Hawai'i have suggested through their work on a guidebook informed by Indigenous views of land and relations that the role of scholars is not only to change what people do but how they think about themselves in order to account for "the intermeshment of life on local and global scales." Tuck and Yang's statement and article title that "decolonization is more than just a metaphor" is crucial here as well. Decolonizing is not merely another kind of social justice cause that media can choose to support or amplify, Tuck and Yang argue that decolonization "implicates and unsettles everyone."[41] Acknowledging relations to place and a history of relations fundamentally transforms by centering the process of remembering and caring for places that are full of story, full of relations, full of history.

In addition to countering settler-colonialism then, how might we begin to think anew about journalists' relations to the lands, peoples, and societal structures they cover—and to ascertaining who speaks for whom? And is it different for Indigenous journalists? Further, to quote one of the journalists we interviewed: what makes Indigenous journalists Indigenous—and how is Indigenous journalism done Indigenously?

There is no single, unified Indigenous point of view that might answer these questions. Watts provides some insight when she suggests that "colonization is not solely an attack on peoples and lands; rather, this attack is accomplished in part through purposeful and ignorant misrepresentations of Indigenous cosmologies."[42] She outlines the divide between Indigenous cosmologies and the Euro-Western view that separates *the what* from *the how and why* such that *the what* becomes both empty and open to interpretation and assigning meaning. Watts describes how her own worldview is in "constant conflict," contending that "it is necessary to tease out what the land's intentions might be, and how she tries to speak through us." Drawing on Anishnaabe and Haudenosaunee cosmologies, she states that

> All elements of nature possess agency, and this agency is not limited to innate action or causal relationships. Thus, habitats and ecosystems are better understood as societies from an Indigenous point of view; meaning that they have ethical structures, inter-species treaties and agreements, and further their ability to interpret, understand and implement. Non-human beings are active members of society. Not only are they active, they also directly influence how humans organize themselves into that society.[43]

In Watts's articulation, there are not levels of agency, but rather all things have spirit and agency and these form organizing principles for governance and formulating human agency. For Watts, the process of decolonization begins at connecting to place and listening to land. What this requires of journalism and journalists is still unclear, similar to what Tuck and Yang argue in relation to activism, and it's this process that makes hearing from Indigenous journalists so important in our view. They are actively experimenting and improving journalism as a tool so that it serves publics that not only include Indigenous communities but that accounts for and is accountable to Indigenous relations with human and nonhuman relatives.

Countering Erasure

In one of the rarely published early accounts of an Indigenous journalist who worked in Canadian media in the early 1990s, Lenape journalist Bud White Eye suggests that for those who venture into the newsroom, the stakes are high and the work is difficult:

Journalists have to assume blame somewhere, somehow, sometime. If they're going to write and report, they *must* know that the way they see something may not be the way others who have a stake in it will see it. And journalists can change or influence the thinking of those who are mere bystanders or news followers.[44]

Echoing the concerns we heard from many journalists, he goes on to describe the difference in coverage of two murders in London, Ontario.

First Nations community members and family easily recognized the different treatment and the subtle message that was conveyed: the white woman's case was worth expanded coverage, the case of the 'dead Indian' had little chance of increasing news sales and did not merit continuing coverage. First Nations children in school playgrounds and high schools suffer from the belief that their lives are of far less worth than those of others, a belief perpetuated by the media in the handling of First Nations stories. Even if a journalist is a member of a First Nation and is available to advise on news coverage, there is no guarantee that news outlets will get their reporting right or that they will want to.[45]

White Eye further describes exchanges he experienced in his time at Canada's public broadcaster, CBC national and regional news shows, where he was told stories he suggested weren't news or that there were enough "Native stories this week" to which he responded: "How many white stories have we done this week?"[46]

In the over 25 years since White Eye wrote about his experiences, more Indigenous journalists have joined the ranks of American and Canadian media. Many we interviewed have come up through Indigenous media outlets and moved to mainstream and sometimes back again; many have started their own media presences through blogs, websites, podcasts, and Twitter accounts. While experiences varied among those we interviewed, challenges White Eye identifies persist both in journalism education and professional practice.[47] Martha Troian is an investigative Anishnaabe journalist who has been published by a range of outlets from CBC to APTN, Vice and *Toronto Star* for the past ten years. She describes her journalism school experience this way:

I remember being in J school where there wasn't enough Indigenous perspective—that's for sure—within the curriculum. It was just certain stereotypes or misconceptions about Indigenous people and the issues because there was no context. And I understand where that comes from. It comes from the fact that Canadians—they don't know their own history; they don't know Indigenous peoples' history. And it's not just our history either, right? It's their history too. And they don't know it. And so I think that that's where the ignorance comes from . . . I think things are changing. For instance, my son is learning. At his school, they embrace the Indigenous perspective. It is within the curriculum; it's on the walls; it's in the homework; it's in the reading books. They have a human rights component in the curriculum as well. So I think it's changing slowly.

Many of the curricular changes that have transformed grade schools across Canada have not trickled up to university settings, where curriculum is not standardized and faculty are vastly white and male like most newsrooms.

Troian's experience is one we heard from many other journalists as well. It begins in journalism school, where there are often no permanent Indigenous faculty and very little curricula that address challenges related to reporting on Indigenous communities or settler-colonialism as a terrain and context for reporting—and for many, this continues on into the newsroom.[48] A recent journalism graduate who anonymously contributed to our research described to us the constant difficulties they faced in the classroom as an Indigenous person. They were only able to address it by volunteering their own time to hold workshops for faculty and students in order to educate them about Indigenous people and issues. Omushkego journalist Lenny Carpenter, during his work with Journalists for Human Rights that we discuss later in the chapter, wrote an op-ed for the *Toronto Star* that many echoed when he stated: "Indigenous people are in fact playing the role of educators to counter the failure of Canada to educate its citizens on accurate Indigenous history, cultures and perspectives."[49]

The onus of this kind of constant education puts a special burden on Indigenous journalists both in the newsroom—and in their storytelling. Gitxsan journalist Angela Sterritt who is a columnist and reporter for CBC said that it's not only that most working journalists don't know the history of Indigenous people in Canada, they also don't know many Indigenous people or communities.

The non-Indigenous journalists I work with generally are not fully aware of the serious ramifications of residential school. Many are still learning about the 60s Scoop and the full implications of foster care today and how it's continuing. Many also do not know about the racism that dark-skinned Indigenous women experience. Some have no idea what a treaty is. And most do not know exactly what the Indian Act spells out. It's all very, very new to most. Their relationships with Indigenous people often only exists through their journalism. That's the only time they connect with Indigenous people is through news gathering, which is going to make it hard to report on something when you're starting off at zero.

What "starting at zero" means for journalists is significant both in terms of how they contact sources, and whether those sources will return their calls, e-mails, or direct messages on Facebook and Twitter. Sterritt also said, "It's important to note that some non-Indigenous journalists are really trying hard and are learning, but it's very very slow and you have to go back often and remind them about for example the impacts of residential school. It's not like our people where we get it, because it is lived." She said she ends up supporting and educating colleagues and that it doesn't mean it's always easier for an Indigenous journalist.

Journalists, not in my newsroom, have come to me and said, 'hey, can you give me access to this community?' Because there's fear. There's a legitimate fear of people feeling they don't know where to start and don't know who to talk to or how to ask for permission. So, there are sometimes barriers that Indigenous journalists don't have. I mean, we have the same journalistic standards but we don't always have the same barriers of mistrust that non-Indigenous journalists have. We still are journalists in the end and just because you're Indigenous, it doesn't give you a free pass. But it helps the storytelling significantly, tremendously.

It's this intention to both represent—and better represent—Indigenous communities that inspires much of the innovations in terms of methods and storytelling by Indigenous journalists. Many of those we interviewed offered up instances of how they had to address prior journalisms and offer sources a different approach in order for them to be willing to sit down for an interview. This was particularly palpable with MMIWG reporting. MMIWG has received significantly more attention in Canada because an official inquiry was underway as we wrote this chapter —an inquiry it's worth pointing out that many of the journalists we talked to worked hard in their reporting to bring about. In cases of trauma, Troian pointed out that many of the families were moving from dealing with police where their cases were mishandled and concerns and complaints went unheeded to dealing with journalists who were Indigenous women but still had to work and earn their trust to tell their stories.

Troian described the process as building a relationship, not dissimilar to how many journalists might describe "cultivating" a source, but for Troian, there's a much more accountable, networked relationship building framework that draws on her own situated knowledge and experiences as an Indigenous journalist.

> It goes back to maintaining that relationship with people because if you build that trust, likely they will always come back to you and they want to reveal the information to you first. And it doesn't always happen. I've interviewed other Indigenous folks out there who had huge mistrust against the media and they would say to me, 'I don't care if you're Indigenous.'. . . I had to let them kind of like scold me. And I know where that comes from because they've been burned so many times by other media outlets. And they're so frustrated and angry. So I'll let them take it out on me because I understand where they're coming from. I understand how they were burned by mainstream media. And then they're ready to talk.

Being Indigenous in Troian's terms doesn't give journalists an "in"—instead the hard work involves listening to the added trauma prior journalisms have wrought for families. There is a quality to reporting on any Indigenous issue, and tragedy in particular, that requires journalists to be aware of sedimentation of representations that their work must counter. Such stories also often require educating audiences and colleagues about the deep context of the stories, lives, and communal experiences of both victims and their families. Sterritt described her experiences and the changes that have happened in reporting over the past five years this way:

> I have a newspaper clipping of a little five-year-old girl who was brutally raped and murdered. And the newspaper, all these clippings from that time, I think that was probably in the 80s . . . And it was just quotes from the RCMP. They named her Nation wrong. I don't think they said her Nation. I think they said her last name wrong. Nothing from the family. It was just based on the RCMP. And then gory details. Nothing about the family loving her or being horrified or traumatized. Nothing. So that woman never talked to media, ever. Until last year. She talked to me. So, today, some Indigenous reporters like myself and Connie Walker, Martha Troian, Tiar Wilson, who is now with the [MMIW] commission have more of an inclination to explicate, 'the family member loves her. This is where she came from. This is who she was.'

Sterritt, Troian, and the Indigenous women reporters they mention were part of a team at CBC that put together a database that has grown to include 306 of the women and girls whose deaths are part of the over 1,200 being investigated by the MMIWG Commission. Sterritt said that her commitment to this story stemmed from several aspects: (1) that she could write "from a perspective of knowledge, care, and understanding," (2) that the stories of trauma and atrocity needed to be balanced with resilience so that the work these families have done is part of the story, and (3) that burying the stories means "more hurt grows"—"we need our stories to bubble up and truth to come out" so that healing can begin.

Configuring journalism as part of healing for families who have suffered tragedies is not likely something mainstream journalists who regularly report on crime would similarly articulate. Crime journalism has become a staple of news entertainment and one that, as we pointed out in Chapter 2 as well, often lacks the historical context for victims from minority communities who have suffered police neglect and brutality as well as major settler-colonial attempts at genocide and assimilation. Though, again, Indigenous journalists are beginning to shift these practices as evident in Cree journalist Connie Walker's award-winning CBC Radio series on Missing and Murdered that features an episode entitled, *Finding Cleo*. The episode has been downloaded over 17 million times, and has been described in *High Country News* as not "focus[ing] on a death for its own sake." Instead, "The story's true mystery lies in systems that dwarf a single event: the Canadian government, child welfare practices, Indian residential schools and the colonial legacies that shadow Indigenous lives."[50]

Indigenous communities still directly and intergenerationally suffer from trauma related to genocidal policies and institutions, and most prominently discussed are residential schools that were first opened in the late 1800s and ran until the 1980s, and "the 60s scoop"—a secondary mass removal event of Indigenous children from homes and families in the 1960s that placed them in foster care, often far from their communities.[51] The challenges Indigenous journalists describe reporting on these issues and others, and similar to scholarly points raised by Simpson's critique of anthropology—and Rao and Wasserman's critique of journalism ethics— are not only in the news practices and routines but also in choice of experts, fairness in coverage, evidence-gathering, conceptual frameworks for interpretation, consideration of relevant historical context, and the styles of storytelling. With platform changes and Internet-fueled transformations, we argue journalistic practices and ideals need to rethink what independence means such that journalists must also employ a *simultaneous* locatedness that accounts for their own situated knowledge and the sedimentations of other, prior journalisms. This is particularly important when journalists recognize their view as coming from somewhere and their position and profession as in relation with humans and non-humans. Yet, instead of being recognized as experts on Indigenous issues, journalists who are Indigenous have often been questioned. In her reporting on Indigenous journalism, Saulteaux Cree-Métis journalist Emilee Gilpin summarized it this way:

> When Indigenous journalists aren't named opinion, they're often named 'advocacy journalists' or 'activists,' or told they are 'too biased' and unable to report without a degree of partiality, or without a conflict of interest, in order to uphold their objectivity.[52]

This is a topic and experience we broached with many journalists we interviewed as well, and which is much and widely discussed. Bias, as we have pointed out in earlier chapters, extends from a belief, commitment, and aim in journalism to be objective. Though it's changing, as Gilpin and many we spoke to elaborate, these kinds of charges in racialized newsrooms and conflicts can have serious implications both for journalists and for narratives about Indigenous issues and people as the next two sections describe.

Perspectives, Expertise, and Knowledges

Shoshone-Bannock journalist Mark Trahant has a 30-plus-year career in journalism that includes positions in Indigenous media and mainstream media. He began his career, without a journalism school education in 1975, working for his tribal newspaper. When we interviewed him, he noted ironically that he was a professor at the University of North Dakota's journalism school and running the blog, *Trahant Reports,* that focused on Indian health care, an underreported issue in the United States.[53] Shortly after that, in early 2018, Trahant was asked to reboot then in-hiatus *Indian Country Today* and is now its full-time editor. In the historic federal election of 2018 where 103 Indigenous candidates were running for office, Trahant partnered with First Nations Experience and Native Voice One to produce the "first ever" live, national election coverage of Indigenous candidates by 40 Indigenous journalists.[54] Trahant subsequently reformed *ICT* into an independent nonprofit entity "owned by the non-profit arm of the National Congress of American Indians." And as of this writing, *ICT* is moving the main newsroom from Washington, DC, and expanding it at the Walter Cronkite School of Journalism and Mass Communication at Arizona State University (ASU). At ASU, Trahant plans to launch another "first-ever" that builds directly on the success of election night coverage: a "national television news program by and about Native Americans" that will air weekly on PBS. Describing these developments, Trahant sees the move as "build[ing] a new kind of news operation, one that could be sustainable and a career path for Native American journalists."[55]

We asked Trahant about the thorny issue of objectivity, and his reply suggested an alternate framework:

> I've never thought in terms of objectivity. They used to accuse me when I was a reporter. They said I couldn't write a straight lead to save my life. I think we choose what to cover. And when we choose what to cover, we distort it from the very beginning. If we were truly objective, a four-hour meeting would be a four-hour story. Just by making that choice now, to me, there are standards. Can we be fair? Can we illuminate in a way that's not one side or the other? Those to me are the standards, not objectivity.

What Trahant signals here is that journalism methods are defined by who is using them and how, and how they situate themselves as truth tellers and seekers. Even as a column writer, Trahant said: "I'm not afraid of it being labeled 'opinion,' but it's much more analytical than opinion, because I really don't try to persuade as much as I do inform and give people options." For Trahant, the keyword is independence, which he defines as not being beholden to anyone by giving or seeking money. Independence however does not mean disconnection or lack of accountability, and in reporting on and within small communities, this gets particularly challenging. Several Indigenous journalists we talked to said that given a choice, they wouldn't report on their own community—and some pointed out that their families suffered when they reported on elections and controversial issues within their own communities. In looking at his own career, Trahant sees community reporting as "very difficult."

> Folks who do our tribal paper now just have an extraordinary challenge trying to walk a line of fairness and keep up a high standard. It gets into relationships with your family. When you find out something that could cause someone to lose employment. In a community of two, or three, or four thousand, it's just very tough.

Trahant also sees a positive side to community reporting in terms of accountability:

> When you write about somebody, you had better be prepared to have coffee with them the next day. And to not just have this arbitrary 'I wrote it, I'm not going to talk to you now,' like you do in the city. You're going to sit down and say, 'Here's why I wrote it. Here's my thinking,' and get reaction and have a conversation. And to me that's what's really good about it. We need more of that.

Trahant brought that approach first to his blog and social media accounts where he often publishes a picture of a working "white board" with his ideas and actively asks for feedback. He has continued that in his role as editor of *Indian Country Today* often posting quotes by Indigenous journalists and leaders.

Instead of cause for declaring crisis as elaborated in Chapter 4, social media in Trahant's formulation is a "copy edit desk" for ideas and analysis, and a way to develop networks of audiences. He summed up his own substantial body of work by saying, "I couldn't do my work without social media." His blog posts are regularly picked up and supported by mainstream media who don't have, for example, the depth and expertise in their newsroom on what the impact of Medicaid changes might be in Alaskan Native communities. Trahant sees this as the big opportunity for individual journalists who develop expertise in a particular area, but a cautionary tale for institutions, even those like *Indian Country Today* who "still get caught up in what's happening right now whether or not a story is significant or not. And if I had a magic wand, I would let them do what they're doing now, but shift just a bit more toward: let's worry about what really matters rather than just every story that's going to get clicks."

Many journalists, both Indigenous and non-Indigenous, complain that turning around same-day stories that run about 500–700 words in length don't allow for broader commentary that might provide insight into systemic inequities and structural challenges. Journalism and journalists' focus on events, what happened, and what's considered "news" follows well-described and studied news values (such as conflict, novelty, timing, location). Scholarship and professional journalists have been slow to gesture at deeper challenges around quick turnaround journalism that lacks deep context and the structural inability of journalism to adequately account for colonial conditions. For some journalists we spoke to, this sparked a deeper conversation about objectivity, independence of the press, and the need for Indigenous journalists—and for others, the problems were structured into the commodification of stories and how they deal with sources.

Mandan-Hidatsa and Lakota journalist Jodi Rave Spotted Bear runs the independent news site, *Buffalos Fire,* which started as a blog and includes a podcast. Spotted Bear also founded the Indigenous Media Freedom Alliance (IMFA) based in North Dakota, a nonprofit media corporation that is "creating a news system that can respond to the news gap of information in American Indian communities in the Great Plains." The IMFA website notes that there are only 12 independent Indigenous media organizations in the United States despite there being 565 federally recognized tribes. Spotted Bear is passionate about educating communities on the need for independent journalism, and part of that stems from the overwhelming role that social media has played—often stepping into the role mainstream media won't or can't.[56]

> How is the lack of the democratic press affecting our communities? I don't think people understand that because we haven't had a free press for so long. So, what I really deplore is the fact that any kind of news going on in the community, because we don't have the traditional method of a newspaper, or a radio station, or a broadcast network, everybody has to get their views on Facebook.

In part because it has played such a major role in Indigenous communities, Spotted Bear was wary about the way in which Facebook can be used for the spread of false information, rumors, and complaints, and said so long before Facebook founder Mark Zuckerberg stood for hearings in the U.S. Senate—or before the term "fake news" was widely used. At the same time, Spotted Bear sees the potential of digital media to democratize media and provide a platform for Indigenous storytellers "to tell our own stories."

Part of Spotted Bear's inspiration stems from her own work as a reporter for the mainstream press for 15 years regionally and nationally. When we discussed objectivity, she described an earlier reporting experience on the repatriation of human remains, and related how a white woman who had been sent from a competing newspaper told her: "You know, sometimes you wouldn't know me and Jodi were at the same event." Spotted Bear described her approach as being "totally from an Indigenous perspective" whereas the other reporter didn't know the issues: "we had a different perspective on the same events." Spotted Bear summed it up this way:

In journalism school that's what they teach you, to be objective. However, you know, the older I get and the longer I do this it's like, we can pretend all we want that we don't have opinions, but we're human beings and we do have opinions and it does affect the way that we tell stories, which is why I think it's important to have American Indian journalists or First Nations journalists.

In some ways, what Spotted Bear is arguing here is that what journalists bring to the story is as important as the story itself—their knowledge, expertise, and perspective matter when considering how to tell stories about, from, and for Indigenous communities but also when considering how to tell stories that *represent* the knowledge, expertise, experiences, perspectives, and deep historical contexts of those communities. This is how situated knowledge can become a form of expertise for journalists, as we also argue in Chapter 2. Trahant described an example of his practices related to climate change and the Internet when we asked him what he thought Indigenous reporters do differently when they report on Indigenous issues.

Let's take climate change, for example. To me part of the story ought to be that if you look at whether it's 50,000- or 100,000-year history, folks have been through this before. Shoshones, my tribe, hunted Mastodon. When that went away there was a transition. Finding out how that transition occurred, whether it's through stories or other scientific methods. And I think both need to be part of that. To know that we've been there. One of the lectures I do in my class is how the Pueblos invented the Internet. And basically, the idea is that if you look at ancient Pueblo villages, they were lined up by this road system that was incredibly straight. And then they communicated with streams of light, and light on, light off, one comma zero. People from that generation would be amazed at the technology, but the way the story was conveyed would probably be really familiar. In fact, I would argue that the Pueblo revolution of 1680 was a social media story, because they took a piece of media — a rope — and had a story told about it. And as the ropes were untangled and that led to the revolution, or signaled the revolution. It tied story and object together in a way that, again, is familiar.[57]

This theme was echoed in many of the discussions we had with journalists about the repetition and countering of typical mainstream narratives about Indigenous communities, and many had similar stories they could point to where their own perspectives, knowledge, and expertise mattered.

Anishnaabe journalist and satirist Tim Fontaine has spent many years at both CBC and APTN, working in film and newspapers. Based out of Winnipeg, he expanded this theme by noting that even between newsrooms in different parts of Canada, the tone and narratives vary in coverage of Indigenous issues.

> There is this real exoticism that exists in newsrooms when it comes to Indigenous communities. Manitoba was different. There was a lot of people that knew people in the community and did a good job of maintaining those relationships. But I know that in a lot of other newsrooms it's not the same . . . to me knowing that history, that deeper history and that context, I think is one of the most important things. Because, you can report on something that happened and shock people like Attawapiskat, right?

Attawapiskat is a northern Cree community that was added to Treaty 9 in 1930, and most of its members only moved to the reserve (a traditional seasonal gathering place) in the mid-1960s. Attawapiskat has been in the news often since the early 2000s due to housing, water, suicides, its agreement with the De Beers diamond mine that operates near their community, financial management, and other issues. Chief Theresa Spence of the Attawapiskat Nation went on a hunger strike in a tipi across from Canada's Parliament during the Idle No More movement in order to protest the subpar conditions of her community, many of which persist despite political promises, public awareness, and media coverage. Fontaine's analysis of media coverage echoes much of the scholarship that found media unable and unwilling to cover Attawapiskat without deploying a deficit view of the community and its chief.[58]

> There is a classic example where it was like, 'oh, look at how horrible they live,' and 'the chiefs that are doing this.' And that was the automatic thing. Well then you realize, there's this whole other thing that's been happening here for years and years and years, and it's a deeper, deeper, deeper sickness that's affecting that community that wasn't one of their own making. And people just refuse to see that, I think. That's where Indigenous journalists were very, very valuable, I think, in guiding some of that coverage.

After our interview, Fontaine launched *Walking Eagle News*, a satirical news blog and Twitter account. He takes a similar approach on a weekly show he formerly hosted and produced for APTN called "The Laughing Drum." In reflecting on his varied roles in journalism, Fontaine talked about how he realized the "why" of journalism's methods was embedded in commercial logics intended to shock as opposed to illuminate structural concerns and the complicated impacts of colonialism:

> I found that why my coverage stood out, I think, or why my work stood out, was because it was more about finding out 'why' . . . Or, understanding 'why' and being able to explain to your readers or your audience 'why,' as opposed to just showing them something that shocks them. Because there still is a lot of that in coverage today, where it's like, 'Oh my god, look at *this*,' right? It's so centered on crisis, and so centered on shocking the audience. 'Look at how these Indians live,' as opposed to 'why is it that it's like this?'

Arguably, journalists are always challenged to report in a way that sheds light on both the impact of structures and conditions for change. Yet, this is particularly compounded when journalists report on Indigenous communities where the history of media is one of propping up a colonial narrative and the current practices revolve around, as we earlier pointed out, framing Indigenous people as tragic and/or expendable victims. This is intensely palpable when considering reporting on MMIWG as we argued in the previous section, but it cuts across reporting on all issues and events related to Indigenous communities, and it becomes markedly evident when considering reporting on major movements and events as our discussions with Indigenous journalists about Standing Rock revealed.

Geographies and Destabilizing "the Local"

Reporting from somewhere, as opposed to nowhere, means that Indigenous journalists are more likely to both unearth their own epistemology (how they know what they know) and epistemological commitments (what methods and evidence are admissible; what matters), and acknowledge the ways in which their stories reflect their own situated knowledges (their view comes from somewhere). In this sense, Indigenous perspectives, expertise, and knowledges are an intervention into both media practices and narratives as well as settler-colonial systems and institutions, and they offer a crucial counter to erasure, ongoing colonial violence, and misrepresentation. Indigenous reporters are more likely not only to provide a deeper context and credible voices on the ground but also to frame their stories as stories of resilience, of historical narratives repeating themselves even while acts of resistance persist. As Monet put it,

What I've been trying to instill in a lot of the conversations that I have when critiquing media and its approach in covering Indian Country is that *the history—the historical narrative—is just as important as what's happening on the ground*. It's just as important as the present in terms of bringing context to any issue happening in tribal life. And I feel strongly about that, particularly in Standing Rock. The historical narrative was the backbone, the very foundation of what brought people there.

Monet points out that historical context was key to understanding what was happening at Standing Rock as the latest installment in "a decades-long history of militarization and environmental racism on this particular tribe, versus just a bunch of people going and camping-out and protesting a pipeline." Without that understanding, mainstream media struggled to see it as a story worthy of attention and ongoing coverage—or the significance of events that occurred there when, for example, dogs were brought in to attack those at the Standing Rock encampment.

There were narratives that came out of Standing Rock in the very beginning back to the dog attack, where this kind of corporate terror was how one of the reporters had framed it. It was seen linked back to this history of militarization with those attack dogs. And it just so happened that on the day that that confrontation unraveled, it happened to be the anniversary of the Whitestone Hill massacre where militarized troops came in and slaughtered hundreds of Dakota and Lakota men and women. And to have that connection made in the historic narrative where this history of militarized torture and terror is nothing new. But it's repeated itself. And, wow, how ironic that it's repeated itself on the day; that dogs used to attack water protectors at the same time that a century and a half ago the same kind of militarized people came in and tortured their ancestors. It was a pretty powerful thing to take in while I was there at the ground. And I don't know that a lot of other journalists [got it]—well, there weren't a lot of journalists there, to be fair.

With Monet's framing, Standing Rock needed to be understood as not new, but a latest event in a history of militarization with attack dogs and environmental racism built on centuries-long histories of massacre and genocide. Historical narratives repeat themselves, and the resources Indigenous journalists bring to the table are not just knowledge of this history: as Monet points out, it is also important to know exactly *when* to bring these historical narratives up.

For Monet, reporting at Standing Rock as one of the first journalists on the ground had particularly high stakes both because of her status as a freelancer and because it was an event that wasn't being covered by mainstream media. She described it this way in an article published afterward: "I self-financed my early reporting [at Standing Rock] and filed my first dispatches for $50 a piece for National Native News, a desperate solution to national media's initial ignoring of the situation—white editors dominated and later determined the narrative that was most comfortable and timely for them."[59] Monet was arrested at Standing Rock along with other protestors when police refused to recognize her press credentials. She was also charged, and later acquitted. Leading up to the trial there were concerns expressed by many about whether she should be standing trial at all. She wrote about the arrest for the *Columbia Journalism Review* (*CJR*), and pointed out:

> When journalists were arrested during the protests in Ferguson, Missouri, their plight was reported by *The New York Times, Time* magazine, CNN, and so on. By comparison, the media that stepped up to share my Standing Rock struggle has largely been independent—fitting, perhaps, since these niche newsrooms invested early in chronicling this moment among the Lakota Sioux and their allies.[60]

In describing both her work as a journalist and why she decided to write about the arrest for *CJR*, a widely read magazine that serves both journalists and scholars, she articulated it this way, raising the issues of objectivity and advocacy:

> I take pride in the fact that I have reported on the movement at Standing Rock from multiple points of view, and with a concerted effort to represent all sides in conflicts. I've formed strong working relationships at both the county and state level, and reached out to leading community voices away from the reservation. Because I am a journalist of Indigenous origin, and because much of my work has been steeped in writing about Indigenous-themed struggles like Standing Rock, I have often felt I've had to overcompensate in my role as a journalist as a way to disprove notions of activism.

Monet said in her interviews with us that she considers herself an advocate in one area only: "If there is one role where I feel like I am an advocate it is for this Indigenous narrative to be embraced in elite, legacy media and to be handled responsibly by legacy media." Monet credits Oglala Lakota journalist Tim Giago with making a huge difference for her and many in the current and rising generations of Indigenous journalists. Giago covered protests at Wounded Knee in the 1970s and was appalled then at the lack of local and national coverage. He left a columnist job at a nearby mainstream newspaper and went on to co-found the Native American Journalists Association and launched a newspaper on the Pine Ridge Reservation that fostered a generation of Lakota journalists and many others across Indian Country in the United States. Monet described the difference this makes in terms similar to many journalists and scholars quoted in this chapter—as countering the typical deficit stories of "poverty, and welfare checks and alcoholism . . . what you get when you have Lakota writers, for instance, writing about Lakota community, it ends up becoming discussions beyond that." There's not ignorance about difficult social conditions but neither is it "the focal point of the story and it's certainly not the headline." In this sense, Simpson's observation is apt here that "when the people we speak of speak for themselves, their sovereignty interrupts" the representations often made about them.[61]

When we interviewed Indigenous journalists from both the United States and Canada who covered Standing Rock, they pointed out that the main difference in coverage of Standing Rock was the Facebook Live feed. You didn't have to rely on mainstream news sources—or the rookie reporter sent from the local *Bismarck Tribune*, as Spotted Bear noted—to get some sense of what was going on. Even President Obama, as Trahant pointed out, learned about Standing Rock from someone in Indonesia who saw it on Facebook Live. In the absence of mainstream news, social media provided a vital platform for understanding what was happening on a day-to-day basis. Much of the infrastructure for the live video feeds from Standing Rock is relatively new, and many pointed out that it wasn't run by Indigenous people. Monet described her own surprise on arriving to report:

> When I first got to Standing Rock . . . I was really surprised to see that the people who were running the media group were a bunch of white kids . . . some were from North Dakota, and some of them were their buddies from Iowa. And they were these kinds of ragtag, hippy types, but they knew what they were doing and they have lots of expensive gear and a lot of media savvy. They were quick on the Internet. They were quick with coding.

Many of those working on media at Standing Rock were experienced with media produced during protests. Unicorn Riot, for example, played an important role in keeping a video feed going and it wasn't without risk. The role this video feed played, and the constancy of it through difficult circumstances, ironically, was what got mainstream media interested.

Difficult circumstances may be an understatement in this case. Métis journalist Dennis Ward, a news anchor with APTN, went to Standing Rock several times over the course of the encampment. He described his own shock about the way protesters and media were treated.

> They were dressed as though they were ready to go into war. I mean, I guess, that was the smart way to go because we didn't even have bottles of water and a granola bar for the treaty raid. And we're getting shot at and pepper sprayed, and out in the heat for nine hours with no water, but I guess they're just used to that. Whereas us in Canada aren't used to having the police come at you that way. They all had—even on the treaty raid—they're all wearing goggles and helmets and stuff. We're like, "What?" My camera person who was pretty young, and was just getting in there and getting every shot, got pepper sprayed, and we all got shot at with rubber bullets and these little pellets. It was nuts. I dreamt about it for months probably afterwards.

The turning point some observed in mainstream media attention came when Amy Goodman, a journalist whose program *Democracy Now* is a popular staple of PBS programming, was also arrested. In other words, the conflict and encroachment on freedom of the press provided the news value rationale required for mainstream media. Our interviews also suggested that while Facebook Live could be a powerful and transformative platform, the odd editorializing commentary from Facebook Live streamers did not address what was missing from mainstream media reporting. It was an addition and an alternative mode for understanding—not a replacement for in-depth reporting and analysis.

Social media, however, also reorients thinking about the audience and the way that journalism gets done. Ward went as far as to say: "Facebook is the new phone book, especially covering Indigenous communities when some of them are remote communities and that's how people connect. And that's how you find stories often." Similar to Trahant's earlier comments, Ward says that it has transformed his journalism practices. He said, "I don't even look at the news wires anymore; Twitter is my news wire." And he further pointed out that these platforms are multi-directional: "It can make you more accountable, you get a lot of feedback."

This accountability and connection—as well as the deeper context—mean that Indigenous audiences are likely to make connections to history but also to related issues. Issues like climate change, for example, suddenly raise other issues such as traditional knowledge, justice, and adaptation measures much like Standing Rock raises issues of development, land rights, sustainability, health, and consultation—all of which are connected. Yet mainstream media is unlikely to make these connections let alone acknowledge the colonial geographies in the United States or Canada. In fact, the term "parachute journalism" has been applied to how mainstream journalists drop into Indigenous communities unaware of the long histories, cultural contexts, and colonial relations at stake in the stories they seek to tell. As Justice pointed out to us, parachuting is a settler-colonial practice and this critique is also equally applicable to many other professions associated with education, church, and the state where individuals drop into Indigenous communities and operate on an extractive logic built on inequitable power relations and dehumanizing presumptions.[62] As Monet put it, "Indian country is not a foreign country . . . and it shouldn't take violence to not be ignored." Yet, for several journalists we interviewed, that is precisely how Indigenous communities are treated—as foreign terrain.

Parachute journalism rests on a kind of journalistic hubris that one can descend into a place, get the lay of the land quickly, and build enough relationships fast enough with sources in order to tell others, back in one's home country or global audiences "what happened"—"what they need to know"—why they should care or be concerned. Much of this storytelling rests on the news values of the journalist's newsroom and editors—so amplification of certain kinds of conflict or what's perceived as unusual often end up as "the story." In this sense the "where" of journalism is a series of dislocations that are constituted as omniscience where distance and objective-seeming approaches are prized. Except, in covering Indigenous lands and concerns, this has often meant an erasure of Indigenous presence, title, geographies, settler, and extractive colonialism in favor of "containment" and an orderly "chain of events" narrative in order to justify a "replacement" according to Brooks.[63] Brooks, Estes, Gilio-Whitaker, and Dunbar-Ortiz are Indigenous scholars who have recently published in-depth histories of Indigenous experiences in the United States that capture both the breadth of experience among Indigenous peoples and the challenge of pushing against dominant American narratives about humans, non-humans, and their relations.[64]

In contrast to parachute journalism, a nuanced articulation of diversity and commonality, as well as the survivance, resilience, and kinship in the face of genocide and settler-colonialism also informs the approaches of many journalists we spoke with. Some of this makes it into texts like *Indian Country Today*'s lead to this story:

> With New Zealand's Southern Alps looming above, about 30 members of the Winnemem Wintu tribe from Northern California sat on the windswept bank of the Rakaia River cradling in their hands dark and wormy salmon fry, a long-lost relative finally found.[65]

Here, salmon are articulated as *relative* and the story, reminiscent of stories of many Indigenous peoples in the Americas, tells of the relocation of salmon from the Klamath River, which flows through Oregon and Northern California in the 1890s and 1900s to the McCloud River system in New Zealand. The salmon are thriving in McCloud River. The Klamath salmon population meanwhile has dwindled to only 1,500 in 2016 due to dams, mercury and other toxins, and climate-change-related impacts. The Winnemem Wintu have obtained a grant to bring back some Klamath descendants from the McCloud River, but they face an uphill battle dealing with bureaucracies, policies, scientists, and continued environmental degradation even while salmon remain central to their culture and lifeways. The article quotes Traditional Chief and Spiritual Leader Caleen Sisk as saying: "I want you to have this relationship with the salmon, to have this in your hearts So you'll . . . understand why we're going to do whatever it takes to bring them back."

Rick Harp is a longtime Cree journalist based in Winnipeg and the force behind the podcast, *Media Indigena*. Reflecting on his work on the podcast and on journalism generally at a symposium on Indigenous communities and climate change held at Princeton University, Harp pointed out that for Indigenous people, "stories literally can be life or death," and that "the status quo is literally deadening and destroying the lives of Indigenous peoples which means that if Indigenous journalism is to be of any service to Indigenous peoples, it must critically engage that status quo." Harp goes on to further argue that work Indigenous journalists do is closer to those covering wars and conflict zones.

> Lately I found myself wondering whether Indigenous journalists ought to regard their work as that of war correspondents. Indigenous lands, Indigenous waters, Indigenous bodies, even Indigenous languages all are

under constant attack in forms both overt and covert, proximate and distal. Think I'm being hypberbolic? Talk to the people at Standing Rock. Talk to the Indigenous journalists who were there covering it . . . How then does a journalists cover a people—their own people—in the face of such relentless existential threats? Somehow the media convention of 'let's hear from both sides of the story' just doesn't cut it.[66]

This push against media conventions, and idealized notions of what it means to do journalism offers a differentiation that puts Indigenous journalism(s) as something beyond the repair and reform we suggest in the previous chapter and instead moves closer to transformation.

Much of the transformation that Harp and others we quote in this chapter suggest stems from having covered events where Indigenous concerns are profoundly and persistently misrepresented and misunderstood by mainstream media. Nehiyaw Iskwew journalist Ntawnis Piapot who is from Treaty 4 Territory located in Saskatchewan, reported on the trial for the killing of Colten Boushie, which we more fully detail in Chapter 2. Piapot later wrote about her experience of reporting for *JSource*, an online news source in Canada similar to *CJR* that is read by journalists and scholars. The headline of her account speaks volumes on its own: "Colten—Our Relative, Our Warrior." In the article, she describes how she considers Colten Boushie as a relative and relates that covering the case changed her:

Covering the Colten Boushie case changed me as a journalist. As an Indigenous woman, I can't sit here and act like I'm not hurt, angry and scared for the future of this province. Saskatchewan is a whole different place in Canada. You can feel the racism towards Indigenous people and it manifests itself insidiously in our workplaces, schools and on our streets. You can witness a fraction of it on social media on a daily basis. Hundreds of everyday people comment and tell people of colour that Colten's death was not a race issue when they haven't experienced any form of racism a day of their lives.[67]

In Piapot's analysis, Indigenous journalists can't separate themselves from the violence they cover and the violence and persistent colonialism they experience as Indigenous people. Navigating this as a journalist requires transformative thinking about both how to tell the story and how to think about the multiple audiences that story will serve.

Yet, none of the journalists we spoke to learned this in a journalism school—rather, they synthesized and often supported one another in working out and articulating their own negotiations with journalism as a craft, profession, responsibility, and additional identity. As Spotted Bear pointed out, there are few journalism programs or courses at Tribal colleges in the United States.[68] Trahant is moving *Indian Country Today* into the Cronkite School at ASU, developing a weekly show for PBS, and creating a dynamic environment that supports young Indigenous journalists as a way to fill that gap. In addition, ICT hosts journalists working in tribal media for stints at ICT as a way to develop more journalism talent. Canada similarly has few Indigenous-focused journalism training programs or courses with significant Indigenous student populations or faculty. First Nations University of Canada is one of these, with a summer institute and two-year program for journalism training.[69] Many journalists, as discussed earlier, also have to educate their colleagues, and a few engage in more formalized peer training about how to report on Indigenous communities. The next section describes a new NGO-led effort to reach out to younger and would-be journalists living and working in rural communities in Canada, enlarging the ranks of Indigenous journalists and supporting them to navigate professional and communal priorities. The event we attended also served to bring together mid-career journalists whose stories are, as this chapter amply demonstrates, not well known.

Sioux Lookout: Training New Journalists

In the summer of 2017, we traveled to Sioux Lookout, a small community in northern Ontario that serves as a regional hub for both nearby Treaty 3 First Nations and fly-in communities in Treaty 9 in northwestern Ontario. Treaty 3 includes 28 communities in Manitoba and Ontario and has a population total of about 25,000 people. Treaty 3 was the first post-Confederation treaty settled on October 3, 1873 and covers 55,000 square miles (roughly the size of Bangladesh and larger than Greece, Iceland, or Cuba). Some communities in this area are also part of Nishnawbe Aski Nation (NAN—formerly known as Grand Council Treaty 9), which represents 49 communities within northern Ontario whose populations are estimated at around 45,000 people.[70]

We went to Sioux Lookout to attend a first conference for newly trained Indigenous community journalists that also included mid-career Indigenous journalists who were there to offer insight, support, and feedback on story pitches. Organized by Journalists for Human Rights, a Toronto-based non-profit organization, the conference—named Mookitaakosi—marked the end of three years of journalism training provided mainly to youth from fly-in communities all over the region covered by Treaty 3 and Treaty 9 who wanted to learn how to tell stories from and about their communities through mixed media (print, audio, video).

The meetings took place about a 30-minute drive outside of Sioux Lookout in the community of Lac Seul. Lac Seul is also one of many Indigenous communities in Canada with a boil water advisory. While the current government has promised to end these advisories, not much has been accomplished as we near press deadline and are close to the end of their mandate. And like many Indigenous communities, these advisories only hint at how the land, water, and people in this region have been impacted by the long tale/tail of colonial disruption and destruction. A historic plaque posted on the roadside of Lac Seul briefly narrates how Treaty 3 required the chiefs and leaders of Obishikokaang Anishinaabeg to choose a place for their reserve. They chose well in 1874, "with a view to preserving their traditional way of life," near "sweet water, and a shoreline that was ideal for cultivating rice" with access to plenty of fish and game. But in the 1920s, the river lake system of Lac Seul was selected for creation of a reservoir for hydroelectric power by the Ontario government. "In 1934, without knowledge or permission of the Obishikokaang Anishinaabeg, the dam was activated and the lake rose by 12 feet (36 m)." They returned from winter trapping to find 82 reserve houses, council houses, farms, barns, powwow grounds, and sacred Midewiwin (Grand Medicine Society of Ojibwe) grounds flooded. Families were left homeless, and rice beds were also destroyed as was the habitat of/for non-human relatives. This story is not atypical in Canada and the United States, and yet most of those who benefit from electricity further south are unaware of how deeply rooted their current modern conveniences are in the long tale/tail of colonialism.

We first learned about the conference via tweets from Sterritt, who was invited to give the keynote address. Here is how the conference website described the event:

> The conference was named 'Mookitaakosi' by Jerry Sawanas, who is a long-time radio broadcaster with Wawatay and renowned Oji-Cree language expert from Sandy Lake First Nation. Mookitaakosi refers specifically to the sound of frogs waking up in the spring after their hibernation and beginning to sound their voices again. The frogs' voices were silent but are now coming out once more and being used again. Animals never change what they're doing, and it's important for humans to listen to their

voices. Mookitaakosi: voice coming out and getting clear, first muffled in the bush while the frogs emerge from their hibernation. The storyteller is named dibaajimo in many Ojibwe and Oji-Cree dialects, and like our relations the frogs, dadibaajimoowininiwag (storytellers) are also sounding out their voices and stories. Journalism is relatively new but necessary in Indigenous communities.[71]

In her panel discussion at the conference, Sterritt situated her own journalism as the modern version of what she termed, "runners": people who were chosen to deliver information on foot between communities where she's from in the Gitxsan Nation (in what is now northwestern British Columbia).[72] Journalism in both of these formulations is therefore not necessarily "new" but a version of storytelling that serves the need for information in order to govern effectively and communicate between communities.

Over the three years of its operation, JHR's program sent community journalism trainers into Indigenous communities for eight months. They were tasked with not only training journalists but also providing local radio programming and community media literacy training. JHR also facilitates internships for Indigenous journalists and has successfully placed 19 of 21 of these interns in journalism jobs. The program was sponsored by the Ontario Trillium Foundation, which is part of the Ontario government. Carpenter, who we reference earlier in the chapter, was the program manager responsible for the conference and described its aims as "increasing the quantity and quality of Indigenous voices in Canadian media."

Carpenter has been a journalist since 2004 when he attended journalism school at Algonquin College. Prior to JHR, he worked primarily with *Wawatay News*, operating since 1974 in print and serving more than 80 First Nations across northern Ontario.[73] Carpenter described the work at JHR as growing out of a study called *Buried Voices*, which examined coverage of Indigenous people in Ontario media between 2010–2013 and then again from 2013–2016. The first study revealed that, on average, 0.28% of all stories in Ontario media were about Indigenous communities. And of those, less than a quarter were considered "positive." This study was conducted during Idle No More, and Carpenter notes many editorials reflected a negative tone at that time. In the 2013–2016 study, the percentage of stories rose to 0.5%, with more positive coverage than negative. But, in our interview with Carpenter he pointed out that this is still a far cry from reflecting the 2% of the population that is Indigenous in Ontario—and regionally, in the northern part of the province, that proportion is much higher, but most media come out of Toronto, the provincial capital or Ottawa, the federal capital. Regarding the disproportionately low coverage, Carpenter stated that "to us that said there needs to more Indigenous journalists." He also noted that many young people from Indigenous families and communities are more likely to go into social services or health care rather than journalism. Yet, Carpenter pointed out that Indigenous journalists bring a different approach to their stories for precisely the reasons that draw them into the other professions, specifically because they:

> Know the nuances of the history, like residential schools, the Indian Act, treaties. They know about community relationships. That's often misunderstood by non-Indigenous people. I think that's really crucial, and I think they bring the understanding because their own families and communities may be affected by those things. There is more sense of respect and understanding and sensitivity to covering a story.

He further pointed out that "non-Indigenous journalists will stick to their hard journalistic standards and ethics. Whereas Indigenous journalists know how to balance that, because . . . ethics aren't universal, they're culturally based." Carpenter used the example of bringing tobacco to an elder when requesting an interview as a sign of respect, a common practice in Indigenous communities in many parts of the continent. Yet, many ethical guidelines for journalists specifically require that journalists refrain from giving or receiving gifts to avoid conflicts of interest—real or perceived and to maintain independence. Not only that, but many non-Indigenous journalists might not be aware of traditions and customs surrounding community leaders, ceremonies, or cultural ways of being and engaging with one another. JHR, in addition to the program we write about here, has trained over 1,200 non-Indigenous journalists across Ontario, Manitoba, and Saskatchewan using two-hour workshops that share best practices for reporting in Indigenous communities.

In setting up Mookitaakosi as a conference, Carpenter said they wanted "to inspire people" and invited those who had participated in the program from communities, trainers, and a number of well-known Indigenous journalists. Mid-career Indigenous journalists who have spent time in both Indigenous media and mainstream media are rare in Canada and the United States. Narration of how Indigenous journalists arrived at this point in their career is important not just to encourage the young journalists attending Mookitaakosi but also because these narrations are not well known. Conference panelists were among the first and few to join the ranks of professional journalism (and the majority of them, it's worth noting, are employed on a freelance basis). One of the first mid-career panelists to speak began her talk by saying she was from a reserve of 250 people that felt remote and disconnected, with only a few channels for TV and radio. In narrating her own journey to journalism, she asked a key question that animated many of the themes that ran through the conference: "Why would anyone ever want to listen to us?"

For her, the deafening silence, the lack of stories that reflected her community represented a kind of oppression. It was, she said, painful not to be heard and to not matter. She went on to point out that 50% of her nation, comprising many similarly small and larger communities, were under age 19. The need for "a voice, and a platform to speak" was a powerful motivator for her to become involved with the training program so that young people could become "empowered [to see] their own worth." Another panelist who freelances for many major outlets and has a large following online pointed out that this is precisely why she tries to get past the usual political "talking heads" and experts who respond to news stories and instead make the community "come alive" in her work.

For Indigenous journalists, where they are speaking from is as important as where and to whom they are speaking—it is what animates careers as well as concerns and approaches. Talaga described her view of Mookitaakosi similarly—in terms of communities as place-based experts:

> At the JHR meeting that we were at, we broke off into groups, and we spoke to the youth who were from the communities talking about the story ideas that interested them. And, every single story idea that came up had to do with where they were living, and what was happening in their community, and how the community could be made a better place if this happened, or that happened. We had everything from mental health wait times to speak to the counsellor to what happens when trauma teams leave a community after a suicide. How do people pick up the pieces when they have been left behind? Who does that? Whose role is that? I think the questions that are being answered in a microscopic way, or looked at in a microscopic way, by the journalists who are part of the JHR program are really vital and integral, because they have a bird's eye view of what's happening in the community around them.

When Indigenous communities are suddenly thrust into the spotlight by a mainstream media rife with stereotypes and sedimentations of representation, it is most often by media less focused on what reflects resilience or deeper structural problems and more on what reflects breakdown, conflict, and tragedy. Questions from the community get shunted off to the side in favor of stories that serve existing frames and other audiences. As Harp pointed out, media are interested in "both sides" and maintaining or propping up a status quo. In many ways, the JHR program seeks to address that by training individuals and communities to counter mainstream narratives.

Conclusion

This chapter draws on the sophisticated and deep expertise that emerged in interviews and fieldwork with Indigenous journalists. Indigenous journalists are actively exposing the methodological partisanship and sedimentation of codified journalistic norms and practices while re-articulating relations with technology, peoples, land, non-humans, cultures, and conditions for settler-colonialism. They are doing this by negotiating and experimenting with journalism methods in order to arrive at culturally appropriate ways of telling stories, dealing with sources, and deciding which contexts matter and when, and in the process decolonizing journalism. In so doing, they are actively transforming the expectations for what stories and representations about Indigenous people should look and sound like, turning to Indigenous experts for insight into Indigenous lifeways, histories, and experiences, advocating for Indigenous audiences to be considered as active engaged publics of all media, and recognizing the deep historical and structural presence of settler-colonialism in the United States and Canada.

The stories mainstream journalists have generally told themselves about journalism are of often getting it right, of figuring out what news audiences needed, and of delivering it. Objectivity—that view from nowhere—is an uncomfortable part of this narrative given that ethical codes abandoned it as an explicit value in 1996, but it persists as an implicit expectation and tacit good in many newsrooms much like its proxies do: independence, unbiased, having enough distance. When we asked Indigenous journalists about the thorny issue of objectivity, what emerged was a differently described practice of journalism where networks of relations form the basis for witnessing, reporting, and intervention via media channels. Indigenous journalists all still identify as journalists but recognize the violence of prior journalisms, cogently re-articulating the epistemology of their journalism as set within a different set of relations with technology, peoples, land, non-humans, cultures and conditions for settler-colonialism.

This active experimentation is what makes this chapter in many ways provisional but also provides a layer that we hope others will build upon. This chapter puts Indigenous journalists into conversation with one another and situates journalism within a longer history of storytelling and governance with newer challenges related to independence. In so doing, there is an implicit and inherent reckoning with the story mainstream professional journalists often tell about their profession and its role in society as the voice of the voiceless that stands against oppression and serves as a watchdog for the state. Professionalization in some ways has provided a thin layer of misattribution as if journalists could, should, and do operate outside of broader cultural norms.

While rural and small-town journalists might share a similar accountability ethic, Indigenous journalists said their burden was much greater because of historical and governance contexts as well as the lack of representation. The ability to see what's happening thus requires locating oneself but also a sensibility about the relations one is a part of—the collective one speaks from, and the audiences who are part of similar and different networks and collectives. Being "in good relations" means that how the "where" and the "why" questions are configured matters immensely. Further, given the volume of reporting on land, resource development, and environment that are caught up in Indigenous rights and concerns, we would argue that proportional representation in newsrooms is not enough.

There is an inherent messiness to this as well in that there is no "neat place" for Indigenous journalisms and journalists who also engage in observing and reporting but from a situated standpoint incorporating Indigenous knowledge and cosmologies.[74] Their work contributes to what we argue are some of the multiple journalisms that are emerging and maturing across new digital platforms. Experimentation, as Fortun, Marcus, and Fischer have pointed out in relation to anthropologies and histories of science, "shape and clarify what the questions are and how they might be asked and answered," and experimental ethnographies intentionally "construct an open system in order to rework and specify questions, examine and extend traditions of thought, and explore possibilities for shifts and displacements so that new insights and analyses might emerge."[75] In this vein, this chapter lays down pathways through an open field of inquiry, experimentation, and hopefulness using ethnographic methods as a mode of exploration and tool for reworking and examining persistent critique and new or emergent methodologies for doing and thinking about journalism.

Many of the journalists we interviewed see themselves as a significant wave of professionals who are beginning to change journalistic stances and methods and demonstrating how their situated knowledge is a form of expertise. Yet conceptions of Indigenous people as an audience or public have yet to be fully appreciated by mainstream news. Harp argues that if Indigenous people were considered a part of the audience, most stories "would start from a very different place." He points out that the old question of "What's in it for me?" normally applied to weighting of news values and assigned to audiences presents a conundrum for Indigenous journalists who must always also ask: "What's in it for settlers? As Indigenous people we have no choice about ignoring that. The inverse is not true."[76]

Conclusion

HOW DO JOURNALISTS KNOW what they know? Who gets to decide what good journalism is and when it's done right? What kind of experts are journalists, and what role should (and do) they play in society?

Until a couple decades ago, these questions were rarely asked by journalists. The assumption by most journalists about how good journalism was defined and who was credible and vital to society remained generally undisputed. When journalists were asked such questions by malcontented publics and critics, often they were easily ignored. Now, if you're on social media, you're likely to see multiple critiques of journalism and media on a weekly, if not daily or hourly, basis. It seems not only convenient but pragmatic to give most of the credit to new media technologies for changes to how journalism does what it does and how relationships between journalists and diverse audiences have changed.

This book rests on a different assumption, however. Namely, that while new technologies have had an enormous impact, they aren't the whole picture. Rather, we contend that technologies offer diagnostics to understand much deeper, persistent, and structural problems confronting journalism—and that new digital technologies have only served to amplify these problems. We argue that you can't talk about journalistic inquiry—and what role journalists and media organizations could, should, and have played in society—without talking about gender, race, intersectional concerns, and settler-colonialism.

This book investigates modern journalism's internal relationship with power and why particular kinds of accountability conversations have not become central to journalism studies as the practice of journalism increasingly confronts wide and sustained criticism—and its crisis. The criticism and/or perceived crisis within journalism have largely been oriented more toward addressing failing economic models, technology, and competition with newer and bigger media platforms such as Facebook and Google. They have not tended to enroll persistent, long-standing questioning of journalism's founding ideals and methods related to who can speak for whom, how and why (particularly in a global world). This terrain is a key part of our focus. We see representational harms as having contributed to a reckoning not addressed or even acknowledged in the vast majority of scholarship or public intellectual discourse about journalism's challenges related to economic and technological changes. Much of the research among journalists in this book reflects the ways in which journalists have been negotiating with professional norms and practices, experimenting and inventing new ways of responding to and contending with these multiple reckonings facing journalism.

A central topic we address and that emerges in both defense and derision of journalism is the durability of objectivity as a central element in methods, ethical codes, and approaches. Few attempts have been made to bring debates about objectivity together with issues related to social order, power, authority, and accountability in journalism.[1] In opening up journalism studies and suggesting that theories must account for persistent critiques, we are suggesting that the crisis in journalism is possibly *more profound,* encompassing not just the economic foundation of the industry but also the ways in which the profession has been historicized and valorized. Digital technologies present a reckoning both to those who practice journalism and those who study journalism in terms of intersectional representations and settler-colonialism. The question of how to "save" journalism might benefit from recognizing what we argue is a long overdue corrective in Chapter 2. The central question needs to shift from saving journalism as we have known it to instead asking what kinds of work, intervention, and transformation one can make with journalism and as a journalist.

Generative answers to that latter question animated our many conversations with and research among journalists working in the United States and Canada, in a variety of news organizations from startups and freelancers to mainstream media—and we've long witnessed as professors how these questions animate the passion and drives of many who are new to the profession. This book offers an alternative roadmap that addresses long-standing concerns about what structures journalism as a means for inquiry *and* as an apparatus for maintaining social order. We contend that journalism has been able to avoid important structural conversations largely because of its loose and paradoxically rigid methods rooted in sedimented power relations, despite thoughtful and rigorous scholarly explorations and critiques of the role of publics, professional methodologies and practices that ultimately haven't gone far enough and/or haven't been taken up.[2]

Instead, journalists have tended to deploy specific kinds of accountability in response to what largely has been seen as a crisis concurrent with the rise of new media platforms and digitalization—and there is no doubt that digitalization has changed the terrain.[3] Journalists have responded to the shifting and increasingly technological landscape by attempting to diversify how they know what they know and do what they do through practices that now include social media in addition to continually evolving ethical codes, ombudspeople and public editors, letters to the editor, opinion columns, and other contested attempts to open up its professional identity to equity and inclusion, audiences, and others. Ultimately, however, these attempts have been internal to the field and often in a way that reinforces existing power relations and the need to protect a single, paternal, modern journalism. This is beginning to change, and there were always alternate modes of operating as a journalist—of making do, in the words of de Certeau—and efforts are emerging and becoming more widespread as is evident in the latter chapters of the book that investigate efforts at repair, reform, and transformation.[4]

In bringing these emergent journalism practices into the scholarly literature on journalism, we also see the need for similar repair, reform, and transformation in scholarship. In Chapter 1, we draw from both journalism studies scholars and historians of science who have been asking questions about how journalists and scientists know what they know for decades. As two fields oriented around objectivity, both have long delved into issues of method, stance, and power, advancing important and necessary critique.[5] Journalism studies scholars have been drawing inspiration, theories, and approaches from STS that involve the social nature of technology and technology's role in organizational change in newsrooms.[6] The two fields, however, diverge on the degree and nature of their critique specifically around issues of power, and the role of gender, race, and colonialism in the production of knowledge. Beginning in the 1980s, feminist science studies scholars like Haraway, Harding, Traweek, and Star destabilized objectivity in scientific methodologies as being less about transcendent facts and methods and more about masculinity and whiteness. These moves had consequences for the field, ultimately supporting a growing and robust area of feminist and postcolonial STS.[7]

Despite a few efforts that we describe in more detail in Chapter 1, journalism studies has not made these critical intellectual turns. We ask in the introduction of the book: why have questions related to gender, race, and colonialism been so hard to ask in a field that studies a profession whose mission is to speak truth to power? Certainly, there have been about three decades of robust scholarship on these topics in the closely adjacent broader (and some would say the "umbrella") field of media studies, which shows how racist, colonial, and gendered coverage in media occurs up to the present. Even as journalism studies scholars are likely to describe and reference the emergence of objectivity in the 1920s, they aren't also likely to point out that concurrently Indigenous people and people of color in the United States and Canada were suffering in myriad of ways that went unreported and were considered part of the normal social order of the time. Nor have these same histories of journalism tended to focus much on the ramifications of white male newsrooms, editors, and publishers. Instead the influence and power of what these newsrooms produced, and (since the 1970s) a focused interest in the mechanics of *how* they produced news has been the focus of those who study journalists and journalism. In some sense, such scholarship contributes to both the narrative journalists tell of their profession *and* the stability of social ordering and interpretive communities that perpetrated harmful representations, ahistorical narratives that ignore the genocidal founding of both Canada and the United States (that were in many cases supported by media of their day), and still persistent exclusions in media based on race and gender. How to narrate the present in a way that accounts for the terrain of settler-colonialism and acknowledges power relations, exclusions, and the harm and sedimentation of mis- and under-representation is a challenge that confronts both journalists and journalism scholars.

Feminist media scholars have in recent decades focused on gender as it relates to content and representations, news norms and practices, the number of women in news, and their progression through the ranks as well as some limited scholarship on issues of economics. There are now NGOs and academic projects that report regularly on how many bylines are women and how many women are expert sources in mainstream media. Yet, very little of this also includes some accounting for or a focus on intersectionality. Following Crenshaw we define intersectionality as the ways in which systems necessary for daily life intersect with race, indigeneity, class, immigration status, disability, age, poverty, gender identity, and sexual orientation.[8] For media, there is a deep history, which we refer to as a sedimentation of representations and a long tail/tale of settler-colonialism that adds to the challenge for scholars and journalists of adopting an intersectional approach. We argue that the persistence of structural oppression and the complicity of journalists in propping up social orders of their day compel scholars and journalists to adopt an intersectional approach to their research and reporting. Indeed, the point we raise in Chapter 6 bears repeating here, too: Too often under settler colonialism, the "fourth estate" has served as the rationalizing propaganda wing of the other three.

When Publics Speak, "Stories are Life and Death"

Social movements have, as we argued in Chapter 2, continually underscored persistent critiques of journalism and continue to do so up to the present. Our analysis of the social movements that grew out of murder trials related to the killings of Tina Fontaine and Colten Boushie feature Indigenous experts whose expertise doesn't just include their knowledge of the failure of government systems for Indigenous youth, women, and communities. The additional dimension of their expertise includes knowing how to talk back and about a media that has also continually failed to represent and/or diagnose where and when systems have failed Indigenous people. Indigenous people like Jesse Wente, a longtime CBC commentator, Pam Palmater, a professor of governance at Ryerson University, and others on #NativeTwitter and elsewhere continually add to public discourse in order to actively challenge media representations. They hold media accountable for their unwillingness to represent Indigenous youth as vibrant survivors of over a century of genocide and settler-colonialism in Canada who are still left to navigate systems that are stacked against them from the outset.

How is it that court reporting as a genre of journalism, the journalists who sat in the courtroom, and the editors who slotted their story and headlined it couldn't see their way through the evidence presented to arrive at the analysis that the foster care system had brutally failed Tina Fontaine and her family and community, and that it continues to fail other youths still fighting to stay alive under similar circumstances? And how is it that they could not see a role for journalism to hold systems of governance accountable on behalf of Indigenous children and youth? How is it that a kid who stops to repair a flat tire and is gunned down point blank in front of his friends and relatives as Colten Boushie was somehow doesn't produce the outrage that media is so famous for fostering in other cases?

Here, Rick Harp's point that for Indigenous people, "stories are life and death" and that "the status quo is literally deadening and destroying the lives of Indigenous peoples" has deep and poignant resonance.[9] Addressing this status quo, as Harp points out and as is so aptly demonstrated through the works of many Indigenous journalists we discuss in Chapter 6, configures accountability quite differently. Tanya Talaga, through her recent lectures and book, *All Our Relations*, has done much to make connections between the kinds of harm, exclusions, and suffering occurring in Indigenous communities dealing with settler-colonial institutions and structures globally.[10]

In the wake of the MMIWG report (released as we finalized this manuscript in mid-2019), Talaga's new column for the *Toronto Star* pushed back against the newspaper's own main editorial that refused the term "genocide" to describe what was happening to Indigenous women and girls in Canada. Talaga was not alone as many Indigenous journalists, public intellectuals, and leaders also spoke out on various platforms, but neither was the *Star* alone as several newspaper editorials challenged the report. The report was prepared by a former judge, drew on 15 community hearings and 2,386 participants in a process that began in Fall 2015—and included a in-depth appendix on why the word "genocide" was appropriate. It is deeply troubling given the critique in this book that Canada's leading newspapers became stuck on whether the word genocide was appropriate instead of using the report to hold systems and institutions accountable for women, girls, and their families who have and continue to suffer.

We also see many parallels to work social movements and journalists have been doing in other communities of color globally, and in the United States particularly—where the intersections of historical relations, race, gender, and colonial systems and structures that dominate daily life produce and reproduce an intolerable present.[11] And we want to explicitly recognize the kinds of emotional labor and education of their colleagues that Indigenous and POC journalists have to do to in their varied newsrooms, the considerations they make about educating diverse publics unaware of the history of settler-colonialism, the kinds of trauma they report on and experience while reporting—and the trolling they also regularly experience online. When we talk about the persistent critiques of gender, race, and colonialism throughout this book that journalism studies and many journalists have dismissed, avoided, or ignored, these are the stakes we consider and the ways in which we see these critiques persisting into the present.

This is in part why the main questions that animate this book are as follows: What structures journalism as a means for inquiry? How do journalists know what they know and how are they practicing journalism in a digital age? Digital technologies are not a rationale that can fully circumscribe the current crisis in journalism nor are these technologies and new platforms an antidote, shiny new tool, or harbinger. Rather, they provide a mirror to help understand and diagnose long-standing and understudied questions of power and structure and what they mean for 21st-century journalism.[12]

STS scholars have long contended that technology reflects and maps onto our beliefs, ideals, values, and webs of practice[13]—in other words, that technologies by themselves don't change anything, and media are no exception in this regard. Instead, technologies are elements of co-production that help assess how and what journalists are doing in the world and what kinds of knowledge are being co-produced by journalists and for whom.[14] In this sense, social media *and* data journalism provide different means by which to understand how technologies enable new forms of accountability and collaboration—and simultaneously shed light on epistemological questions related to journalism's methodologies, dominant interpretations and framing, and conceptions of which publics it seeks to serve and/or prioritize. How to establish validity (and whether there are multiple truths), and how journalism knowledge production relates to larger systems—and who benefits from these narratives and frames—are now questions on the table for journalists on a daily basis, arguably, in ways they haven't been in modern histories of the profession as evidenced in Chapters 1 and 2.

Journalism studies has been less interested in the deep existential questions that practicing journalists have been both forming in memoirs and fomenting in high-profile resignations and speculative memoir fragments as we describe in Chapter 3. We are recommending that there is much generativity and work to do in bringing Indigenous studies and feminist and postcolonial STS scholarship to bear on these questions. For example, TallBear has been suggesting that accounting for whose meanings and interpretations are prioritized matters in a myriad of ways; Nelson, Pollock, TallBear, Reardon, and Benjamin, for example, have shown how stereotypes and racial hierarchies are durable and malleable in medicine, drug discovery, and genomics.[15] It's this scholarship that helps to understand and situate such high-profile apologies as the one we described and analyzed in Chapter 1 from *National Geographic*.

This book contributes to journalism studies and the practice of journalism particularly because professional journalism's reliance on objectivity as a dominant method despite decades of critique both in practice and journalism education remains relatively stable. With resources like this book and others that might follow, our hope is that journalism education might produce greater innovation by helping future journalists to enter the profession with a more accurate accounting of the sedimentation of harms journalism has actively participated in and perpetuated in its framing, narratives, and methodologies. Journalists have done extraordinary things—that we're not questioning. This book seeks to diagnose and historicize the deep dissonance in methods, newsroom cultures, and interpretive communities that we experienced as working journalists and that we still hear from our students who enter the profession and our colleagues who remained "in the business" long after we departed for academia. In part this is why there is a chapter on speculative memoir, since we have heard many of what Joe Sacco has called "the dinner table conversations," and we see journalists actively grappling with how to do better, what their stories are doing in the world, what their obligations are, and to whom are they accountable.[16]

On Not Saving Objectivity

What we hope becomes clear in this book, with evidence and argumentation, is that what journalists think happened is deeply related to who they are and where they're coming from in broad and specific senses—and that there are multiple truths and perspectives that contribute to understanding what "really" happened. Recognizing individual and collective social and historical location needs to become part of the methodology for journalists in order to situate themselves, their knowledge, and expertise within a wider web of relations and entanglements. We are not thinking here of conflicts of interest in the formal sense, nor are we thinking of so-called bias that rests on a commitment to objectivity. Even while journalists recognize the flaws of objectivity and it was removed from SPJ's code of ethics in the 1990s, it remains a standard at public broadcasters and private news organizations formally and informally. And perhaps most importantly, publics have bought it, too, and are polled on whether they think the news media are biased.

Given the critique and wide variety of sources now available with digital media, it's not so surprising that the veil of objectivity has been summarily ripped off by publics who by and large think news media are biased. Of course, the current U.S. president would heartily agree, as his pronouncements on Twitter and treatment of journalists at the White House amply demonstrate. While we denounce that prestige and elite journalism would be called "fake," we might also say that this moment calls attention to the ways in which we talk about journalism methods and how they contribute to social order. If an elected politician is seeking to shift the social order, going after journalists and undermining their credibility and authority reflects a tacit knowledge about the power of journalism to describe the world and to name enemies and allies.

According to Star, this power to decide whose metaphor brings worlds together is why we seek to expand the crisis facing journalism such that it encompasses how journalism does what it does—its methods, stance, and commitments. Digital media and the global crisis of climate change will continue to present journalists, journalism, and scholars with new layers of challenges. Getting to the deeper questions then, we would argue, is that much more pressing such that journalism might be able to pursue and claim more ethical, transformative, and diagnostic work.

Indigenous journalists offer an example of how to pursue transformation in journalism methodologies both by offering up situated knowledge as expertise and by recognizing that their obligations are to land/waters, nonhuman relatives, ancestors, and Indigenous peoples who have been under-represented and harmed by media. Many have pointed out that reporting on Indigenous issues as an Indigenous journalist is not easier. Rather, they are well aware of what missteps and mistakes can be and have been made by journalists—and they are tacitly operationalizing a relational framework in articulating how, to whom, and why they are accountable. It's vital to note the immense diversity of Indigenous people in the United States and Canada, and the majority of the journalists we talked to said that reporting on their own nation or communities is challenging.

The Indigenous journalists we spoke with are aware of the limits of the profession and its dominant methodologies and actively synthesize new approaches that draw from their situated knowledge and their obligations to communities, nonhumans, and lands/waters. We see this approach as potentially transformative to journalistic methods and approaches. The history of journalism is not only one of triumphs as many seeking to "save journalism" might want to retell. Rather, journalism is a strong, powerful set of tools that can and do intervene in systems. And at the same time, interpretive communities of editors and journalists have and continue to exclude, contribute to an ossification of forms and styles, and perpetrate harm. Indeed, the coverage by many mainstream media outlets of Standing Rock, MMIWG, and other recent Indigenous protests provide too many examples of this.

This is what makes this book important. As former journalists and journalism professors, and after years of cobbling together resources to teach what we argue for in this book, we have come to think of the task of formalizing our critique as an ethical and intellectual obligation. We recognize in the introduction that there are external and internal to journalism adjudications of what kind of "good" journalism offers and what kinds of knowledge it produces. In light of this, we seek to bring internal and external conversations together in this book in order to suggest that external critiques offer generative questions and to highlight persistent exclusions and incomplete histories of the profession that drive both how the current economic crisis is circumscribed and what kinds of solutions should be entertained. In this sense, we see the crisis as also a rupture and reckoning between journalists, their organizations and publics, and the timing of this book is important in this respect.

Addressing Rupture, Critique, and Crisis

From the 2009 U.S. Senate hearings on the state of media to the nearly $600 million funding package for media announced by the Canadian government and many other indicators and reports, it's clear that the digitalization of North American life is rapidly developing into a new infrastructure for how we live and run our daily lives. The consequent impact on news consumption, production, and distribution has been cataclysmic. There is no doubt that news organizations have multiple economic and technological shocks to contend with. Yet, deeming this moment in journalism a narrowly circumscribed crisis ignores the ways in which technology reflects our beliefs, values, structures, and relations and the commercial context of modern journalism in North America. That a rupture has occurred in business-as-usual for news organizations shouldn't preclude asking broader questions starting with, we argue, for whom and where is this a crisis.[17]

If we take seriously the contention that stories are life and death, then crises of mis- and non-representation might be understood as happening for much longer as newsrooms maintained the ability to narrate and parse reality such that social ordering and hierarchies remained stable. However, the more we've talked to those working to repair and transform journalism, and the more we've studied articulations by social movements, the more we see how much these broader narratives of suffering and harm have been submerged even while incidences like Oka, Gustafsen Lake, Wounded

Knee, Standing Rock (to name a few) demonstrate exactly how powerful journalism can be in reinforcing and mutating stereotypes, demonstrating a total lack of accountability to those they cover, and a narrow racialized sense of for whom and to whose benefit is journalism a watchdog.[18] Black, Latinx, and other scholars of color would likely add many more additional events and issues some of which are recent and top of mind like Ferguson protests and racial violence at Charlottesville. Bringing alongside race, gender, and colonialism to re-consider journalism's claims and histories is how we arrive at broadening the crisis in journalism—in order to recognize its profundity and the ways in which digital media hasn't supplanted journalism so much as it has called it to account in a reckoning that plays out amidst the noise and signals occurring on and through social media. These counterpublics, as many have argued, have always voiced challenges to mainstream media, but never have their voices joined forces nor been heard quite so loudly.

Legacy media are employing multiple tactics to stem the rupture to the foundations of their business and to address reckonings with multiple and diverse publics. However, in underplaying the reckoning, legacy media as a whole hasn't quite been able to move to repair or reform in the same ways that a mission-driven startup that we profile in Chapter 5 does, nor do either types of organizations suggest the wider transformative changes that Indigenous journalists discuss. This is a time of experimental thinking in journalism, and here we see parallels to the field of anthropology in the 1980s both in terms of declarations of crisis and rapidly globalizing audiences and collapsing hierarchies of knowledge and power.

In their seminal interventionist book, Marcus and Fischer articulate the challenges confronting anthropology as part of a broader "crisis of representation" in the humanities where metanarratives, grand theories, disciplinary boundaries, and "specific totalizing visions" have given way to an "uncertainty about adequate means of describing social reality."[19] They detail an important period of experimental ethnography, one that is still continuing: building both on Geertz's innovations and the critiques of these innovations. In other words, instead of doubling down on the methods that had secured anthropology a place in the academy, Marcus and Fisher propose a reckoning with how much the terrain for describing and comparing the world had changed—and propose listening to voices outside of academia, some of whom were sharply critical at that time of the usually Western white gaze employed by anthropologists.

Contrary to journalism studies, which has often lamented the decline in journalism's authority, Fortun notes that Marcus and Fischer sought "not for ethnography to regain an authority that was lost, but to recast ethnographic authority in ways responsive to both critiques of past ethnographic work and to a changing world."[20] Marcus and Fischer suggest formalizing many of the tools we now take for granted in anthropologies of media, science, and technology: multi-sited ethnography, collaboration with informants, reflexivity, and juxtaposition of and close attention to the circulation of media and other representations. They suggest that the aim of anthropology should be seeking to understand the complex, layered social processes at work in a vastly interconnected and increasingly global web of social realities. The object is to reveal, if even temporarily, the constructedness inherent in everyday life at the micro and macro level in an effort to understand the processes of profound change ongoing in cultures around the world, revealing sociohistorical contexts and connections.

This is a robust edict even for anthropologists who spend years working on research projects (as we have on this one), and we're not suggesting journalists become anthropologists or vice versa. What Marcus and Fischer argue for and about is applicable to journalism and its profound crisis: namely that ways of thinking about, approaching, and narrating a dynamic, constantly evolving world must be reassessed in order to account for *both* critique and for systems, both macro and micro, that govern what's possible in daily life as well as the limits of journalism and its available forms and styles. They define systems as:

> The political and economic processes spanning different locales, or even different continents . . . these processes are registered in the activities of dispersed groups or individuals whose actions have mutual, often unintended consequences for each other, as they are connected by markets and other major institutions that make the world as a system.[21]

In adopting an open approach and systems thinking, narratives are "purposefully partial rather than masterfully comprehensive descriptions, aware of possible complicities with colonial practices and imaginations."[22] Fischer's latest work on "anthropology in the meantime" is also instructive here in that he acknowledges that "new social structures and new 'forms of life' (both biological and social, sometimes quite intertwined) are emergent in ways we cannot quite forsee, despite confident prediction."[23] Acknowledging partiality, uncertainty, and potential complicity in the face of complexity might seem paradoxical to journalists intent on fostering credibility and maintaining authority, but it is both an acknowledgment of the sedimentations and structures we live with and how systems intersect and interact in ways that aren't always entirely visible or stable. As Haraway elegantly writes with a nod to Clifford: "We need stories (and theories) that are just big enough to gather up the complexities and keep the edges open and greedy for surprising new and old connections."[24]

Situated, Systems Journalism

In suggesting systems journalism as a newly emergent approach, we build on our observations in Chapter 3 regarding speculative memoir fragments, *the Discourse* in Chapter 5, and Indigenous journalists in Chapter 6. All of these chapters provide examples of journalists who are actively opening up the "internalist" epistemology of journalism, questioning long-held methodological imperatives and practices in order to address persistent critiques and exclusions. Like Fischer and Marcus suggested for anthropology, these chapters show how journalists are actively experimenting with collaboration and employing reflexivity. Journalists have been reckoning with the deficiencies and crisis in their own ways from memoir fragments that point to how race, gender, and colonialism impact their abilities to do journalism and (especially in the case of Sunny Dhillon, Minelle Mahtani, and Jenni Monet) would suggest that journalism needs to be practiced differently.

We propose in Chapter 1 that journalists employ strong objectivity and incorporate the concept of situated knowledge. This is something we have taught at the UBC School of Journalism for many years now as a possible counter to objectivity. It offers journalists a view of themselves as participants in the stories they tell and narratives they devise in order to navigate complex situations. Knowledge, we argue, is always produced from somewhere, and journalism is no different in this respect even while good methods are required to produce good facts and interpretations. We suggest this so that journalism might repair, reform, and possibly transform its potential to live up to its own ideals and hopefully intervene at the intersections of systems that continue to perpetuate injustice and suffering.

Here we suggest that situated knowledge—the view from somewhere—can be a form of expertise rather than a bias. Bias suggests that there is an outside place of knowing that journalists must arrive at in order to produce objective facts, rationalizing what they do and their stories as requiring a "view from nowhere" in order to arrive at a usefulness for democratic participation and diverse audiences. Given the rapid shifts in audiences and technologies, considering situated knowledge as a form of expertise in our view reflects the increasingly globalized systems and diverse audience contexts that journalists are required to navigate even as the ideals of accountability and accurate diagnoses of multi-local problems and potential solutions remain. We view the *Discourse* as moving in this direction with its efforts at repair; however, there are economic challenges that require more reform. Indigenous journalists point to a differently configured address of reckoning because they consider the enmeshment and intersection/interaction of systems. They are not looking to replicate or re-create the industry of old; instead, they enfold both an accounting of journalism's history and possibilities for transformation.

In observing, participating, and relaying experiences from one place to another, journalism has, continues to, and can contribute to a future that we want to live and flourish in. Systems journalism asks what we might expect of the worlds we inhabit—of the intersections, interferences, interactions, resistances that are recorded, mapped, and tracked in the stories that get circulated and realities that get described. We also see a core question emerging in the kind of systems journalism that Indigenous journalists are already practicing, and given that varied sorts of settler-colonialism exist globally, it's worth asking in relation to journalism more broadly: What might good relations look like for journalists and media organizations? And how are journalists related to the worlds they inhabit?

"Being in good relations" is a term many Indigenous scholars use to provide a framework for thinking about what kinds of worlds we want to live and participate in. Here, we might think about what confronts both scholars and journalists as a constant reckoning where the questions become when, where, how to intervene and participate in the systems that govern, stifle, and manage the worlds we inhabit. Good journalism in this sense depends on what systems it is part of, whose social order matters, and what kinds of counter-narratives are possible. Indigenous journalism ends up being a good example of how to respond to critiques around voice, expertise, knowledge, and methods. Indigenous journalists are likely to have a clear and coherent view of who they are, what they are doing, and when, how, and why they are doing it. Indigenous reporters are more likely then not only to provide a deeper context and more credible voices on the ground but to frame their stories as stories of resilience and of historical narratives repeating themselves even while acts of resistance persist. We suggest that this work of locating oneself and one's knowledge is necessary, if not crucial, to how journalism might consider its role in this era of digital reckoning.

In closing, this book suggests there is much to be learned from considering systems, multiple journalisms, multiple knowledges, and the social orders they co-produce. Journalism in our current highly connected set of platforms and social networks potentially plays a potent role in connecting its audiences to stories that represent the fullness of our relations to land, water, humans, and non-human relatives. Whether, when, and how journalism plays that role remains worthy of ongoing care.

NOTES

Introduction

1. Rector & Bogel-Burroughs, 2018.
2. *Capital Gazette* editorial, 2018.
3. *Capital Gazette* editorial, 2018.
4. See a number of scholars on this topic: McChesney, 2015; Siles & Boczkowski, 2012.
5. Zelizer, 2015, p. 1. See Reuters Institute for the Study of Journalism 2019 digital news report for the most recent data on a range of challenges facing journalism globally (Newman, 2019).
6. See Robinson (2005) who identified a gap in feminist journalism studies scholarship with respect to research on media economics and structure. See also Deuze (2005), one of the few journalism studies scholars to link the shared concerns of technological change and multiculturalism.
7. Carey, 1974.
8. Sullivan, 2018.
9. Sullivan, 2018.
10. Nielsen, 2018.
11. Gans, 1979, p. 61, referenced in Durham, 1998, p. 131.
12. Hallin & Mancini, 2004.
13. Picard, 2014.
14. Rosen, 2006.
15. Carey, 1974; Gans, 1979; Schudson, 1989; Tuchman, 1972.
16. Carey, 1974, p. 88.
17. See Anderson & Robertson (2011) for one of the few contributions to historical analysis of journalism and settler-colonialism. Also see Benjamin (2019), Noble (2018), Tufecki (2014) for powerful emerging critiques of technology as implicated and constitutive of social structures.
18. Durham, 1998; Haraway, 1997; Herman & Chomsky, 1988; Rhodes, 1993; Shapin & Schaffer, 1985; Steiner, 2018.
19. Baiocchi et al., 2014; Jenkins, Ford & Green, 2013; Papacharissi, 2015.

20. Posetti, 2018.

21. Rhodes, 1993.

22. Anderson & Robertson, 2011.

23. Steiner, 2018.

24. See for example Jenkins, 1992; Justice, 2018; Mahtani, 2001; Pollock, 2012; TallBear, 2013.

25. Jasanoff, 2003, p. 391. For situated knowledge, see Haraway (1988).

26. Jasanoff, 2003, pp. 393–394.

27. Lewis & Westlund, 2015, p. 452.

28. Tuchman, 1978.

29. Ericson, 1998, p. 83.

30. Ericson, 1998, p. 93. See also Borges-Rey, 2017.

31. Justice uses the term "other than human" instead of "non-human" in order to suggest that there is subjectivity outside of human contexts. See Justice (2018) for more.

32. Waldman, 2018.

33. Anderson & Robertson, 2011; Stabile, 2006.

34. Goldberg, 2018.

35. Spivak, 1988.

36. Byrd, 2011, p. xxxi.

37. Jones & Ritter, 2018.

38. Broersma, 2010.

39. Parasie & Dagiral, 2013.

40. Anderson & Robertson, 2011; Hall, 1990; Jiwani, 2009; Rhodes, 1993, 1999; Robinson, 2005; Squires, 2009, 2014; Stabile, 2006; van Dijk, 1987.

41. Callison, 2017; Whyte, 2017; Wildcat, 2013.

42. Carey, 1974; Zelizer, 1993.

43. Felt, 2017, p. 253.

44. Foucault & Ewald, 2003; Ginsberg, Abu-Lughod, & Larkin, 2002; Maaka & Andersen, 2006.

45. See, for example, Boczkowski, 2005; Usher, 2013, 2014.

46. Fortun, 2003; Marcus & Fischer, 1999.

47. Fischer, 2009.

48. Marcus, 2000, p. 3.

49. Marcus, 2009, p. 184.

50. For example, see Boczkowski, 2005; Schudson, 1995; Zelizer, 1993.

51. For example, see Dumit, 2004; Jasanoff, 2004; Shapin, 1995; TallBear, 2013.

52. Dumit, 2003, p. 40.

53. Barthel, 2015.

54. Barthel, 2015.

55. Gertz, 2013.

56. Barthel, 2015.

57. Media Matters, 2017.

58. Quote from Callison & Young, 2018. See also Cukier et al., 2011; Pritchard & Sauvageau, 1998.

59. Gertz, 2013.

60. Carey, 1974.

61. Dumit, 2012; Haraway, 2016.

62. Callison & Hermida, 2015; Hermida, Lewis, & Zamith, 2014; Papacharissi & de Fatima Oliveira, 2012.

63. Küng, 2015.

64. See Anderson (2018) for a discussion of data journalism's recent growth and a genealogy of the relationship between data and journalism.

65. Benson, 2017; Graves & Konieczna, 2015.

66. Jackson, 2014.

67. Benson, 2017; Cagé, 2016.

Chapter 1

1. Anderson, 2018.

2. Schudson & Anderson, 2009, p. 96.

3. Callison, 2014.

4. Brennan & Kreiss, 2014; Turner, 2013; Zelizer, 1993.

5. STS scholars—some of whom are also anthropologists and/or use ethnographic methods—have tended to ask questions like how are experts made, under what conditions, what language must be used to become an expert (Callison, 2014; Dumit, 2004, 2006; Fortun, 2001; Jasanoff, 2005), who is allowed to know and speak (Ellis et al., 2009; Irwin & Wynne, 1996), how is knowledge and credibility produced (Haraway, 1997; Latour, 1993; Shapin, 1995; Shapin & Schaffer, 1985), and what structures expert testimony (Collins & Evans, 2002; Jasanoff, 2003, 2009).

6. Jasanoff, 2003; Rhodes, 1993.

7. Dumit, 2012; Haraway, 2016.

8. Posetti, 2018.

9. Goldberg, 2018.

10. Hawkins, 2018.

11. Edwards, 2018.

12. Demby, 2018.

13. See Rao (2018) for tweet thread.

14. TallBear, 2013; TallBear, 2018. "Sorry for the Racism" segment of Episode 108. *Media Indigena*, Mar 30. Author Callison was part of this *Media Indigena* discussion.

15. TallBear, 2018.

16. Ward, 2014.

17. Goldberg, 2018.

18. "In writing about Indigenous people for the ILO, Errico uses the term 'social situation' to describe the context that many Indigenous people face with regards to their land and human rights as well as ongoing and historical ecological changes associated with climate change" (Callison, 2017, p. 10).

19. Hall, 1990; Said, 1979.

20. Tuchman, 1972, p. 668.

21. These range from: necessary foundation, professional ideology and flawed method (Reese, 1990; Schudson, 1978, 2001; Singer, 2007; Ward, 2004), to worthy and/or complicated goal that can include an account for subjectivity (Ryan, 2001; van Zoonen, 1998a), performative routine (Broersma, 2010a, b), and gendered impossibility (Durham, 1998; Steiner, 2018).

22. Carey, 1974, p. 91.

23. Boczkowski & Anderson, 2017; Peters & Broersma, 2013, 2017; Zelizer, 2017.

24. Ward, 2011, p. 138. Early studies of bloggers by Singer (2007, 2008) indicate that this is broadly applicable to digital media contributors and audiences as well. Bloggers are likely to evaluate the moral and/or ethical shortcomings of journalists against traditional norms like objectivity even as they also pursue their own "new" modes of journalistic engagement. Zuckerman's notion of bridgebloggers (2008) provides a helpful counterpoint where he argues that bloggers from other parts of the world are essential "to mediate between these cultures and languages—play an increasingly crucial role in connecting these disparate spheres of conversation and argument together." While Zuckerman doesn't address objectivity in this article, the underlying premise is that language, national communities, and place matter in terms of interpretive frameworks for understanding the world.

25. Ward, 2011, p. 153.

26. Ward, 2011, pp. 153–154. Ward suggests that this can be achieved through a combination of an "objective stance" (loosely defined as critical distance, openness to evidence and counter-arguments, disinterestedness, fair representation) and a five-part criteria that tests stories for objectivity: empirical validity, completeness and implications (similar to balance), coherence with existing knowledge, self-consciousness about frames, sources and representations, and inter-subjectivity or openness to dialogue and varied perspectives (in this sense, a broader "interpretive community") (2011, pp. 154–155).

27. Ward, 2011, p. 155.

28. Ward, 2011, p. 157.

29. Ryan, 2001; Deuze, 2005, p. 448.

30. Deuze, 2005, p. 448.

31. Anderson & Robertson, 2011; TallBear, 2018. Notably, even in the acknowledgment of racist coverage, Goldberg mobilizes her personal context as a Jewish woman as being part of her motivation to undertake the hiring of a historian to study the magazine's archives. She doesn't employ this reasoning and discuss whether she hired writers and editors of color in this issue devoted to race nor does she offer a sense of who is in her newsroom.

32. Schudson, 2001.

33. Schudson, 2001; Ward, 2004.

34. Ward, 2004, pp. 236–237.

35. Ward, 2011, p. 131.

36. Ward, 2011, p. 131.

37. Ward, 2011, p. 132 quoting from Baughman, 1987.

38. Prenger & Deuze, 2017. See also Culver (2017) for historical and comparative overview of development of ethical codes and discussion of role (or lack thereof) of publics in drafting and approving these codes.

39. Schudson, 2001, p. 150.

40. Deuze, 2005.

41. Deuze, 2005, p. 448.

42. See, for example, Anderson & Robertson, 2011; Herman & Chomsky, 1988; Mullen & Klaehn, 2010; Rhodes, 1993; Robinson, 2005; Stabile, 2006.

43. Broersma, 2010a.

44. See, for example, Kovach & Rosenstiel, 2014. Robinson (2017) suggests that the problem is much broader when it comes to race by focusing on media ecology, power, privilege, and spaces for dialogue and deliberation.

45. Journalists have, as Zelizer (1993) argues, formed interpretive communities in the 20th century. Coming at journalism less as a profession and more as a loosely organized community of practitioners, Zelizer argues, drawing on de Certeau (1978), that events do not exist "objectively" but "are projections of the individuals and groups who give meaning in discourse" and that "professional consciousness emerges at least in part around ruptures where the borders of appropriate practice need renegotiation" (1993, p. 224). Zelizer considers this especially apparent in communal recollections of high marker journalistic events such as Watergate. Zelizer has further argued for the role of imagination because of the way in which journalism is conducted as a method: "The very essence of journalism is creating an imagined engagement with events beyond the public's reach. How that is accomplished is also imagined because journalism operates largely out of the public eye. Journalists gather their information in ways and from domains that remain largely invisible. Acting much like shamans who journey to inaccessible worlds and return with some critical insight, journalists act as 'stabilizing agents who solidify consensus and reinstate social order on their return'" (Zelizer, 2017, pp. 12–13).

46. Shapin & Schaffer, 1985.

47. See Anderson (2018) for a periodization of journalism studies and its relations with STS scholarship and approaches.

48. See Pollock & Subramaniam (2016) for an overview, as well as emerging engagement with settler-colonialism and Indigenous studies in, for example, Reardon & TallBear, 2012; TallBear, 2013; TallBear & Whyte, 2013.

49. Fischer, 2003; Haraway, 1988, 1997; Latour, 1993; Shapin & Schaffer, 1985; TallBear, 2014.

50. Shapin & Shaffer, 1985.

51. Haraway, 1997, p. 24.

52. Haraway, 1997; Shapin & Schaffer, 1985; Traweek, 1988.

53. Haraway, 1997, p. 24.

54. Haraway, 1997, p. 26.

55. Haraway, 2004, p. 224.

56. Haraway, 1997, p. 235.

57. Gill, 2007; Robinson, 2005; Ross & Carter, 2011; van Zoonen, 1998.

58. Haraway, 1988, pp. 194–195.

59. See Takenaga (2019) for the *New York Times* response to the critique and its recognition that "there are people in the newsroom who felt in retrospect that we shouldn't have run the Nairobi photo."

60. See Fischer, 2003, 2018.

61. Zelizer, 2000, p. 9.

62. Benson & Neveu, 2005; Hall, 1990; Rhodes, 1993, 1999; Robinson, 2017; Robinson, 2005; Squires, 2009, 2014; Stabile, 2006; van Dijk, 1987.

63. For example, Herman & Chomsky, 1988; McChesney, 2015; Mullen & Klaehn, 2010.

64. Hall, 1990; Jiwani, 2009; Squires, 2009, 2014.

65. Jiwani & Young, 2006.

66. Ericson, Baranek & Chan, 1991.

67. Stabile, 2006.

68. Anderson & Robertson, 2011.

69. Rhodes, 1993.

70. Rhodes, 1993, p. 185.

71. Rhodes, 1993, p. 185.

72. Rhodes, 1993, p. 186.

73. Rhodes, 1993, p. 186.

74. Rhodes, 1993, p. 186.

75. Rhodes, 1993, pp. 186–187.

76. Rhodes, 1993, p. 185.

77. Jiwani, 2009, p. 735.

78. Hall, 1990, pp. 12–13.

79. Jiwani, 2009, p. 738.

80. Squires. 2014, p. 12.

81. Squires, 2014, pp. 12–13.

82. Callison & Young, 2018.

83. On civic imagination, see Baiocchi et al (2014); for counter-narratives, see, for example, Jackson & Welles (2015, 2016).

84. Silva, 2004.

85. See Alia (2011) on northern media in Canada. See David (2012) and Roth (2005) on APTN specifically. Scholars of Canadian media have yet to include APTN in many studies, deeming it "alternative" media even as it wins mainstream awards for investigative journalism.

86. Daley & James, 2004, p. 4.

87. Daley & James, 2004, p. 13.

88. Daley & James, 2004, p. 17.

89. Duarte, 2017, p. 130.

90. Brooks, 2018, p. 346.

91. de Certeau, 1984.

92. Jenkins (1992) is primarily discussing fictional work in media (i.e., Star Trek fan communities), but we find his framework useful in considering how social movements respond to journalism.

93. See Jenkins, Shresthova & Peters-Lazaro, 2019.

94. Big Noise Films, 2000.

95. Ananny, 2018; Anderson, 2018; Boczkowski, 2004; Kreiss, 2012; Usher, 2014.

96. Carey, 1974; Gans, 1979; Schudson, 1978; Tuchman, 1978.

97. Brennan & Kreiss, 2014.

98. Brennan & Kreiss, 2014. See also Boczkowski & Lievrouw, 2007.

99. See Boczkowski, 2004, 2005. See also other journalism technology literature that focuses on legacy media such as Parasie & Dagaril, 2013; Usher, 2014.

100. For example, see Benjamin, 2013, 2019; Nelson, 2016; Pollock, 2012; Reardon, 2009; TallBear, 2013.

101. For example, see Ellis, Waterton & Wynne, 2010; Irwin & Wynne, 1996; Jasanoff, 2003.

102. Ananny, 2018; Anderson, 2018.

103. Anderson, 2018, p. 1 in proofs.

104. Anderson, 2018, p. 1 in proofs.

105. Ananny, 2018, p. 1.

106. Ananny, 2018, p. 4.

107. Ananny, 2018, p. 2.

108. Ananny, 2018, p. 4.

109. See Dumit (2012) or Haraway (2016).

110. For example, Fischer, 2003; Haraway, 1997; Latour, 2000.

111. Dumit, 2012; Hayden, 2003; Jasanoff, 2004; Reardon, 2009.

112. Rosen, 2006.

113. Baiocchi et al, 2014; Jasanoff, 2005.

114. Choy, 2005, 2011; Tsing, 2015.

115. Fischer, 2003; Fortun, 2001.

116. Choy, 2005.

117. Durham, 1998; Steiner, 2012, 2018.

118. Durham, 1998, p. 125.

119. Durham, 1998, p. 127.

120. Durham, 1998, p. 128.

121. Durham, 1998, pp. 125–126; see also Steiner, 2012, 2018.

122. Harding, 1998.

123. Haraway, 1988.

124. Star, 1990.

125. Durham, 1998, p. 118.

126. Steiner, 2018, p. 1854.

127. Butler, 1988, p. 519.

128. Spivak's (1988) questions about the role of women and the subaltern and whether they can speak are particularly relevant to concerns about journalism authority given journalists' presumptive stance that they can shine a light on the powerless.

129. Simpson (2016) provides an instructive take on the different ways that colonized and marginalized groups and their knowledges have been limited, annihilated, and instrumentalized in service of nation building, "settler statecraft" and white masculinity.

130. Spivak, 2004, p. 87.

131. The Global Media Monitoring Project in 2015 found that women accounted for only 32% of experts in the news in NA, while a new 2019 gender tracking tool that uses computational linguistics found that women are only 25% of sources in mainstream media outlets in Canada (Taboada & Torabi Asr, 2019). Research by anthropologist and STS scholar Tim Choy (2005) on discursive strategies related to environmental conflicts and debates is relevant with respect to the "extralinguistic effects" of "ritualized" and repeated media events and speech (p. 10)—in this case the repeated disproportion of gendered sources. He draws from Bauman (2004) who makes the point that mediated speech can result in a range of authority generation for both the original speaker and the mediator, which raises questions about the effects of these source inequities on power relations and journalism authority.

132. Jasanoff, 2003, p. 394.

133. Jasanoff, 2005.

134. Following Crenshaw (1991) we define intersectionality as the ways in which systems necessary for daily life and structural oppression intersect with race, indigeneity, class, immigration status, disability, age, poverty, gender identity and sexual orientation. Costanza-Chock, Shweidler & the Transformative Media Project, 2017.

135. Arvin, Tuck, & Morrill, 2013, p. 10.

136. Arvin, Tuck, & Morrill, 2013, p. 10.

137. Arvin, Tuck, & Morrill, 2013, p. 10.

138. Bell, 2014, 2016; Boczkowski & Papacharissi, 2018; Hamilton & Tworek, 2017; Tworek, 2019.

139. In relation to labor, economic, and technological challenges, see Siles & Boczkowski (2012) for a thorough review of the gaps in the literature on the newspaper crisis. See also Papacharissi (2015) on new "journalism(s)."

140. Anderson & Robertson, 2011; Callison, 2017; Pollock & Subramaniam, 2016.

141. Star, 1991, p. 52, emphasis in original.

Chapter 2

1. Callison & Hermida, 2015; Hermida, Lewis & Zamith, 2014; Jackson & Welles, 2016; Papacharissi & de Fatima Oliveira, 2012.

2. Picard, 2014, p. 278.

3. Callison & Hermida, 2015; Hermida, Lewis, & Zamith, 2014; Papacharissi & de Fatima Oliveira, 2012.

4. Christensen et al., 2013.

5. Tworek, 2018.

6. Jackson & Welles, 2016, p. 399.

7. Palmater, 2018.

8. Palmater, 2018.

9. CBC News, 2018.

10. Wente, 2018.

11. Callison is one of ten members of the Advisory Council for the Indigenous Screen Office.

12. Lambert, 2018.

13. Lambert, 2018.

14. Anderson & Robertson, 2011; Callison & Young, 2018.

15. Callison & Hermida, 2015.

16. Wente, 2018.

17. Wente, 2018.

18. Balkissoon, 2018.

19. Ettema (2009) referenced in Papacharissi & de Fatima Oliveira (2012).

20. Papacharissi & de Fatima Oliveira, 2012, p. 275.

21. Callison & Hermida, 2015.

22. FineDay, 2019.

23. Fontaine, 2018.

24. RCMP, 2014, 2015.

25. Reclaiming Power and Place: The Final Report of the National Inquiry into Missing and Murdered Indigenous Women and Girls, 2019.

26. CEDAW, 2015, pp. 23–24.

27. Pember, 2018.

28. Hunt (2015/2016, pp. 35–36) makes an important intervention in the complexity and stakes for repositioning representations of Indigenous women who "trade or sell sex." She examines recent law enforcement approaches in Canada and argues that the latest strategies, which identify Indigenous women as victims of human trafficking as opposed to individual women who "trade or sell sex," are a double-edged sword. They improve safety and accountability within the justice system as they raise the stakes for the severity of the violation and its enforcement compared to previous regimes that undermined the systemic oppression faced by Indigenous women in the sex trade, while concurrently "further entrench[ing] . . . violent relations with the state" (2015/2016, pp. 35–36). She argues that for policies to be just and effective they need to consider Indigenous women's multiple histories of colonial violence, their "position as rightful subjects," and the complex role of enforcement strategies in their safety and relationship to the state (pp. 35–36). This is something that Hunt has spoken about in media interviews, but the layered complexity and nuance provides a challenging terrain as we will cover in Chapter 6 in part because it requires an acknowledgment of colonialism and its specific impacts on women.

29. Daschuk, 2013; See also Dhillon, 2017; Hunt & Stevenson, 2016.

30. DaughtersDOC, 2017.

31. Wente, 2018.

32. Callison & Young, 2018.

33. Callison & Young, 2018.

34. Broersma, 2010a.

35. Ericson, Baranek, & Chan, 1987, 1989, 1991.

36. Ericson, Baranek, & Chan, 1987, p. 351.

37. Zelizer, 1993.

38. Phillips, 2010.

39. Wahl-Jorgensen, 2012, p. 2.

40. Wahl-Jorgensen, 2012, p. 2.

41. Wahl-Jorgensen, 2012, p. 2.

42. Nielsen, 2017, p. 1251.

43. Ericson, Baranek, & Chan, 1991.

44. Anderson, 2018; Barnhurst & Mutz, 1997; Reiner, Livingstone, & Allen, 2000.

45. Swisher, 2015.

46. Pao, 2017, p. 5.

47. Swisher, 2015.

48. Swisher, 2015.

49. Pao, 2017, p. 8, italics in original.

50. Pao, 2017, p. 9.

51. Couldry, 2000.

52. Haraway & Goodeve, 2000, p. 159.

53. Swisher, 2015.

54. Alba, 2017.

55. Landsbaum, 2017.

56. Bullock, 2016.

57. Domonoske, 2016.

58. Olivarius, 2018.

59. Schrode, 2018.

60. Lederman, 2017.

61. "Kelly Oxford talks," 2017.

62. See Onwuachi-Willig (2018) and her article "What about #UsToo? The invisibility of race in the #MeToo Movement." See also Pember (2018) and her article, "Sherman Alexie and the Longest Running #MeToo Movement in History."

63. Onwuachi-Willig, 2018, p. 105.

64. Onwuachi-Willig, 2018, p. 106.

65. Onwuachi-Willig, 2018.

66. Traditional newspaper and television research on media trust and credibility has tended to focus on two types of studies: studies of journalism source credibility and studies comparing the credibility of various mediums. In the process of trying to assess credibility, researchers developed numerous media credibility scales. Gaziano & McGrath (1986) developed a scale identifying 12 dimensions of newspaper and television news credibility. These dimensions included fairness, bias, completeness, accuracy, respect for privacy, watch for people's interests, concern for community, separation of fact and opinion, trust, sensationalism, concern for public interest, factual and level of training. Other scales include Meyer's (1988) believability and community affiliation indexes. Media scholars, such as Ericson, Baranek, & Chan (1989), have been critical of industry studies of media credibility. This is particularly with respect to television news, suggesting these studies are flawed conceptually because they are constructed to solely benefit media economics through understanding the "strategic staging" required for managing audiences and not focused on broader notions of the public good.

67. Choy, 2005, p. 6.

68. Choy, 2005, p. 7.

69. Choy, 2005, p. 7.

70. Choy, 2005, p. 7.

71. Rosen, 2006.

72. Rosen, 2006.

73. Jenkins, 1992; Rosen, 1999.

74. Chan-Olmsted, 2018.

75. Deuze, 1999, p. 385.

76. Singer et al., 2011.

77. Domingo, 2008.

78. Domingo, 2008, p. 681.

79. Domingo, 2008, p. 697.

80. Domingo, 2008, p. 697.

81. Hermida, 2014; Papacharissi & de Fatima Oliveira, 2012.

82. Hermida, 2014, p. 361.

83. Hermida, 2014, p. 361.

84. Hardey quoted in Hermida, 2014, p. 361.

85. Lankshear & Knobel, 2011, p. 76, quoted in Hermida, 2014, p. 365.

86. Papacharissi & de Fatima Oliveira, 2012, p. 266.

87. Papacharissi & de Fatima Oliveira, 2012, p. 267.

88. See Wahl-Jorgensen (2012) for her research on emotions, news and Pulitzer Prize journalism.

89. Ananny, 2018; Ellis, Waterton, & Wynne, 2009; Jasanoff, 2005.

90. Boczkowski, 2004.

91. Ellis, Waterton, & Wynne, 2009, p. 2.

92. Ellis, Waterton, & Wynne, 2009, p. 2.

93. Ellis et al., 2009, p. 2.

94. Haraway (1997, p. 36) quoted in Ellis et al., p. 3.

95. Ellis, Waterton, & Wynne, 2009, p. 3.

96. Ellis et al., pp. 8–9.

97. Jasanoff, 2005, p. 247.

98. Jasanoff, 2005, p. 247.

99. Leonard, 1995.

100. Jasanoff, 2005. See also Ananny, 2018.

101. Hunt, 2015/2016, p. 36.

102. See Stabile (2006) for her study of crime news in the United States and journalism's historic role in the criminalization of Black men.

103. Haraway, 2000.

104. Callison & Hermida, 2015; Jackson & Welles, 2016; Rhodes, 1993.

105. Dahlgren, 1996; Tuck & Yang, 2012.

106. Bauman, 2013.

107. Hunt, 2015/2016, p. 33.

108. Zelizer, 1993.

109. Byrd, 2011, p. xvii.

110. Byrd, 2011.

111. Byrd, 2011, pp. xxxiv–xxxv.

Chapter 3

1. Ching, 2018.

2. Ching, 2018.

3. Ching, 2018.

4. In Canada, journalists Kai Nagata (2011) and Sunny Dhillon (2018) both used essays circulated via Twitter to explain their quitting of jobs at CTV and *The Globe and Mail* respectively. We explore Dhillon's essay later in this chapter.

5. Mcdonald (2007, p. 82) also uses this term "speculative memoir," but we are using it quite differently. Mcdonald is analyzing the genre-bending memoir *Never Let Me Go* by Kazuo Ishiguro and writes, "Utilizing the tropological framework of the autobiography in a discourse of an imagined world and environment, Ishiguro invites us to abandon the veil of authenticity and bear witness to a memoir from another reality, an imagined past that could represent a real future, where Science Fiction again calls on our imaginations to act as a lens by which to scrutinize contemporary social dilemmas."

6. *Correspondent Confidential*, 2013–2014.

7. Deuze & Witschge, 2018.

8. Broersma, 2010a.

9. Broersma, 2010, p. 22.

10. Malcolm, 1990, p. 1.

11. Sacco, 2013, p. xiii.

12. Sacco, 2013, p. xiii.

13. Sacco, 2013, p. xiii.

14. Sacco, 2013, p. xiii.

15. Sacco, 2013, p. xiii.

16. The first-person exploits of Hunter S. Thompson's investigative journalism in the 1970s was referred to as a genre of long-form journalism known as "gonzo journalism" in which the writer is involved in events "from the inside" (Caron, 1985, p. 2).

17. Coward, 2009, 2010; Smith & Watson, 2010.

18. Spurr, 1993, p. 10.

19. Coward, 2009.

20. Coward, 2010, p. 224.

21. Smith & Watson, 2010, p. 6.

22. Smith & Watson, 2010, p. 10.

23. Smith & Watson, 2010, p. 6.

24. We draw from rhetorical genre theory to understand genre as more about motive within a specific "sphere of activity," than form. See Young & Giltrow (2015), who explore journalism education using genre theory, drawing from Burke (1969) and Bakhtin (1986).

25. van Zoonen, 2012, pp. 56–57.

26. Smith & Watson, 2010, pp. 12–13.

27. Picard, 2014.

28. Roger Alton quoted in Broersma, 2010a, p. 22.

29. Broersma, 2010a; Coward, 2009, 2010.

30. Vice Media, 2013a.

31. Stanley, 2014.

32. In 2017, Chakarova spoke to a Vancouver audience of mostly journalism students and professors as part of a panel on sex trafficking, which was assembled in a small black box theater behind a popular Cuban restaurant. The panel, which was organized by the Global Reporting Centre, included a Vancouver-based activist, a human rights lawyer, and a Seattle-based FBI agent. Black box theaters are used as adaptable, experimental spaces where performers and the audience engage with each other on a more intimate and level plane. Behind the theater space was a smaller space where a photo exhibit associated with the film and also titled *The Price of Sex* had been set up.

33. Vice Media, 2013a.

34. Ching, 2018.

35. Barnhurst & Mutz, 1997; *Correspondent Confidential*, 2103–2014.

36. Vice Media, 2014d.

37. Vice Media, 2014c.

38. Vice Media, 2013b.

39. Vice Media, 2014a.

40. Vice Media, 2014b.

41. Entman (1993, p. 52) defines framing as "to select some aspects of a perceived reality and make them more salient in a communicating text, in such a way as to promote

a particular problem definition, causal interpretation, moral evaluation, and/or treatment recommendation."

42. For our analysis, *Correspondent Confidential* videos were transcribed verbatim and then coded thematically using NVivo 10, a qualitative data analysis computer software package (CAQDAS).

43. Deuze, 2007.

44. Vice Media, 2013b.

45. Klein & Plaut, 2017.

46. Vice Media, 2014a.

47. Vice Media, 2014a.

48. Vice Media, 2014b.

49. Vice Media, 2013a.

50. Awad, 2006.

51. Haraway, 1997; Marcus & Fischer, 1999.

52. Fischer, 2003; Fortun, 2001; Haraway, 1997; Harding et al, 2011; TallBear, 2014.

53. Choy, 2005; Dumit, 2006, 2012.

54. Vice Media, 2013b.

55. Vice Media, 2013b.

56. Vice Media, 2013a.

57. Vice Media, 2014d.

58. Vice Media, 2014b.

59. Vice Media, 2013b

60. Vice Media, 2013b.

61. Vice Media, 2014c.

62. Vice Media, 2014c.

63. Hamilton & Jenner, 2004, p. 313.

64. Ibrahim, 2003, p. 98.

65. Schultze, 2000.

66. Schultze, 2000, p. 8.

67. Vice Media, 2014c.

68. Vice Media, 2014c.

69. Vice Media, 2014d.

70. Ibrahim, 2003.

71. Spurr, 1993, p. 9.

72. Ching, 2018.

73. Spurr, 1993.

74. Haraway, 1997.

75. Broersma, 2010; Singer, 2008.

76. Rao & Wasserman, 2007.

77. Ibrahim, 2003.

78. Monet, 2019.

79. Monet, 2019.

80. Monet, 2019.

81. Dhillon is a graduate of the UBC School of Journalism and was taught by author Young.

82. Dhillon, 2018. In another example of quit lit in Canadian journalism, Kai Nagata in 2011 quit his job as the CTV Quebec bureau chief stating in his widely read and tweeted blog post: "I have serious problems with the direction taken by Canadian policy and politics in the last five years. But as a reporter, I feel like I've been holding my breath. Every question I asked, every tweet I posted, and even what I said to other journalists and friends had to go through a filter, where my own opinions and values were carefully strained out. Even then I'm not sure I was always successful, but I always knew at the CBC and subsequently at CTV that there were serious consequences for editorial."

83. Dhillon, 2018.

84. Mahtani, 2019.

85. TallBear, 2014a.

86. Haraway, 1997, p. 36. See also Harding, 1992.

87. Picard, 2014, p. 277.

88. Picard, 2014, p. 277.

89. Hallin & Mancini, 2004.

90. Steel, 2017.

91. Steel, 2017.

92. Küng, 2015, p. 75.

93. Norris, 2016.

94. Küng, 2015, p. 89.

95. Küng, 2015, p. 84.

96. *The Islamic State*, 2014.

97. Martinson, 2015.

98. Martinson, 2015.

99. Norris, 2016.

100. Picard, 2014, p. 280.

101. See Carlson, 2014, p. 14.

102. Chadwick, 2013.

103. Picard, 2014.

104. Deuze, 2017.

105. Jenkins et al, 2013.

106. Hodapp, 2015.

107. Wolf, 2000, p. 280.

108. Moran, 1999, p. 270.

109. Sacco, 2013.

110. Mehta & Mukherji, 2015, p. 2.

111. McCloud, 1993, p. 41.

112. Miller & Shepherd, 2009, p. 265.

113. Picard, 2014; Singer, 2008.

114. See Couser quoted in Jolly (2011, p. 819) "forms like confession, apology, testimony, conversion, and coming-of-age narrative reflect the relation between the narrator and his or her early self, whether critical or defensive."

115. Ching (2019) notes in a follow up e-mail that Vice Media's editorial vision was evident in the final product, which emerged out of a number of "competing influences" that included her goals of "emphasizing the internal conflict of the journalist" and the organization's focus on "entertainment value and bravado." According to Ching, the fact

that she was largely able to produce the series in her living room compared to the norm for Vice Media content, which tends to be "directed and produced in-house," increased her editorial control.

116. Fischer, 2003; Fortun, 2001.

117. Hamilton & Jenner, 2004.

118. Greer & Reiner, 2015; Ibrahim, 2003.

119. Deuze, 2005.

120. See, for example, Rasmussen's (2015, p. 118) examination of the development of the 21st-century breast cancer memoir in which she finds a "de-evolution" into post-feminist consumerism that ultimately disempowers the narrator.

121. Meyrowitz, 1986.

Chapter 4

1. According to an article in *Muskrat Magazine*: "The word 'Toronto' itself, originates from the Kanienke'haka word 'Tkaronto' which translates to, 'the place in the water where the trees are standing.' The reference is said to come from Haudenosaunee and Huron-Wendat fishers posting stakes for fishing weirs in the narrows of the river systems, many of which are now mostly paved over with concrete" (DaCosta, 2014). Ryerson University, located in Toronto, makes this statement in their land acknowledgment: "Toronto is in the 'Dish With One Spoon Territory.'" The Dish With One Spoon is a treaty between the Anishinaabe, Mississaugas, and Haudenosaunee that bound them to share the territory and protect the land. See the full land acknowledgment at https://www.ryerson.ca/aec/land-acknowledgement/. For further discussion of this land acknowledgment that was written by Anishnaabe writer and Ryerson Professor Hayden King, read or listen to *CBC Unreserved* at https://www.cbc.ca/radio/unreserved/redrawing-the-lines-1.4973363/i-regret-it-hayden-king-on-writing-ryerson-university-s-territorial-acknowledgement-1.4973371

2. Siles & Boczkowski, 2012, pp. 4–5. See also Angelucci & Cagé, 2017; Shirky, 2009; Winseck, 2010.

3. Plener, 2017.

4. Plener, 2017. See also Rendell, 2017.

5. Iqbal, 2017.

6. Iqbal, 2017.

7. Paradkar, 2016.

8. Plener, 2017.

9. Küng, 2018.

10. Küng, 2018.

11. Küng, 2018.

12. Bozckowski & Lievrouw, 2008.

13. Callison, 2017.

14. TallBear, 2014, p. 175.

15. See Siles & Bozckowski, 2012; Roitman, 2013; Zelizer, 2015.

16. Zelizer, 2015, p. 7.

17. McChesney & Pickard, 2011; Picard, 2014.

18. Hallin & Mancini, 2004; Raboy & Taras, 2005.

19. Skelton, 2018. Retrieved from http://www.chadskelton.com/2018/02/there-are-fewer-journalists-in-canada.html

20. PPF report, 2017, p. 17. Taylor Owen, a former professor and colleague at the UBC School of Journalism, was one of four of the PPF Report's main academic researchers.

21. PPF Report, 2017, p. 11.

22. Greenspon, 2017; Greenspon, 2017a; Greenspon & Owen, 2017.

23. See, for example, an article by Hudes (2017) in the *Star* in which Greenspon is quoted: "one of the main challenges moving forward will be coming up with a sustainable strategy while media companies continue to deal with increasing pressures that . . . further erode their ability to connect with consumers. "It's just a downward spiral," he said. "How you break that spiral, that's what we're trying to address." For journalism organizations such as the *Star*, Facebook, and Google have decimated their advertising revenue, which remains an ongoing concern. See Owen (2018) for insight into how platforms are reorienting journalism in Canada.

24. PPF Report, 2017, pp. 101.

25. Campion-Smith, 2016; Honderich, 2016; Honderich, 2018.

26. Reguly, 2001.

27. Compton & Dyer-Witheford, 2014, p. 1201. They are part of a small group of political economists and communications scholars of media in Canada who comment regularly on media ownership, competition and concentration in Canada (see also Edge, 2014; Hackett, Gruneau & Gutstein, 2000; Mosco & McKercher, 2006; Skinner, Compton & Gasher, 2005; Winseck, 2010), while the media economics/management literatures have been underdeveloped (Picard in Young, 2016).

28. Whyte, 2017.

29. Whyte, 2017.

30. Roitman, 2013.

31. Felt, 2017.

32. Felt, 2017, p. 253.

33. Honderich, 2016.

34. PPF report, 2018.

35. Deuze, 2017, p. 14.

36. See Byerly (2011) for a discussion of the difficulties faced by the few women media owners in the United States. Robinson (2005) identified scholarship and research combining feminist and economic approaches to journalism as a significantly underdeveloped area of study.

37. Callison is a regular contributor to *MediaIndigena*.

38. Yu, 2016.

39. Zelizer, 2015, p. 2.

40. CBC and CTV (Canada's national broadcasters), *The Globe and Mail* and the *National Post* (Canada's two national newspapers, as well as the *Toronto Star* organization, which has become a national media player after integrating four Star Metro bureaus in Vancouver, Edmonton, Calgary and Halifax) are headquartered in Toronto. In the Canadian news business, Toronto is commonly referred to in a serious-joking way as "the center of the earth." Worthy of more study is the fact that many prominent news startups, such as *the Discourse, National Observer*, and *The Tyee*, were all started in Vancouver.

41. "Sharing the stories only we can tell," no date.

42. APTN, 2009.

43. Owen, 2017; Young & Hermida, 2018.

44. Honderich, 2016.

45. Winseck, 2010, pp. 367–368.

46. Winseck, 2017.

47. See Picard's 2016 submission to the House of Commons Standing Committee on Canadian Heritage where he outlines the importance of local news, and the "unique challenges" facing Canadian communities "because of the extraordinary consolidation of news enterprises, reductions in local staffing, and the increasing shift of news and information production outside communities. Such issues should not be addressed merely as media and communication policy concerns, but also as cultural and social policy concerns."

48. Compton & Dyer-Witheford, 2014; Edge, 2014; Winseck, 2010.

49. Paradkar, 2017.

50. English, 2017.

51. Cole, 2017.

52. Domise, 2017.

53. J-Source, 2015.

54. 2016 Census Backgrounder, City of Toronto, 2017.

55. Paradkar, 2016.

56. Henry, 1999; Jiwani, 2016; Mahtani, 2001; Miller, 1998; Pritchard & Sauvageau, 1998.

57. Pritchard & Sauvageau, 1998.

58. See Dhillon's 2018 article in *Medium*.

59. For example, CBC-Radio Canada's 2017 Employment Equity Annual Report indicates slight to no increases in inclusion among its staff from 2016: women (48.4%, up 0.2% from 2016), Indigenous peoples (2%, similar to 2016), visible minorities (11.5%, up 1% from 2016), persons with disabilities (2.6%, up 0.1% from 2016). See also (Cukier et al., 2011) and (Miller, 1998, 2006).

60. Zelizer, 1993.

61. Zelizer, 1993, p. 219.

62. Zelizer, 1993, p. 220.

63. Zelizer, 1993, p. 220.

64. Dewey, 1927; Ward, 2004.

65. Zelizer, 1993, p. 220.

66. Zelizer, 2017, p. 181.

67. Picard, 2013.

68. Cole, 2017.

69. Ahmed, 2012.

70. Kreiss, 2019.

71. Young, Hermida, & Fulda, 2017.

72. Borges-Rey, 2017; Coddington, 2015; Hermida & Young, 2019; Usher, 2016.

73. Borges-Rey, 2017, p. 2.

74. Heravi, 2017.

75. Bozckowski & Lievrouw, 2008; Bozckowski & Mitchelstein, 2013.

76. "History of the *Toronto Star*," n.d.

77. Deuze, 2017, p. 11.

78. Honderich, 2016.

79. Popplewell, 2018. Unlike the issues-based particulars of diverse publics outlined by Choy in Chapter 2, according to Popplewell (2018) there are a range of market research categories at the *Star*: "Among the types of humans *Star* reporters now understand to be the desired readership: the 'wise elders' (older, culturally active, and generous with their money), who represent 9.7% of the audience, and 'future managers' (socially progressive up-and-comers with large media appetites). Less appealing in the modern era are the 'lunch at Tim's' crowd (socially conservative bargain hunters) or, worse, the 'hillside hobbyists' who, at 11% of the Canadian audience, have strong traditional values, live largely outside the urban centres, and have almost no willingness to pay for any online news whatsoever."

80. Rankin, 2019.

81. Heravi, 2017. Heravi found that the "vast majority (70%) of organizations with data teams" have small groups of between one to five people, with 22% supporting "data teams of six to ten people."

82. Hermida & Young, 2017.

83. Anonymous, 2016b.

84. Anonymous, 2016a.

85. Bozckowski & Lievrouw, 2008, p. 966.

86. According to Picard (2014, p. 278) "news providers of all sizes are now employing multiple platforms for reaching and engaging with the public. They are reconceiving the nature of audiences and rethinking what information the public needs in different places, at different times, and the methods in which that information is conveyed. These are all indications of the appearance of new journalistic relations and practices."

87. Zelizer, 1993.

88. Boczkowski, 2004; Fink & Anderson, 2015; Hermida & Young, 2017; Nielsen, 2012.

89. Anonymous, 2016b.

90. Eschner, 2016.

91. Bozckowski & Lievrouw, 2007, p. 963.

92. Heravi, 2017.

93. Anonymous, 2016f.

94. Young & Giltrow, 2015.

95. Felt, 2017, p. 254.

96. Anonymous, 2016b.

97. Anonymous, 2016f.

98. Anonymous, 2016f.

99. Zelizer, 1993, p. 222.

100. They include a series on racial profiling and police (2002), which was recognized with one of the highest awards in Canadian journalism. See "Singled out," *Toronto Star*, 2002. Retrieved from https://www.thestar.com/news/gta/knowntopolice/singled-out. html). Others include investigations on racial bias in marijuana arrests (See "Toronto marijuana arrests," *Toronto Star*, 2017. Retrieved from https://www.thestar.com/news/insight/2017/07/06/toronto-marijuana-arrests-reveal-startling-racial-divide.html) and racial disparities in child apprehension (2014) (See "Why are so many black children in foster and group homes," *Toronto Star*, 2014. Retrieved from https://www.thestar.com/

news/canada/2014/12/11/why_are_so_many_black_children_in_foster_and_group_
homes.html). Jim Rankin, who we interview in this chapter, was the lead journalist on the
first two investigations and a member of the team of journalists on the third.

101. $32,000 and a 3-year wait: Star reporters share what it's like trying to access public documents in Canada, 2018.

102. "Atkinson Principles," n.d.

103. *Toronto Star*, n.d.

104. Atkinson Principles, n.d.

105. Simpson, 2014; TallBear, 2014.

106. Simpson, 2014, p. 98.

107. Vimalassery, Pegues, & Goldstein, 2016, p. 1.

108. Anderson & Robertson, 2011.

109. Craig, 2016.

110. Küng, 2015.

111. Felt, 2017.

112. Anonymous, 2016b.

113. Anonymous, 2016b.

114. Anonymous, 2016b.

115. Rankin, 2019.

116. See also Tworek, 2019.

117. Robinson, 2005.

118. Acker quoted in Ahmed, 2012, p. 9.

119. Acker, 2006, p. 443.

120. Talaga, whose work we discuss in Chapter 6, began her column in early 2019 as we were finalizing this manuscript, following a national lecture series, *All Our Relations,* and a 2017 book, *Seven Fallen Feathers*.

121. Anderson, 2018.

122. Millar, 2019a.

123. Picard, personal communication, 2016.

124. Felt, 2017; Zelizer, 2015.

125. Tworek, 2019, p. 5.

126. Tworek, 2019, p. 5.

Chapter 5

1. An earlier version of this chapter has been published as "When gender, colo-nialism, and technology matter in a journalism startup" in *Journalism*. See Young & Callison, 2017.

2. Author Callison's father, aunt and uncles are all residential school survivors as are many Indigenous people across Canada over the age of 60. Though most schools were closed by the 1970s, the last school was not shuttered until the mid-1990s. See the Truth and Reconciliation Commission's website and final report for detailed descriptions of the impact and timelines related to these schools.

3. Fleck, 1979.

4. When it launched in 2014, *the Discourse* was identified at that time as a digital and data journalism innovator in North America; however, their identity as "a startup" has shifted as a result of their longevity. While we refer to the organization as "the startup," it

has since our fieldwork in 2016 passed early stages as a company even as it continues to stay nimble and experimental in terms of the work it produces and how it maps onto the media landscape regionally and nationally.

5. Gender, as we suggest, is an undeveloped area of the startup literature in North America, although a 2017 study by SembraMedia, an NGO focused on providing support for digital journalism entrepreneurs, found that women accounted for 38% of founders of journalism startups in four Latin American countries—Argentina, Brazil, Colombia, and Mexico.

6. *the Discourse* newsletter, Summer 2018.

7. Our ethnographic practice draws from anthropological approaches to studying media, science, and technology and a long history of ethnographic approaches to journalism organizations, newsrooms, agency and identity (see Usher, 2013 for a recent study of a public radio news show). For this research, we spent several months attending periodic story meetings as participant-observers (Fortun, 2003; Marcus & Fischer, 1999), attending events where employees were speaking (including at our own journalism school and at our university), and interviewing most of the full-time employees, several freelancers, and one of the former co-founders of the startup. As journalism professors teaching in the same city as this startup, our social and professional overlap is not insignificant and created continual ethical plateaus. Not only have students we supervised and taught worked with this startup, but we attend many of the same media industry events. It is in this sense that ethnographic practice operates within what Marcus and Fischer (1999) consider to be an "open system" where investigators must seek to understand the complex, layered social processes at work in a vastly interconnected and increasingly global web of social realities (Fortun, 2003). Our practice and analyses are thus informed by our discussions with the startup employees and interpolated with scholarship, teaching, contributing, and working in a settler-colonial media context in Canada.

8. Benson, 2017; Graves & Konieczna, 2015.

9. Millar, 2016. See Jackson (2014) for a discussion of repair.

10. Benson, 2017; Cagé, 2016.

11. Discussed extensively in Chapter 4.

12. Millar, personal communication, 2017.

13. We draw from Harding's critique of science (1998, p. 2) and Turkle & Papert (1990, p. 128).

14. Bruno & Nielsen, 2012; Carlson & Usher, 2016; Deuze, 2017; Powers & Zambrano, 2016; Wagemans et al., 2016.

15. Wagemans et al., 2016, p. 160.

16. Carlson & Usher, 2016, p. 12.

17. Bruno & Nielsen, 2012, p. 2.

18. Wagemans et al., 2016.

19. Royal, 2012; Usher, 2018; Young & Hermida, 2015.

20. Wagemans et al., 2016.

21. Powers & Zambrano, 2016.

22. Powers & Zambrano, 2016, p. 872.

23. Deuze, 2017.

24. Deuze, 2017, p. 10.

25. See PPF, 2017; Zelizer, 2015. Others have found similar concerns with respect to the impact of financial models. In interviews with 10 leaders of U.S. nonprofit journalism organizations, Coates Nee found that accessing diverse revenue streams is difficult, and relying on philanthropy "tenuous" (2014, p. 338). In their 2011 study of U.S. online startups, Funabiki & Yoshihara (2011) found the top the revenue streams were foundations (68.8%), individual donations (62.5%), and advertising (53.1%). No similar studies exist in Canada.

26. Cagé, 2016.

27. Cagé, 2016, p. 5.

28. Cagé, 2016, p. 1.

29. Benson, 2017, Ferrucci, 2017; Graves & Konieczna, 2016.

30. Ferrucci, 2017, p. 358.

31. Benson, 2017, p. 16.

32. Graves & Konieczna, 2016, pp. 1978–1979.

33. See Naldi & Picard (2012) on startups in the United States. Author Young is co-founder of *The Conversation Canada*, a nonprofit national journalism startup and affiliate of the global Conversation journalism network. Author Callison is on the board of *The Narwhal*, a nonprofit environmental journalism startup in Canada.

34. Naldi & Picard, 2012, p. 71.

35. Millar, 2018a.

36. Millar, 2018a.

37. Millar, 2018a.

38. Jackson, 2014.

39. Jackson, 2014, p. 223.

40. Millar, personal communication, 2017.

41. Personal essay published on *Medium*, 2016.

42. Hermida & Young, 2019.

43. Byerly, 2011.

44. According to an unpublished study by Taylor Owen (2017) conference paper by Hermida & Young (2019).

45. PPF, 2017.

46. Schmidt, 2017.

47. Millar, 2019b.

48. Schaffer, 2007 quoted in Naldi & Picard, 2012, p. 72.

49. Anonymous, 2016i.

50. PPF Report, 2017.

51. PPF, 2017.

52. Wajcman, 2010.

53. Millar, 2016.

54. Millar, 2016.

55. Byerly, 2013; Young & Beale, 2013.

56. Freeman, 2016; Mahtani, 2001, 2005; Robinson, 2005; Smith, 2015; Young & Beale, 2013.

57. Feminist media studies scholars have approached gender through a few main lenses. They include: content and media representations (see recent examples, GMMP, 2010; Ross & Carter, 2011), news norms and practices (Robinson, 2005; van Zoonen,

1998) and the number of women in news, their progression through the ranks (Franks, 2013; Robinson, 2005; Young & Beale, 2013), as well as some limited scholarship on issues of economics (Byerly, 2011; Robinson, 2005). Theoretically there have been a range of orientations from liberal feminist to standpoint (Durham, 1999; Steiner, 2012). Similar to feminist science and technology studies, much of the literature sets "women in news" apart and distinct from "gender and news," which examines gender as socially constructed as opposed to essentialized understandings of men/women, and journalism actively involved in producing gender (see, e.g., Faulkner, 2001, p. 79 on the differences between "women and technology" and "gender and technology"). A main question has been why there are so few women in the profession and in the news, with insufficient attention paid to the lack of minority women in countries with large immigrant and/ or Indigenous populations, despite the fact that there have been important contributions in this area (Mahtani, 2005; Steiner, 2012). For instance, the Global Media Monitoring Project (2010) found women largely under-represented in news internationally. The professionalization literature suggests that gendered working techniques and practices are part of a professional knowledge system in journalism. For example, van Zoonen (1998) has questioned the neutrality of the news category in general, claiming news itself as masculinist, which is reflected in competition, crime news, and the hard/soft news binary.

58. Byerly, 2011.
59. Byerly, 2011, p. 35.
60. Byerly, 2011, p. 39.
61. Anonymous, 2016h.
62. Anonymous, 2016h.
63. Faulkner, 2009, p. 173.
64. Millar, 2016.
65. Anonymous, 2016h.
66. Millar, 2016.
67. Leonard, 1995.
68. Anonymous, 2016k.
69. Young, 2005; Zelizer, 1993.
70. Anonymous, 2016k.
71. See Canadian Journalism Foundation, 2016, and *the Discourse*, 2015.
72. Appelgren & Nygren, 2014.
73. Royal, 2012.
74. Royal, 2012; Faulkner, 2001, p. 79.
75. For example, Gillespie et al., 2014; Turner, 2013.
76. Wajcman, 2010, p. 8. See also Nielsen (2012) on the growing importance of studying technologists as shapers of the nature of legacy media organizations.
77. Appelgren & Nygren, 2014; Royal, 2012; Young & Hermida, 2015.
78. Faulkner, 2001, p. 81.
79. Faulkner, 2001, p. 173.
80. Faulkner, 2009, p. 184.
81. Faulkner, 2001; Lohan & Faulkner, 2004.
82. Turkle & Papert, 1990, p. 129.
83. Turkle & Papert, 1990, p. 147.
84. Turkle & Papert, 1990, p. 148.

85. Rao & Wasserman, 2007, p. 37.

86. Rao & Wasserman, 2007, p. 38.

87. Anderson & Robertson, 2011; Callison & Hermida, 2015; Simpson, 2014; TallBear, 2014.

88. Coulthard, 2014.

89. Anderson & Robertson, 2011.

90. *The Discourse*, 2018.

91. *The Discourse*, 2018.

92. DeJarnette, 2016.

93. Schudson, 2001; Ward, 2004.

94. Anderson & Robertson, 2011.

95. Haraway, 1988.

96. Callison, 2014.

97. Anderson & Robertson, 2011; Bein, 2017; Cukier et al., 2011; Henry, 1999; Mahtani, 2001; Pritchard & Sauvageau, 1998.

98. Robinson, 2005.

99. Kirkness & Barnhardt, 2001, p. 15.

100. Millar, personal communication, 2017. Hamilton is a graduate of the UBC School of Journalism and was taught by author Callison.

101. Millar, 2018a.

102. Millar, 2017.

103. Callison, 2014; TallBear, 2014.

104. Carlson & Usher, 2016.

105. Byerly, 2011.

106. Haraway, 1997, 1988; Harding, 2011.

107. Millar, 2019c.

108. Jackson, 2014, p. 222.

Chapter 6

1. A note on terminology. In this chapter, we use the terms "native," "Indigenous," "Indian," "Native American," "Métis," and "First Nations" interchangeably. Wherever possible, we note the Nation/people that journalists are part of; however, we do not do the same for scholars (following the conventions in the rest of the book and in most scholarship) we refer to by last name only. Nearly all of the scholars we utilize in this chapter are Indigenous.

2. See, for example: Ahtone, 2019; Gilpin, 2018; Martin, 2019; Monet, 2019.

3. Cram, 2019.

4. The number of Indigenous journalists in mainstream media in North America does not reflect Indigenous peoples' likely proportion of the audience. In the United States, the American Society of Newsroom Editors (ASNE) is the main source of longitudinal data on minorities in newsrooms with an annual survey that it has completed since 1978. Its most recent survey in 2018 found that people of color accounted for 22.6% of journalists (employees and managers)—with 0.37 American Indian and 0.13% Hawaiian/Pacific Islander. These percentages amount to an increase in people of color from 13.52% a decade ago in 2008—and 3.95% three decades ago when the survey began in 1978. Longitudinal data for Indigenous journalists is complicated as methods have changed over time, are self-reported, and don't account for enough data from states with a high

percentage of Indigenous peoples. For example, only 17% of newsrooms responded to the annual survey for 2018. Year over year who responds changes with more tribal media responding in 2008, for example. Conversely, it's notable in 2018 that media from Alaska did not participate in the survey and there is only one source from Hawaii; Alaska has an over 15% Indigenous population and Hawaii a 21% Indigenous population.

Other data emerges from publicly funded broadcasters in Canada and the United States, which are required to gather diversity data. NPR's 2018 annual report indicated that 27% of its employees were people of color (an increase of 2% from 2017), with 0.25% of those American Indian. This is compared to the most recent census data from the United States in which American Indian and Alaska Native populations are 1.7% (over 5.2 million) and Native Hawaiian or other Pacific Islanders are 0.2% (over 1.2 million) of the country's population. The most recent annual report from Canada's public broadcaster, the CBC, shows that people of color are 10.5%, and Indigenous people make up 2% of permanent staff. In Canada, 4.3% are Indigenous people who identify as First Nations, Métis or Inuit, with Indigenous peoples among the fastest growing and the youngest in both the United States and Canada.

In the United States, another source of data on the number of indigenous journalists is the U.S.-based Native American Journalists Association (NAJA). It has 562 members, but as the current president and Kiowa journalist Tristan Ahtone pointed out in an email: "many of our members are Associate Members (non-native) and there are still a number of Native journalists that aren't members" so the list is not complete but provides another data point. It's important to note that the commercial and freelance situation of Indigenous journalists is not adequately reflected in the data. Given the increasing prevalence of the so-called gig economy and precarity of labor in journalism, how many are working outside of mainstream media, and how much and whether Indigenous journalists are getting bylines and/or are able to make a living wage is not known.

5. Haraway, 1988; Harding, 1998; TallBear, 2013, 2014.

6. Anderson & Robertson, 2011; Simpson, 2014.

7. Ethnographic and paraethnographic methods include attending and participating in the first conference of newly trained Indigenous community journalists and mid-career Indigenous journalists held by Journalists for Human Rights in Canada, and in-depth semi-structured interviews with Indigenous journalists from the United States and Canada. In addition, we brought some of these journalists in as guest speakers to our classes, larger gatherings at the UBC School of Journalism and public venues at UBC, and panels at other universities and conferences on Indigenous journalism. Callison's involvement with the podcast *Media Indigena* alongside fellow contributor Kim TallBear and produced and hosted by Rick Harp has also served as a kind of paraethnographic exercise adjacent to fieldwork, as has an op-ed column we jointly authored for *The Conversation* in the wake of the deaths of Colten Boushie and Tina Fontaine (Callison & Young, 2018). Finally, while at Princeton, Callison co-convened an International Symposium on Indigenous Communities and Climate Change that brought together Indigenous scholars and journalists, several of whom are quoted in this chapter.

8. TallBear states "Decolonizing methods begin and end with the standpoint of Indigenous lives, needs, and desires, engaging with academic lives, approaches and priorities along the way" (2013, p. 20).

9. Anderson & Robertson, 2011; Simpson, 2014; White Eye, 1996.

10. While this book chapter focuses primarily on Indigenous journalists who have worked in mainstream media, and the challenges of negotiating with journalism norms and practices, Indigenous media has a long history in both the United States and Canada. Indeed, from the beginning of settler-colonialism, Indigenous people began using media in vital ways to defend their homelands and express concerns, beginning with the *Cherokee Phoenix* in 1828, which fought removal from their homelands (Dunbar-Ortiz, 2014). Cherokee scholar Daniel Justice pointed out to us that the starting point could be considered much earlier with works like Garcilaso de la Vega's *Comentarios Reales de los Incas* and Fernando de Alva Cortés Ixtlilxóchitl's *Historia chichimeca*. Both are examples of 16th- and 17th-century mestizo writers who took up the media of their time to address Indigenous and first-generation mestizo concerns. See recent scholarship on the legacy of Ixtlilxóchitl in particular in Brokaw and Lee (2016).

The website for the Indigenous Media Freedom Alliance founded by Mandan-Hidatsa and Lakota journalist Jodi Rave Spotted Bear notes that as of early 2019, there are only 12 independent Indigenous media organizations in the United States despite there being 565 federally recognized tribes. And in a 2018 report commissioned and released by Democracy Fund, Rave points out that there has been a steep decline in Indigenous print sources (700 newspapers in 1998 to 200 in 2018; 100 magazines in 1998 to 8 in 2018) and a steep rise in radio (from 30 stations to 59 in 20 years). What's most challenging is the dearth of journalism programs in tribal colleges and universities and the lack of independence amongst tribal media where tribes control 72% of newspapers and radio stations. Rave argues that independent media that serve Indigenous communities needs to become the norm—and not the exception.

11. Peryer (2019) provides interview excerpts with several Kānaka Maoli (Native Hawaiian) leaders that offer critique of how mainstream media are covering (and have covered) their work to protect Mauna Kea.

12. Native American Journalists Association (NAJA) used to have many Canada-based Indigenous journalists, but according to discussions with longtime members, this shifted in the late 1990s for various individual and institutional reasons. NAJA has primarily focused on the U.S. context throughout the 2000s, but as of this writing, there are plans afoot to once again join with Indigenous journalists working in the Canadian media landscape. Canada has no association of its own like NAJA though a recent Facebook group was formed to support Indigenous journalists working primarily in Canada.

13. When we first began writing, some U.S.-based journalists and activists tagged their posts with #MMIWG on Twitter, reframing the experiences of Indigenous women as continent-wide when 22-year-old and pregnant Savannah Greywind who was Spirit Lake Dakota and Turtle Mountain Chippewa went missing and was later found murdered (Manning, 2017). Other less high-profile cases have similarly been tagged, and statistically, Indigenous women and girls as we pointed out in chapter two are more likely to suffer violence and assault than any other women in North America. See Pember (2018) for more on the U.S. context. As of this writing, new U.S. Congresswomen Deb Haaland who is a tribal citizen of the Pueblo of Laguna Pueblo held hearings for the first time "to address the epidemic of missing and murdered Indigenous women" in March 2019.

14. Following the Facebook Senate hearings, Monet (2018) wrote an op-ed for *Yes!* where she pointed out that giving up Facebook is not an option for Indigenous people— and journalists. And as Duarte has argued about the use of social media during Idle No

More: "Tracing the information that flows through these networks of individuals and the networks of devices that they build reveals the sociotechnical strata through which Native and Indigenous peoples work against the forces of colonialism" (2017, p. 25).

15. Nagle, 2018.

16. In Canada, the Canadian press has a specific section in its widely used style guide for writing about Indigenous people. Journalists for Human Rights, which we write about later in this chapter, has also issued a style guide for reporting on Indigenous people. Some of those we interviewed were consulted about both style guides.

17. Talaga, 2017.

18. In her second book, *All Our Relations*, Talaga (2018) continues with this framework extending it to global Indigenous social situations, pointing out the ways that relations with land and settler-colonialism are directly linked to the distressing prevalence of youth suicides and other health disparities in Indigenous communities.

19. Anderson, 1991.

20. Tuck & Yang, 2012, p. 5.

21. Anderson & Robertson, 2011.

22. Ahtone, 2019. Ahtone is also an associate editor for *High Country News* where he has been pioneering a model for integrating Indigenous journalism and journalists into a mainstream news organization through a Tribal Affairs desk. See https://www.hcn.org/topics/tribal-affairs.

23. See also Navajo/Yankton Dakota Sioux writer Jacqueline Keeler writing on this event including notably "Land Gets Stolen. That's How It Works" (2019) for *Sierra*. Keeler was also in conversation with Ahtone on WBUR's *On Point* (Chakrabarti & Hardzinski, 2019).

24. In their reporting on the issues in Wet'suwet'en territory and Thunder Bay, Indigenous journalists for a variety of outlets, such as Chantelle Bellrichard (CBC Indigenous), Willow Fiddler (APTN), Ryan McMahon (*Canadaland*), are reframing complex stories on the ground, addressing persistent stereotypes and distinct, complex settler-colonial contexts for audiences. During the eruptions of Kilauea in the past several years, Facebook has become a key source for ensuring community safety and updates from Kānaka Maoli who perceived the eruption in spiritual and cultural terms—and not exclusively as mainstream media framed it: property loss and destruction.

25. Nixon, 2019.

26. Rhodes, 1993, p. 185.

27. Anderson & Robertson, 2011; Zelizer, 1993.

28. Haraway, 1997, p. 24.

29. Carey, 1974.

30. Wolfe, 2006, p. 402.

31. See for example, Byrd, 2011; Coulthard, 2012, 2014; Simpson, 2014; TallBear, 2013; Whyte, 2016.

32. Simpson, 2014, p. 95.

33. Simpson, 2014, p. 96.

34. Simpson, 2014, p. 97.

35. See also Dowell, 2013.

36. See Whyte (2016) for a discussion of erasure and Nagle (2018) for journalism on erasure as a concept and problem.

37. TallBear, 2013, p. 176.

38. Subramaniam et al., 2017, p. 418.

39. Roy, 2004.

40. TallBear, 2016, p. 423.

41. Tuck & Yang, 2012, p. 7.

42. Watts, 2013, p. 22.

43. Watts, 2013, p. 23.

44. White Eye, 1996, p. 92.

45. White Eye, 1996, p. 93.

46. White Eye, 1996, p. 96. Much of White Eye's narrative resonates with Author Callison, who was a young Indigenous journalist in the mid-1990s and later chose to shift to an academic career in 2000.

47. Todorova, 2016.

48. In the last several years, Anishnaabe journalist Duncan McCue has taught as an adjunct professor at UBC. McCue is a longtime CBC journalist who pioneered a course titled "Reporting in Indigenous Communities (RIIC)," which he has since also brought to Ryerson University in Toronto in part to address problems in education and practice. In the UBC class on Ethics, Callison taught for nearly a decade, giving a three-hour seminar devoted to the challenges of reporting on Indigenous issues. To graduate all master's journalism students must take this ethics course that includes this seminar. And in order to do so, they must read Anderson & Robertson (2011) and write a short response paper on the book. UBC is one of the few—if not the only—journalism schools in the United States and Canada to require *all* students to develop awareness of the history of journalism in relation to Indigenous people through scholarship, teaching, and opportunities for applied practice. Despite these albeit minor advances, the sedimentation of mis- and non-representation remains an ongoing challenge. McCue refers to this routinized coverage as W4Ds—Indigenous people are either depicted as warriors, dancing, drumming, drunk, or dead. See http://riic.ca for more.

49. Carpenter, 2017.

50. Buckley, 2019.

51. Notably, child removal and foster care systems persist into the present as recent investigative reporting by Sterritt and others have shown in Canada. Similarly in the United States, in the wake of removals of Indigenous children from their families and communities in the 1960s and 1970s, the Indian Child Welfare Act was implemented to give preference for adoption and foster care to family and tribal members. Yet, this policy has recently been challenged in the courts and much of the mainstream news coverage of it has come under intense criticism, prompting some to point out just how few Indigenous journalists there are at mainstream news organizations—and just how much it matters on complex, historically rooted issues like child removal.

52. Gilpin, 2018. Author Callison is also quoted in this article.

53. Trahant has also authored four books—and is working on a fifth—and puts together a weekly radio commentary.

54. See Trahant, 2019; ICT Editorial Team, 2018.

55. ICT Editorial Team, 2019.

56. Spotted Bear underscored that this is a major challenge for communities where even uneven accountability mechanisms like Freedom of Information requests, for

example, can't be made for tribal governments. As of this writing, in conjunction with IMFA and several other journalism and philanthropic organizations, NAJA has launched the Red Press Initiative (2019) in order to study the perception of press freedom among journalists and editors working in tribal media. A preliminary 2019 survey of NAJA members found that "83 percent responded that stories about tribal government affairs sometimes, frequently or always go unreported due to censorship."

57. See Dunbar-Ortiz (2014) for an overview of Indigenous histories in the United States.

58. See Simpson, 2016, for example.

59. Monet, 2019. In this article, Monet describes why she has chosen to publish on her own website, an "Indigenous versions" of her articles that are published by mainstream news sources. We discuss this in more detail in Chapter 3.

60. Monet, 2017.

61. Simpson, 2014, p. 97.

62. Justice, 2019.

63. Brooks, 2018.

64. Brooks, 2018; Dunbar-Ortiz, 2014; Estes, 2017, 2019; Gilio-Whitaker, 2019.

65. Dadigan, 2017, emphasis added.

66. Harp, 2018.

67. Piapot, 2018.

68. See Rave, 2018.

69. Beaudin-Herne, 2018.

70. In Canada, there are numbered treaties from the mid-late 1800s that cover the southern provinces up until you reach British Columbia, which still doesn't have treaties for two-thirds of the province. The northern territories (Yukon, Northwest Territories, Nunavut) have all reached agreements with Indigenous people beginning in the 1980s.

71. This website is no longer available.

72. Ahtone (2019) has made a similar argument: "The practice we call 'journalism' has deep roots in Indigenous communities. From calendars to quipus, codices to songs, record keeping and storytelling have been part of Indigenous life since time immemorial. One of the most influential and enduring forms of documentation has been the ledger drawing: a genre created in the mid-1800s by Plains artists using grease pencils and ledger books—people like Silver Horn, Mad Bull and Zotom."

73. It is the only newspaper that publishes stories in English, Ojibway, OjiCree, and Cree. *Wawatay* went online in 2007, and also operates a radio network and produces programming for APTN.

74. Simpson, 2016.

75. Callison, 2014, p. 48; Fischer, 2018; Fortun, 2001; Marcus and Fischer, 1996.

76. Harp, 2018.

Conclusion

1. Broersma, 2010a, 2010b; Durham, 1998; Ettema & Glasser, 1994; Lipari, 1996; Rao & Wasserman, 2007; Steiner, 2018; Zelizer, 1993, 2015.

2. For example, Durham, 1998; Rhodes, 1993; Rao & Wasserman, 2007; Steiner, 2012, 2018; Zuckerman, 2008, 2014.

3. According to the Pew Research Center's annual survey of media in the United States (there is no equivalent in Canada), as of 2017, almost half of U.S. adults (45%) access their news on mobile devices, with people increasingly getting their news online (43% who say they often get their news online) as compared to television (50%), where people have been largely mainly accessing their news for half a century. As of 2018, the economic context for U.S. newsrooms was difficult to say the least, with employment declining by 23% between 2008 and 2017 across five industries: newspaper, radio, broadcast, cable and other information services (a proxy for digital). The losses were largely by fueled by newspapers.

4. De Certeau, 1984.

5. Broersma, 2010a; Schudson, 2008; Tuchman, 1997; Ward, 2004.

6. Ananny, 2018; Anderson, 2013; Anderson & Kreiss, 2013; Boczkowski, 2004, 2005; Gillespie et al., 2014; Kreiss, 2012; Lewis & Usher, 2014; Turner, 2005; Usher, 2013, 2015.

7. See Pollock and Subramaniam (2016) for an overview, as well as emerging engagement with settler-colonialism and Indigenous studies in, for example, TallBear (2013), Reardon and TallBear (2012), Whyte (2013), Todd (2016).

8. Crenshaw, 1991. See also Costanza-Chock & Schweidler, 2017.

9. Harp, 2018.

10. Talaga, 2018.

11. See in particular Jackson and Welles (2016) for analysis of media related to Ferguson and other major protests associated with Black Lives Matter. See also Benjamin (2019) and Noble (2018) for in-depth discussions of race and new digital technologies that also advance STS frameworks.

12. Dumit, 2014.

13. For example, Latour, 2000; Fischer, 2003; Haraway, 1997.

14. Jasanoff, 2004; Reardon, 2009; Dumit, 2012.

15. Benjamin, 2013, 2019; Nelson, 2016; Noble, 2018; Pollock, 2012; Reardon, 2009; TallBear, 2013.

16. Sacco, 2013.

17. Roitman, 2013.

18. Anderson & Robertson, 2011; Dunbar-Ortiz, 2014; Estes, 2017; Lambertus, 2004; Smith & Warrior, 1996.

19. Marcus & Fischer, 1999, p. 8.

20. Fortun, 2003, p. 174.

21. Marcus & Fischer, 1999, p. 91.

22. Fortun, 2003, p. 176.

23. Fischer, 2018, pp. 1–2.

24. Haraway, 2015, p. 160.

REFERENCES

$32,000 and a 3-year wait: Star reporters share what it's like trying to access public documents in Canada. (2018, March 30). Retrieved from https://www.thestar.com/news/gta/2018/03/30/32000-and-a-3-year-wait-star-reporters-share-what-its-like-trying-to-access-public-documents-in-canada.html

Ahmed, S. (2012). *On being included*. Durham, NC: Duke University Press.

Ahtone, T. (2019, January 25). The mishandling of the MAGA teens story shows why I gave up on mainstream media. *Washington Post*. Retrieved from https://www.washingtonpost.com/nation/2019/01/25/mishandling-maga-teens-story-shows-why-i-gave-up-mainstream-media/?utm_term=.8bfa88ff7ff5

Ahtone, T. (2019, February 4). Journalism is rooted in Indigenous communities. *High Country News*. Retrieved from https://www.hcn.org/issues/51.2/editors-note-journalism-is-rooted-in-indigenous-communities

Alia, V. (2011). *Un/covering the north: News, media, and aboriginal people*. Vancouver, BC: UBC Press.

Alba, D. (2017, September 23). Ellen Pao's story is messier than her book makes it sound. *Buzzfeed*. Retrieved from https://www.buzzfeed.com/daveyalba/the-plaintiff-of-techs-biggest-sex-bias-suit-is-a?utm_term=.vdKY1J7am0#.ln2PwZJo6q

Ananny, M. (2018). Read an excerpt from Mike Ananny's new book, Networked Press Freedom. *Culture Digitally*. Retrieved from http://culturedigitally.org/2018/07/networked-press-freedom/.

Ananny, M. (2018). *Networked Press Freedom: Creating Infrastructures for a Public Right to Hear*. Cambridge, MA: MIT Press.

Anderson, B. (1991). *Imagined communities: Reflections on the origin and spread of nationalism*. London: Verso.

Anderson, C.W. (2018). *Apostles of certainty*. New York: Oxford University Press.

Anderson, C., & Robertson, M. (2011). *Seeing red: A history of natives in Canadian newspapers*. Winnipeg, MB: University of Manitoba Press.

Anderson, C.W. (2013). *Rebuilding the news: Metropolitan journalism in the digital age*. Philadelphia, PA: Temple University Press.

Anderson, C. W., & Kreiss, D. (2013). Black boxes as capacities for and constraints on action: Electoral politics, journalism, and devices of representation. *Qualitative Sociology, 36*(4), 365–382.

Angelucci, C., & Cage, J. (2017). Newspapers in times of low advertising revenues. CEPR Discussion Paper #11414. https://sites.google.com/site/juliacagehomepage/research

Appelgren, E., & Nygren, G. (2014). Data Journalism in Sweden: Introducing new methods and genres of journalism into 'old' organizations. *Digital Journalism, 2*(3), 394–405.

APTN. (2009). Report to the Standing Committee of Canadian Heritage.

Arvin, M., Tuck, E., & Morrill, A. (2013). Decolonizing feminism: Challenging connections between settler colonialism and heteropatriarchy. *Feminist Formations*, Baltimore, *25*(1), 8–34.

Atkinson Principles. (n.d.). *Toronto Star* website. Retrieved from https://www.thestar.com/about/atkinson.html

Awad, I. (2006). Journalists and their sources: Lessons from anthropology. *Journalism Studies*, *7*(6), 922–939.

Baiocchi, G., Bennett, E., Cordner, A., Klein, P., & Savell, S. (2014). *Civic imagination: making a difference in American political life*. New York: Routledge.

Bakhtin, M. (1986). The problem of speech genres. In Caryl Emerson & Michael Holquist (Eds.), *Speech genres and other late essays*, Vern W. McGee (Trans.) (pp. 60–102). Austin: University of Texas Press.

Balkissoon, D. (2018, February 1). Even after death Canada denies Tina Fontaine dignity. *The Globe and Mail*. Retrieved from https://www.theglobeandmail.com/opinion/even-after-death-canada-denies-tina-fontaine-dignity/article37821254/

Barnhurst, K., & Mutz, D. (1997). American journalism and the decline of event-centered reporting. *Journal of Communication*, *47*(4), 27–53.

Barthel, M. (2015, August 4). In the news industry, diversity is lowest at smaller outlets. Pew Research. Retrieved from http://www.pewresearch.org/fact-tank/2015/08/04/in-the-news-industry-diversity-is-lowest-at-smaller-outlets/

Baughman, J. (1987). *Henry R. Luce and the rise of the American news media*. Boston, MA: Twayne.

Bauman, R. (2004). *A world of others' words: Cross-cultural perspectives on intertextuality*. Cambridge, MA: Blackwell.

Bauman, Z. (2013). *Liquid times: Living in an age of uncertainty*. Chichester, UK: John Wiley.

Beaudin-Herne, J. (2018, October 14). How indigenous journalists learn new techniques to tell First Nations stories. *The Globe and Mail*. Retrieved from https://www.theglobeandmail.com/business/careers/article-how-indigenous-journalists-learn-new-techniques-to-tell-first-nations/

Bein, S. (2017, September 8). Here's what CBC staff told their bosses about the need for diversity. *Canadaland*. Retrieved from https://www.canadalandshow.com/cbc-staff-told-bosses-about-need-for-diversity/

Bell, E. (2014). Silicon Valley and journalism: Make up or break up? Reuters Memorial Lecture 2015. Retrieved from http://reutersinstitute.politics.ox.ac.uk/events/silicon-valley-and- journalism-make-or-break.

Bell, E. (2016). The end of the news as we know it: How Facebook swallowed journalism. *Columbia Journalism Review*. Retrieved from https://www.cjr.org/analysis/facebook_and_media.php?

Benjamin, R. (2013). *People's science: Bodies and rights on the stem cell frontier*. Stanford, CA: Stanford University Press.

Benjamin, R. (2019). *Race after technology: Abolitionist tools for the new jim code*. Cambridge and Oxford, UK: Polity Press.

Benson, R. (2017). Can foundations solve the journalism crisis? *Journalism*. doi: 10.1177/1464884917724612

Benson, R., & Neveu, E. (Eds.). (2005). *Bourdieu and the journalistic field*. Cambridge, UK: Polity Press.

Bialik, K., & Matsa, K. (2017, October 4). Key trends in social and digital news media. Pew Research Center. Retrieved from http://www.pewresearch.org/fact-tank/2017/10/04/key-trends-in-social-and-digital-news-media/

Big Noise Films. (2000). *This is what democracy looks like* [film]. Oakland, CA: PM Press.

Boczkowski, P. J. (2004). The processes of adopting multimedia and interactivity in three online newsrooms. *Journal of Communication, 54*(2), 197–213.

Boczkowski, P. J. (2005). *Digitizing the news: Innovation in online newspapers*. Cambridge, MA: MIT Press.

Boczkowski, P. J., & Lievrouw, L. A. (2007). Bridging STS and communication studies: Research on media and information technologies. In E. J. Hackett, O. Amsterdamska, M. E. Lynch, & J. Wajcman (Eds.), *The handbook of science and technologies studies* (3rd ed., pp. 949–977). Cambridge, MA: MIT Press.

Boczkowski, P. J., & Mitchelstein, E. (2013). *The news gap: When the information preferences of the media and public diverge*. Cambridge, MA: MIT Press.

Boczkowski, P. J., & Anderson, C. W. (Eds.). (2017). *Remaking the news: Essays on the future of journalism scholarship in the digital age*. Cambridge, MA: MIT Press.

Boczkowski, P. J., & Papacharissi, Z. (Eds.). (2018). *Trump and the media*. Cambridge, MA: MIT Press.

Borges-Rey, E. (2017). Towards an epistemology of data journalism in the devolved nations of the United Kingdom: Changes and continuities in materiality, performativity and reflexivity. *Journalism*. Retrieved from https://journals.sagepub.com/doi/10.1177/1464884917693864

Brennan, S., & Kreiss, D. (2014, September 8). Digitalization and digitization. *Culture Digitally*. Retrieved from http://culturedigitally.org/2014/09/digitalization-and-digitization/

Broersma, M. (2010a). The unbearable limitations of journalism: On press critique and journalism's claim to truth. *The International Communication Gazette, 72*(1), 21–33.

Broersma, M. (2010b). Journalism as performative discourse: The importance of form and style in journalism. In V. Rupar (Ed.), *Journalism and meaning-making: Reading the newspaper* (pp. 15–35). New York: Hampton Press.

Brokaw, G., & Lee, J. (2016). *Fernando de Alva Ixtlilxochitl and his legacy*. Tucson, AZ: University of Arizona Press.

Brooks, L. (2018). *Our beloved kin: A new history of King Philip's War*. New Haven, CT: Yale University Press.

Bruno N., & Nielsen, R.K. (2012). *Survival and success: Journalistic online startups in Western Europe*. Reuters Institute for the Study of Journalism, Oxford University. Retrieved from http://reutersinstitute.politics.ox.ac.uk/sites/default/files/Survival%20is%20Success%20 Journalistic%20Online%20Start-Ups%20in%20Western%20Europe.pdf.

Buckley, E. S. (2019, January 2). How indigenous reporters are elevating true crime. *High Country News*. Retrieved from https://www.hcn.org/issues/51.1/tribal-affairs-how-indigenous-reporters-are-elevating-true-crime

Bullock, P. (2016, October 8). Transcript: Donald Trump's taped comments about women. *New York Times*. Retrieved from https://www.nytimes.com/2016/10/08/us/donald-trump-tape-transcript.html

Burke, K. (1969). *A rhetoric of motives*. Berkeley, CA: University of California Press.

Butler, J. (1988). Performative acts and gender constitution: An essay in phenomenology and feminist theory. *Theatre Journal, 40*(4), 519–531.

Byerly, C. (2011). Behind the scenes of women's broadcast ownership. *Howard Journal of Communications, 22*(1), 24–42.

Byrd, J. A. (2011). *The transit of empire: Indigenous critiques of colonialism*. Minneapolis: University of Minnesota Press.

Cagé, J. (2016). *Saving the media*. Cambridge, MA: Harvard University Press.

Callison, C. (2014). *How climate change comes to matter: The communal life of facts*. Durham, NC: Duke University Press.

Callison, C., & Hermida, A. (2015). Dissent and resonance:# Idlenomore as an emergent middle ground. *Canadian Journal of Communication, 40*(4), 695–716.

Callison, C. (2017). Climate change communication and indigenous publics. *Oxford Research Encyclopedia of Climate Science*. Retrieved from http://climatescience.oxfordre.com/view/10.1093/acrefore/9780190228620.001.0001/acrefore-9780190228620-e-411

Callison, C., & Young, M.L. (2018, February 15). Stanley trial highlights colonialism of Canadian media. *The Conversation Canada*. Retrieved from https://theconversation.com/stanley-trial-highlights-colonialism-of-canadian-media-91375

Campion-Smith, B. (2016, September 29). Canadian media crisis puts democracy at risk says Torstar chair John Honderick. *Hamilton Spectator*. Retrieved from https://www.thespec.com/news-story/6886777-canadian-media-crisis-puts-democracy-at-risk-says-torstar-chair-john-honderich/

Canadian Journalism Foundation. (2016). CJF Innovation Award. Retrieved from http://cjf-fjc.ca/awards/cjf-innovation-award

Capital Gazette editorial. (2018, July 6). Our say: Please help stop the madness that killed five at Capital Gazette newsroom. *Capital Gazette*. Retrieved from http://www.capitalgazette.com/opinion/our_say/ac-ce-our-say-20180706-a-20180705-story.html

Carey, J. W. (1974). The problem of journalism history. *Journalism History, 1*(1), 3.

Carlson, M., & Usher, N. (2016). News startups as agents of innovation: For-profit digital news startup manifestos as metajournalistic discourse. *Digital Journalism 4*(5), 563–581.

Carlson, M. (2014). When news sites go native: Redefining the advertising-editorial divide in response to native advertising. *Journalism, 16*(7), 849–865.

Caron, J. (1985). Hunter S. Thompson's 'Gonzo' journalism and the tall-tale tradition in America. *Studies in Popular Culture, 8*(1), 1–16.

Carpenter, L. (2017, May 18). The emotional exhaustion of debating Indigenous views. *The Toronto Star*. Retrieved from https://www.thestar.com/opinion/commentary/2017/05/18/the-emotional-exhaustion-of-debating-indigenous-views.html

CBC News. (2018, February 27). Canadians divided on Gordon Stanley verdict: Poll. Retrieved from http://www.cbc.ca/news/canada/saskatchewan/angus-reid-boushie-stanley-1.4553952

CBC News. (2017, May 6). Kelly Oxford talks. Retrieved from https://www.youtube.com/watch?v=IvaAH8Lg3OQ.

CBC-Radio Canada. (2017). Employment Equity Annual Report. Retrieved from http://www.cbc.radio-canada.ca/_files/cbcrc/documents/equity/2017-employment-equity-report-en.pdf

Chadwick, A. (2013). *The hybrid media system: Politics and power.* New York: Oxford University Press.

Chakrabarti, M., & Hardzinski, B. (2019, January 22). In our viral world, a closer look at teen's confrontation with Native American elder. *On Point*. Retrieved from https://www.wbur.org/onpoint/2019/01/22/native-american-maga-teen-confrontation-washington-dc

Chan-Olmsted, S. (2018, May). *Saving Journalism and Media in the Age of Tech Giants: Collaboration or Co-Opetition with the Frenemy?* Keynote at the World Media Economics and Management Conference, Cape Town, South Africa.

Ching, C. (2018). Personal communication.

Ching, C. (2019). Personal communication.

Choy, T. (2005). Articulated knowledges: Environmental forms after universality's demise. *American Anthropologist, 107*(1), 5–18.

Choy, T. (2011). *Ecologies of comparison: An ethnography of endangerment in Hong Kong.* Durham, NC: Duke University Press.

Christensen, M., Nilsson, A. E., & Wormbs, N. (Eds.). (2013). *Media and the politics of Arctic climate change: When the ice breaks.* London: Palgrave Macmillan.

City of Toronto. (2017). 2016 Census backgrounder. Retrieved from https://www.toronto.ca/wp-content/uploads/2017/12/8ca4-5.-2016-Census-Backgrounder-Immigration-Ethnicity-Housing-Aboriginal.pdf

Coates Nee, R. (2014). Social responsibility theory and the digital nonprofits: Should the government aid online news startups? *Journalism, 15*(3), 326–343

Coddington, M. (2015). Clarifying journalism's quantitative turn: A typology for evaluating data journalism, computational journalism, and computer-assisted reporting." *Digital Journalism, 3*(3), 331–348.

Cole, D. (2017). I choose activism for black liberation. Cole's Notes Blog. Retrieved from https://thatsatruestory.wordpress.com/2017/05/04/i-choose-activism-for-black-liberation/

Collins, H. M., & Evans, R. (2002). The third wave of science studies: Studies of expertise and experience. *Social Studies of Science, 32*(2), 235–296.

Compton, J., & Dyer-Witheford, N. (2014). Prolegomenon to a theory of slump media. *Media, Culture & Society, 36*(8), 1196–1206.

Convention on the Elimination of all Forms of Discrimination Against Women (CEDAW). (2015, March 30). Report of the inquiry concerning Canada of the Committee on the Elimination of Discrimination against Women under article 8 of the Optional Protocol to the Convention on the Elimination of All Forms of Discrimination against Women. United Nations. C/OP.8/CAN/1 http://tbinternet.ohchr.org/Treaties/CEDAW/Shared%20Documents/CAN/CEDAW_C_OP-8_CAN_1_7643_E.pdf

Correspondent Confidential (2013–2014). Vice Media. Retrieved from https://video.vice.com/en_ca/show/correspondent-confidential

Costanza-Chock, S., & Schweidler, C. (2017). Toward transformative media organizing: LGBTQ and Two-Spirit media work in the United States. *Media, Culture & Society, 39*(2), 159–184.

Couldry, N. (2000). *The place of media power: Pilgrims and witnesses of the media age.* New York: Routledge.

Coulthard, G. (2012, December 24). #IdleNoMore in historical context. *Decolonization: Indigeneity, Education, Society.* Retrieved from https://decolonization.wordpress.com/2012/12/24/idlenomore-in-historical-context/

Coulthard, G. (2014). *Red skin, white masks: Rejecting the colonial politics of recognition.* Minneapolis: University of Minnesota Press

Coward, R. (2009). Me, me, me: The rise and rise of autobiographical journalism. In S. Allan (Ed.), *The Routledge companion to news and journalism* (pp. 234–244). New York: Routledge.

Coward, R. (2010). Practice review: J ethics and confessional journalism. *Journalism Practice, 4*(2), 224–233.

Craig, S. (2016, August 19). The dark side of The Star: In aftermath of reporter's death, concerns about newspaper's "toxic" workplace culture raised. *Financial Post.* Retrieved from http://business.financialpost.com/news/the-dark-side-of-the-star-in-aftermath-of-reporters-death-concerns-about-newspapers-toxic-workplace-culture-raised

Cram, S. (2019, January 11). Shooting past stereotypes: Photojournalist challenges expectations with contemporary images. *CBC Unreserved.* https://www.cbc.ca/radio/unreserved/iconic-indigenous-imagery-how-photos-shape-movements-and-connect-us-to-history-1.4963770/shooting-past-stereotypes-photojournalist-challenges-expectations-with-contemporary-images-1.4972071

Crenshaw K. (1991). Mapping the margins: Intersectionality, identity politics, and violence against women of color. *Stanford Law Review, 43*, 1241–1299.

Cukier, W., Miller, J., Aspevig, K., & Carl, K. (2011). Diversity in leadership and media: A multi-perspective analysis of the Greater Toronto Area, 2010. Proceedings for the 11th International Conference on Diversity in Organisations, Communities and Nations. University of the Western Cape, South Africa. https://www.ryerson.ca/.../Diversity%20in%20Leadership%20and%20Media_2011.pdf.

Culver, K. B. (2017). Disengaged ethics: Code development and journalism's relationship with "the public." *Journalism Practice, 11*(4), 477–492.

DaCosta, J. (2014, April 11). Toronto aka Tkaronto passes new city council protocol. *Muskrat Magazine.* Retrieved from http://muskratmagazine.com/toronto-aka-tkaronto-passes-new-city-council-protocol/

Dadigan, M. (2017, July 9). Winnemem Wintu work to bring salmon home from New Zealand. *Indian Country Today.* https://newsmaven.io/indiancountrytoday/archive/winnemem-wintu-work-to-bring-salmon-home-from-new-zealand-Lsv8cyI9mUGoZh0A4yccgQ/

Dahlgren, P. (1996). Media logic in cyberspace: Repositioning journalism and its publics. *Javnost-the public, 3*(3), 59–72.

Daley, P. J., & James, B. A. (2004). *Cultural politics and the mass media: Alaska Native voices* (Vol. 139). Urbana: University of Illinois Press.

Daschuk, J. W. (2013). *Clearing the plains: Disease, politics of starvation, and the loss of Aboriginal life* (Vol. 65). Regina: University of Regina Press.

David, J. (2012). *Original people, original television: The launching of the aboriginal peoples television network.* Ottawa, ON: Debwe Communications.

Daughters DOC. [VanishedWomen]. (2017, March 1). There's no such thing as being a voice to the voiceless. Everyone has a voice, you just need to pass the mic. #MMIW #NoDAPL #AMINEXT. [Tweet]. Retrieved from https://twitter.com/ vanishedwomen/status/836984375447339008

de Certeau, M. (1978). *The writing of history.* New York: Columbia University Press.

de Certeau, M. (1984). *The practice of everyday life*, trans. Steven Rendall. Berkeley: University of California Press.

DeJarnette, B. (2016). Article (title removed for anonymity). *Mediashift.*

Demby, G. [geedee215]. (2018, March 12). Is Nat Geo's cover story finna be the shocking revelation that race is socially constructed? [Tweet]. Retrieved from https://twitter. com/geedee215/status/973200946896490496?lang=en

Deuze, M. (1999). Journalism and the web: An analysis of skills and standards in an on-line environment. *Gazette, 61*(5), 373–390.

Deuze, M. (2005). What is journalism? Professional identity and ideology of journalists reconsidered. *Journalism, 6*(4), 442–464.

Deuze, M. (2007). Journalism in liquid modern times: An interview with Zygmunt Bauman. *Journalism Studies, 8*(4), 671–679.

Deuze, M. (2017). Considering a possible future for digital journalism. *Revista Mediterránea de Comunicación/ Mediterranean Journal of Communication, 8*(1), 9–18. https://www.doi.org/10.14198/MEDCOM2017.8.1.1

Deuze, M., & Witschge, T. (2018). Beyond journalism: Theorizing the transformation of journalism. *Journalism, 19*(2), 165–181.

Dhillon, J. (2017). *Prairie rising: Indigenous youth, decolonization, and the politics of intervention.* Toronto: University of Toronto Press.

Dhillon, S. (2018). Journalism while brown and when to walk away. *Medium.* Retrieved from https://medium.com/s/story/journalism-while-brown-and-when-to-walk-away-9333ef61de9a

Domingo, D. (2008). Interactivity in the daily routines of online newsrooms: Dealing with an uncomfortable myth. *Journal of Computer-Mediated Communication, 13*(3), 680–704.

Domise, A. (2017). The 'benevolent liberal racism' behind Desmond Cole's Star exit. *Macleans.* Retrieved from https://www.macleans.ca/news/canada/the-benevolent-liberal-racism-behind-desmond-coles-star-exit/

Domonoske, C. (2016). One Tweet unleashes a torrent of stories of sexual assault. NPR. Retrieved from https://www.npr.org/sections/thetwo-way/2016/10/11/497530709/ one-tweet-unleashes-a-torrent-of-stories-of-sexual-assault

Dowell, K. L. (2013). *Sovereign screens: Aboriginal media on the Canadian West coast.* Lincoln: University of Nebraska Press.

Duarte, M. E. (2017). *Network sovereignty: understanding the implications of tribal broadband networks*. Seattle: University of Washington Press.

Dumit, J. (2003). Is it me or my brain? Depression and neuroscientific facts. *Journal of Medical Humanities*, *24*(1–2), 35–47.

Dumit, J. (2004). *Picturing personhood: Brain scans and biomedical identity*. Princeton, NJ: Princeton University Press.

Dumit, J. (2006). Illnesses you have to fight to get: Facts as forces in uncertain, emergent illnesses. *Social Science & Medicine*, *62*(3), 577–590.

Dumit, J. (2012). *Drugs for life: How pharmaceutical companies define our health*. Durham, NC: Duke University Press.

Dumit, J. (2014). Writing the implosion: Teaching the world one thing at a time. *Cultural Anthropology*, *29*(2), 344–362.

Dunbar-Ortiz, R. (2014). *An indigenous peoples' history of the United States* (Vol. 3). Boston: Beacon Press.

Durham, M. G. (1998). On the relevance of standpoint epistemology to the practice of journalism: The case for 'strong objectivity.' *Communication Theory*, *8*(2), 117–140.

Edge, M. (2014). *Greatly exaggerated: The myth and death of newspapers*. Vancouver, BC: New Star Books.

Edwards, B. (2018, March 12). National Geographic snatches its own wig over racist past. *The Root*. Retrieved from https://www.theroot.com/national-geographic-snatches-its-own-wig-over-racist-pa-1823708177

Elders and Leaders of Sacred Stones Camp. (2016, August 24). We've always 'occupied the prairie' and we're not going anywhere. *Native News Online*. Retrieved from https://nativenewsonline.net/currents/weve-always-occupied-prarie-not-going-anywhere/

Ellis, R., Waterton, C., & Wynne, B. (2010). Taxonomy, biodiversity, and their publics in twenty-first-century barcoding. *Public Understanding of Science*. doi:10.1177/0963662509335413

English, K. (2017, May 4). Journalists shouldn't become the news. *Toronto Star*. Retrieved from https://www.thestar.com/opinion/public_editor/2017/05/04/journalists-shouldnt-become-the-news-public-editor.html

Entman, R. M. (1993). Framing: Toward clarification of a fractured paradigm. *Journal of Communication, 43*(4), 51–58.

Ericson, R. (1998). How journalists visualize fact. *The Annals of the American Academy of Political and Social Science*, *560*, 83–95.

Ericson, R. V., Baranek, P. M., & Chan, J. B. (1987). *Visualizing deviance: A study of news organization*. Toronto: University of Toronto Press.

Ericson, R. V., Baranek, P. M., & Chan, J. B. (1989). *Negotiating control: A study of news sources*. Toronto: University of Toronto Press.

Ericson, R. V., Baranek, P. M., & Chan, J. B. (1991). *Representing order: Crime, law, and justice in the news media*. Milton Keynes, UK: Open University Press.

Eschner, K. (2016, March 24). Out of touch. *Ryerson Review of Journalism*. Retrieved from http://rrj.ca/out-of-touch/

Estes, N. (2017). Fighting for Our Lives:# NoDAPL in historical context. *Wicazo Sa Review, 32*(2), 115–122.

Estes, N. (2019). *Our history is the future: Standing Rock versus the Dakota Access Pipeline, and the long tradition of indigenous resistance*. New York: Penguin Random House.

Ettema, J. S., & Glasser, T. L. (1994). The irony in—and of—journalism: A case study in the moral language of liberal democracy. *Journal of Communication, 44*(2), 5–28.

Ettema, J. S. (2009). New media and new mechanisms of public accountability. *Journalism, 10*(3), 319–321.

Faulkner, W. (2001). The technology question in feminism: A view from feminist technology studies. *Women's Studies International Forum, 24*(1), 79–95.

Faulkner, W. (2009). Doing gender in engineering workplace cultures. II. Gender in/authenticity and in/visibility paradox. *Engineering Studies, 1*(3), 169–189.

Felt, U. (2017). Making knowledge, people and societies. In U. Felt, R. Fouché, C. A. Miller, & L. Smith-Doerr (Eds.), *The handbook of science and technology studies* (pp. 253–258). Cambridge, MA: MIT Press.

Ferrucci, P. (2017). Exploring public service journalism: Digitally native news nonprofits and engagement. *Journalism & Mass Communication Quarterly, 94*(1), 355–370.

FineDay, M. (2019). LinkedIn. Retrieved from https://ca.linkedin.com/in/max-fineday-a32a34100

Fink, K., & Anderson, C. W. (2015). Data journalism in the United States: Beyond the usual Suspects. *Journalism Studies, 16*(4), 467–481.

Fischer, M. M. J. (2003). *Emergent forms of life and the anthropological voice*. Durham, NC: Duke University Press.

Fischer, M. M. J. (2009). *Anthropological futures*. Durham, NC: Duke University Press.

Fischer, M. M. J. (2018). *Anthropology in the meantime: Experimental ethnography, theory, and method for the twenty-first century*. Durham, NC: Duke University Press.

Fleck, L. (1979). *Genesis and development of a scientific fact*. Chicago: University of Chicago Press.

Fontaine, N. (2018, March 13). Tina Fontaine is further proof that missing and murdered Indigenous women and girls need justice: She was 15 years old when she was killed. *Teen Vogue*. https://www.teenvogue.com/story/tina-fontaine-is-further-proof-that-missing-and-murdered-indigenous-women-and-girls-need-justice

Fortun, K. (2001). *Advocacy after Bhopal: Environmentalism, disaster, new global orders*. Chicago: University of Chicago Press.

Fortun, K. (2003). Ethnography in/of/as open systems. *Reviews in Anthropology, 32*(2), 171–190.

Foucault, M., & Ewald, F. (2003). *'Society must be defended": Lectures at the Collège de France, 1975–1976* (Vol. 1). New York: Macmillan.

Franks, S. (2013). *Women and Journalism*. Oxford: Oxford University Press. Retrieved from http://reutersinstitute.politics.ox.ac.uk/publication/women-and-journalism 18

Freeman, B. (2016, Fall). 'You will have a good career here, but not a great career:' Male mentoring and the women journalists of the Canadian Press News Cooperative, 1965–2000. *Labour/Travail, 78*, 237–264.

Funabiki, J., & Yoshihara, N. (2011). Online journalism enterprises: From startup to sustainability. *Renaissance Journalism Center*. Retrieved from http://renjournalism.org/wp-content/uploads/2012/04/StartuptoSustainability.pdf

Gans, H. J. (1979). *Deciding what's news: A study of CBS Evening News, NBS Nightly News, Newsweek and Time*. New York: Pantheon Books.

Gaziano, C., & McGrath, K. (1986). Measuring the concept of credibility. *Journalism and Mass Communication Quarterly, 63*(3), 451–462.

Gertz, M. (2013, June 25). Stagnant American newsroom diversity in charts. *Media Matters for America*. Retrieved from https://www.mediamatters.org/blog/2013/06/25/stagnant-american-newsroom-diversity-in-charts/194597

Gilio-Whitaker, D. (2019). *As long as grass grows: The indigenous fight for environmental justice, from colonization to Standing Rock*. Boston: Beacon Press.

Gill, R. (2007). *Gender and the media*. Cambridge, UK: Polity Press.

Gillespie, T., Boczkowski, P., & Foot, K. A. (2014). *Media technologies: Essays on communication, materiality, and society*. Cambridge, MA: MIT Press.

Ginsburg, F. D., Abu-Lughod, L., & Larkin, B. (Eds.). (2002). *Media worlds: Anthropology on new terrain*. Berkeley: University of California Press.

Gilpin, E. (2018, December 11). Indigenous journalists speak up. *The National Observer*. Retrieved from https://www.nationalobserver.com/2018/12/11/indigenous-journalists-talk-about-past-present-and-future-journalism

Global Media Monitoring Project. (2010). *Who makes the news? Global Media Monitoring Project 2010*, World Association for Christian Communication (WACC).

Goldberg, S. (2018, April). For Decades our coverage was racist. To rise above our past, we must acknowledge it. *National Geographic*. Retrieved from https://www.nationalgeographic.com/magazine/2018/04/from-the-editor-race-racism-history/

Graves, L., & Konieczna, M. (2015). Sharing the news: Journalistic collaboration as field repair. *International Journal of Communication*, 9, 1966–1984.

Greenspon, E. (2017a, January 26). How to fix the ever-weakening state of the news media. *The Globe and Mail*. Retrieved from https://www.theglobeandmail.com/report-on-business/how-to-fix-the-ever-weakening-state-of-the-news-media/article33771186/

Greenspon, E. (2017b, January 26). Shoring up the civic function of journalism in Canada. *Policy Options*. Retrieved from http://policyoptions.irpp.org/magazines/january-2017/shoring-up-the-civic-function-of-journalism-in-canada/

Greenspon, E., & Owen, T. (2017, May 28). 'Fake news 2.0': A threat to Canada's democracy. *The Globe and Mail*. Retrieved from https://www.theglobeandmail.com/opinion/fake-news-20-a-threat-to-canadas-democracy/article35138104/

Greer, C., & Reiner, R. (2015). Mediated mayhem: Media, crime and criminal justice. (5th ed.) In M. Maguire, R. Morgan & R. Reiner (Eds.), *Oxford handbook of criminology* (pp. 245–278). Oxford: Oxford University Press.

Haaland Taking Historic Steps to Address Epidemic of Missing and Murdered Indigenous Women. (2019, March 13). Retrieved from https://haaland.house.gov/media/press-releases/haaland-taking-historic-steps-address-epidemic-missing-and-murdered-indigenous

Hackett, R. A., Gruneau, R. S., & Gutstein, D. (2000). *The missing news: Filters and blind spots in Canada's press*. Toronto: University of Toronto Press.

Hacking, I. (1990). *The taming of chance*. Cambridge, UK: Cambridge University Press.

Hall, S. (1990). The whites of their eyes: Racist ideologies and the media. In M. Alvarado & J.O. Thompson (Eds.), *The media reader* (pp. 9–23). London: British Film Institute.

Hallin, D. C., & Mancini, P. (2004). *Comparing media systems: Three models of media and politics*. Cambridge, UK: Cambridge University Press.

Hamilton, J., & Jenner, E. (2004). Redefining foreign correspondence, *Journalism*, 5(3), 301–321.

Hamilton, J. M., & Tworek, H. J. (2017). The natural history of the news: An epigenetic study. *Journalism, 18*(4), 391–407.

Haraway, D. (1988). Situated knowledges: the science question in feminism and the privilege of partial perspective. *Feminist Studies, 14*(3), 575–599.

Haraway, D. (1997). *Modest_Witness@Second_Millenium. FemaleMan©_Meets_OncoMouse™.* London: Routledge.

Haraway, D. (2004). *The Haraway reader.* New York: Routledge.

Haraway, D. (2015). Anthropocene, capitalocene, plantationocene, chthulucene: Making kin. *Environmental Humanities, 6*, 159–165.

Haraway, D. J. (2016). *Staying with the trouble: Making kin in the chthulucene.* Durham, NC: Duke University Press.

Haraway, D., & Goodeve, T. (2000). *How like a leaf: An interview with Donna Haraway.* New York: Routledge.

Harding, S., ed. (2011). *The postcolonial science and technology studies reader.* Durham, NC: Duke University Press.

Harding, S. (1992). *Whose science? Whose knowledge? Thinking from women's lives.* Ithaca, NY: Cornell University Press.

Harding, S. (1998). *Is science multicultural? Postcolonialisms, feminisms and epistemologies.* Bloomington: Indiana University Press.

Harp, R. (2018, December 9). International Symposium on Indigenous Communities and Climate Change, Episode 144. *Media Indigena.* Retrieved from https://mediaindigena.libsyn.com/ep-144-international-symposium-on-indigenous-communities-and-climate-change

Hawkins, E. (2018). *National Geographic* confronts its past: 'For decades, our coverage was racist. *The Washington Post.* Retrieved from https://www.washingtonpost.com/news/morning-mix/wp/2018/03/13/national-geographic-confronts-its-past-for-decades-our-coverage-was-racist/?noredirect=on&utm_term=.3b19cbb1dff9

Hayden, C. (2003). *When nature goes public: The making and unmaking of bioprospecting in Mexico.* Princeton, NJ: Princeton University Press.

Henry, F. (1999). The racialization of crime in Toronto's print media: A research project. Toronto: School of Journalism. Ryerson Polytechnic University.

Heravi, B. (2017, August 1). State of data journalism globally: First insights into the Global Data Journalism Study. *Medium.* Retrieved from https://medium.com/@Bahareh/state-of-data-journalism-globally-cb2f4696ad3d

Herman, E. S., & Chomsky, N. (1988). *Manufacturing consent: The political economy of the mass media.* New York: Pantheon Books.

Hermida, A. (2014). Twitter as an ambient news network. In K. Weller, A. Bruns, J. Burgess, M. Mahrt, & C. Puschmann (Eds.), *Twitter and Society* (pp. 359–372). New York: Peter Lang.

Hermida, A., Lewis, S. C., & Zamith, R. (2014). Sourcing the Arab Spring: A case study of Andy Carvin's sources on Twitter during the Tunisian and Egyptian revolutions. *Journal of Computer-Mediated Communication, 19*(3), 479–499.

Hermida, A., & Young, M. L. (2016). Finding the data Unicorn: A hierarchy of hybridity in data and computational journalism. *Digital Journalism, 5*(2), 159–176. doi: 10.1080/21670811.2016.1162663

Hermida, A., & Young, M. L. (2019)."Transition or transformation? The precarity of responses to journalism market failure." The Future of Journalism Conference, Cardiff, Wales. September 11–13, 2019.

History of the Toronto Star. (n. d.). *Toronto Star* website. Retrieved from https://www.thestar.com/about/history-of-the-toronto-star.html

Hodapp, J. (2015). The postcolonial Joe Sacco. *Journal of Graphic Novels and Comics, 6*(4), 319–330.

Honderich, J. (2016). Mr. John Honderich (Chair, Torstar Corporation), at the Canadian Heritage Committee. Retrieved from https://openparliament.ca/committees/canadian-heritage/42-1/27/john-honderich-1/only/

Honderich, J. (2018, January 26). We should be very concerned by the crisis facing quality journalism. *Toronto Star.* Retrieved from https://www.thestar.com/opinion/2018/01/26/john-honderich-we-should-all-be-very-concerned-by-the-crisis-facing-quality-journalism.html

Hudes, S. (2017, January 26). Canadian journalism urged to tackle the culture of free to survive. *Toronto Star.* Retrieved from https://www.thestar.com/news/gta/2017/01/26/canadian-journalism-urged-to-tackle-the-culture-of-free-to-survive.html

Hunt, D., & Stevenson, S.A. (2016). Decolonizing geographies of power: Indigenous digital counter-mapping practices on turtle Island. *Settler Colonial Studies*

Hunt, S. (2015/2016). Representing colonial violence: Trafficking, sex work, and the violence of law. *Atlantis, 37.2*(1), 25–39.

Ibrahim, D. (2003). Individual perceptions of international correspondents in the Middle East. *Gazette, 65*(1), 87–101.

ICT Editorial Team. (2018, September 21). We'll do it live! Native election night coverage will be coast to coast. *Indian Country Today.* Retrieved from https://newsmaven.io/indiancountrytoday/news/we-ll-do-it-live-native-election-night-coverage-will-be-coast-to-coast-dV0e-h5MC0SSIXo2aV-hRw/

ICT Editorial Team. (2019, April 3). *Indian Country Today* to open newsroom at Arizona State; goal is to create national TV news program. *Indian Country Today.* Retrieved from ttps://newsmaven.io/indiancountrytoday/news/indian-country-today-to-open-newsroom-at-arizona-state-goal-is-to-create-national-tv-news-program-6ZwULKc8DEuDNrL97qw0ow/

Iqbal, M. (2017, November 6). Portrait of a journalist: Shree Paradkar. *Ryerson Review of Journalism.* Retrieved from http://rrj.ca/portrait-of-a-journalist-shree-paradkar/

Irwin, A., & Wynne, B. (Eds.). (1996). *Misunderstanding science? The public reconstruction of science and technology.* Cambridge, UK: Cambridge University Press.

J-Source. (2015). Desmond Cole on writing about the skin he's in. *J-Source.* Retrieved from http://j-source.ca/article/desmond-cole-on-writing-about-the-skin-hes-in/

J-Source. (2016, April 24). Think there aren't any journalism startups in Canada? Think again. Retrieved from: https://twitter.com/jsource/status/724319564188684288.

J-Source. (2016, September 30). Memo: David Skok joining *Toronto Star* as associate editor and head of editorial strategy. *J-Source.* Retrieved from http://j-source.ca/article/memo-david-skok-joining-toronto-star-as-associate-editor-and-head-of-editorial-strategy/

Jackson, S. J. (2014). Rethinking repair. In T. Gillespie, P. J. Boczkowski, & K. Foot (Eds.), *Media technologies: Essays on communication, materiality, and society* (pp. 221–239). Cambridge, MA: MIT Press.

Jackson, S. J., & Foucault Welles, B. (2015). Hijacking# myNYPD: Social media dissent and networked counterpublics. *Journal of Communication, 65*(6), 932–952.

Jackson, S. J., & Foucault Welles, B. (2016). # Ferguson is everywhere: Initiators in emerging counterpublic networks. *Information, Communication & Society*, *19*(3), 397–418.

Jasanoff, S. (2003). Breaking the waves in science studies: Comment on HM Collins and Robert Evans, The third wave of science studies'. *Social Studies of Science*, *33*(3), 389–400.

Jasanoff, S. (Ed.). (2004). *States of knowledge: The co-production of science and the social order*. London: Routledge.

Jasanoff, S. (2005). *Designs on nature: Science and democracy in Europe and the United States*. Princeton, NJ: Princeton University Press.

Jasanoff, S. (2009). *The fifth branch: Science advisers as policymakers*. Cambridge, MA: Harvard University Press.

Jenkins, H. (1992). *Textual poachers: Television fans and participatory culture*. London: Routledge.

Jenkins, H., Ford, S., & Green, J. (2013). *Spreadable media: Creating value and meaning in a networked culture*. New York: NYU Press.

Jenkins, H., Shresthova, S., & Peters-Lazaro, G. (Eds.). (2019). *Popular culture and the civic imagination*. New York: NYU Press.

Jiwani, Y. (2009). Report: Race and the media: A retrospective and prospective gaze. *Canadian Journal of Communication*, *34*, 735–740.

Jolly, M. (2011). Reading autobiography: A guide for interpreting life narratives, and memoir: An introduction (review). *Biography*, *34*(4), 817–821. https://doi.org/10.1353/bio.2011.0072

Jones, J. M., & Ritter, Z. (2018). Americans' perceptions of news media bias have increased significantly over the past generation. Gallup. Retrieved from https://news.gallup.com/poll/225755/americans-news-bias-name-neutral-source.aspx

Justice, D. (2019). Personal Communication.

Katz, E. (1980). Media events: The sense of occasion. *Studies in Visual Communication*, *6*(3), 84–89.

Keeler, J. (2019, January 23). Land gets stolen. That's how it works. *Sierra*. Retrieved from https://www.sierraclub.org/sierra/land-gets-stolen-s-how-it-works-native-covington-catholic-lincoln-memorial

Kirkness, V., & Barnhardt, R. (2001). First nations and higher education: The four R's—respect, relevance, reciprocity, responsibility. In R. Hayoe & J. Pan (Eds.), *Knowledge across cultures: A contribution to dialogue among civilizations*. Hong Kong: Comparative Education Research Centre, The University of Hong Kong.

Klein, P. K., & Plaut, S. (2017). Fixing the journalist fixer relationship. *Nieman Reports*. Retrieved from https://niemanreports.org/articles/fixing-the-journalist-fixer-relationship/

Kovach, B., & Rosenstiel, T. (2014). *The elements of journalism: What newspeople should know and the public should expect*. New York: Three Rivers Press.

Kreiss, D. (2012). *Taking our country back: The crafting of networked politics from Howard Dean to Barack Obama*. Oxford: Oxford University Press.

Kreiss, D. [KreissDaniel]. (2019, February 5). It's a hell of a lot easier talking about fake news than identity and race though. [Tweet]. Retrieved from https://twitter.com/kreissdaniel/status/1092823533556776962

Küng, L. (2015). *Innovators in digital news*. London: I. B. Tauris.

Küng, L. (2015, July 14). What should legacy media do? Never waste a good crisis. Lucy Kung blog. Retrieved from http://www.lucykung.com/blog/what-should-legacy-media-do-never-waste-a-good-crisis

Küng, L. (2018, April). Cultural change in large journalism organizations. Keynote presented at the Perugia Journalism Festival, Perugia, Italy.

Lambert, S. (2018). Expert tells Winnipeg murder trial he could not determine cause of Tina Fontaine's death. *The Globe and Mail*. Retrieved from https://www.theglobeandmail.com/news/national/tina-fontaine-had-drugs-alcohol-in-system-when-she-was-killed-toxicologist/article37798349/

Lambertus, S. (2004). *Wartime images, peacetime wounds: The media and the Gustafsen Lake standoff*. Toronto: University of Toronto Press.

Landsbaum, C. (2017). Ellen Pao says male reporters were 'skeptical' of her case. *The Cut*. https://www.thecut.com/2017/09/ellen-pao-book-male-journalists-responded-differently-sexism.html

Lankshear, C., & Knobel, M. (2011). *New literacies*. Berkshire, UK: Open University Press.

Latour, B. (1993). *We have never been modern*. Cambridge, MA: Harvard University Press.

Latour, B. (2000). When things strike back: A possible contribution of 'science studies' to the social sciences. *The British Journal of Sociology, 51*(1), 107–123.

Lederman, M. (2017). How Calgary mom Kelly Oxford tweeted her way to Hollywood. *The Globe and Mail*. Retrieved from https://www.theglobeandmail.com/life/how-calgary-mom-kelly-oxford-tweeted-her-way-to-hollywood/article10659378/

Leonard, T. (1995). *News for all: America's coming-of-age with the press*. New York: Oxford University Press.

Lewis, S., & Usher, N. (2014). Code, collaboration, and the future of journalism: A case study of the Hacks/Hackers Global Network. *Digital Journalism, 2*(3), 383–393. doi:10.1080/21670811.2014.895504.

Lewis, S. C., & Westlund, O. (2015). Big data and journalism: Epistemology, expertise, economics, and ethics. *Digital Journalism, 3*(3), 447–466.

Lipari, L. (1996). Journalistic authority: Textual strategies of legitimation. *Journalism & Mass Communication Quarterly, 73*(4), 821–834.

Lohan, M., & Faulkner, W. (2004). Masculinities and technologies. *Men and Masculinities 6*(4): 319–329.

Maaka, R., & Andersen, C. (2006). *The indigenous experience: Global perspectives*. Toronto: Canadian Scholars' Press.

Mahtani, M. (2001). Mapping the meanings of 'racism' and 'feminism' among women television broadcast journalists in Canada. In F. Winddance Twine & K. Blee (Eds.), *Feminism and anti-racism: International struggles for justice* (pp. 349–366). New York: New York University Press.

Mahtani, M. (2005). Gendered news practices: The experiences of women journalists in different national contexts. In S. Allan (Ed.), *Journalism: Critical issues* (pp. 299–310). London: Open University Press.

Mahtani, M. (2019). Risk, relation, revolution, repair: Refusing closure, accepting ambivalence. Public Lecture. Vancouver, BC: Simon Fraser University.

Malcolm, J. (1990). *The journalist and the murderer.* New York: Vintage Books.

Manning, S. S. (2017, August 28). Our collective grieving for Savanna Greywind, a beautiful sister lost. *Indian Country Today*. Retrieved from https://newsmaven. io/indiancountrytoday/archive/our-collective-grieving-for-savanna-greywind-a-beautiful-sister-lost-k51QE3OKb0iWF-89n3vfWw/

Marcus G. (2000). *Para-sites: A casebook against cynical reason*. Chicago: University of Chicago Press.

Marcus G. (2009). Multi-sited ethnography: Notes and Queries. In M. A. Falzon (Ed.), *Multi-sited ethnography theory, praxis and locality in contemporary research*. Burlington, VT: Ashgate Publishing Company.

Marcus G. E., & Fischer M. M. (1999). *Anthropology as cultural critique: An experimental moment in the human sciences*. Chicago: University of Chicago Press.

Martin, N. (2019, February 19). It's Time to Finally Listen to Native Journalists. *Splinter News*. Retrieved from https://splinternews.com/its-time-to-finally-listen-to-native-journalists-1832375168.

Martinson, J. (2015, January 1). The virtues of Vice: How punk magazine was transformed into media giant. *The Guardian*. Retrieved from http://www.theguardian.com/media/2015/jan/01/virtues-of-Vice-magazine-transformed-into-global-giant

McChesney, R. W., & Pickard, V. (Eds.). (2011). *Will the last reporter please turn out the lights: The collapse of journalism and what can be done to fix it*. New York: The New Press.

McChesney, R. W. (2015). *Rich media, poor democracy: Communication politics in dubious times*. New York: New Press.

McCloud, S. (1993). *Understanding comics: The invisible art*. Northampton, MA: Kitchen Sink Press.

McDonald, K. (2007). Days of past futures: Kazuo Ishiguro's *Never Let Me Go* as 'Speculative Memoir.' *Biography*, *30*(1), 74–83.

Media Matters Staff. (2017, August 20). *Reliable Sources* highlights the importance of newsroom diversity in the context of race coverage. *Media Matters for America*. Retrieved from https://www.mediamatters.org/video/2017/08/20/reliable-sources-highlights-importance-newsroom-diversity-context-race-coverage/217703

Mehta, B., & Mukherji, P. (Eds.). (2015). *Postcolonial comics: Texts, events, identities*. New York: Routledge.

Meyer, P. (1988). Defining and measuring credibility of newspapers: Developing an index. *Journalism Quarterly*, *65*(3), 567–574.

Meyrowitz, J. (1986). *No sense of place: The impact of electronic media on social behavior*. Oxford, UK: Oxford University Press.

Millar, E. (2016, February 12; March 29). Interview.

Millar, E. (2017, August 7). Personal communication.

Millar, E. (2018a, June 16). Journalists are getting better at reporting on Indigenous issues, but 'we're still at the beginning stages.' *the Discourse* newsletter.

Millar, E. (2018b, November 3). How *the Discourse* is reinventing the local newspaper to fight polarization. *J-Source*. Retrieved from https://j-source.ca/article/how-the-discourse-is-reinventing-the-local-newspaper-to-fight-polarization/

Millar, E. (2018c, November 23). What does the feds' $595M journalism package mean for news innovation. *the Discourse*. Retrieved from https://www.thediscourse.ca/media/feds-595m-journalism-package-news-innovation

Millar, E. (2019a, March 22). Liberals' journalism funding makes it harder to launch news startups. *the Discourse*. Retrieved from https://www.thediscourse.ca/communities/journalism-funding-startups

Millar, E. (2019b, May 21). The Discourse's do-or-die moment. *the Discourse* newsletter. Retrieved from https://www.thediscourse.ca/media/the-discourse-2019-spring-campaign

Millar, E. (2019c, July 6). Our campaign fell short. Here are our next steps. *the Discourse* newsletter. Retrieved from https://www.thediscourse.ca/media/campaign-fell-short-next-steps.

Miller, C., & Shepherd, D. (2009). In J. Giltrow (Ed.), *Genres of the Internet*.

Miller, J. (1998). *Yesterday's news: Why Canada's daily newspapers are failing us*. Halifax: Fernwood Publishing.

Mindich, D. T. (2000). *Just the facts: How 'objectivity' came to define American journalism*. New York: NYU Press.

Missing and Murdered Aboriginal Women. (2014). RCMP website. Retrieved from http://www.rcmp-grc.gc.ca/en/missing-and-murdered-aboriginal-women-national-operational-overview

Missing and Murdered Aboriginal Women: 2015 update to the national operational overview. (2015). RCMP website. Retrieved from http://www.rcmp-grc.gc.ca/en/missing-and-murdered-aboriginal-women-2015-update-national-operational-overview

Monet, J. (2017, February 16). A reporter's arrest crystallizes her commitment to cover Standing Rock. *Columbia Journalism Review*. Retrieved from https://www.cjr.org/local_news/reporter_standing_rock_pipeline.php

Monet, J. (2018, March 23). #DeleteFacebook? Not in Indian Country. Yes! Retrieved from https://www.yesmagazine.org/peace-justice/deletefacebook-not-in-indian-country-20180323

Monet, J. (2019, January 18). Why I started publishing an 'indigenous version' of my articles: Jenni Monet on fighting erasure in colonized newsrooms. *Literary Hub*. Retrieved from https://lithub.com/why-i-started-publishing-an-indigenous-version-of-my-articles/

Moran, J. M. (1999). Bone of contention: Documenting the prehistoric subject. In J. Gaines & M. Renov (Eds.), *Collecting visible evidence* (Vol. 6, pp. 255–273). Minneapolis: University of Minnesota Press.

Mosco, V., & McKercher, C. (2006). Convergence bites back: Labour struggles in the Canadian communication industry. *Canadian Journal of Communication*, *31*(3), 733–751.

Moving Forward. (2015). *the Discourse*. Retrieved from https://www.thediscourse.ca/series/moving-forward

Mullen, A., & Klaehn, J. (2010). The Herman–Chomsky propaganda model: A critical approach to analysing mass media behaviour. *Sociology Compass*, *4*(4), 215–229.

Nagata, K. (2011). Why I quit my Job. KaiNagata.com. Retrieved from https://kainagata.com/2011/07/08/why-i-quit-my-job/

Nagle, R. (2018, October 23). Invisibility is the modern form of racism against native Americans. *Teen Vogue*. Retrieved from https://www.teenvogue.com/story/racism-against-native-americans

Naldi, L., & Picard, R. (2012). 'Let's start an online news site': Opportunities, resources, strategy, and formational myopia in startups. *Journal of Media Business Studies, 9*(4), 69–97.

Nelson, A. (2016). *The social life of DNA: Race, reparations, and reconciliation after the genome.* Boston: Beacon Press.

Newman, N. (2019). Overview and key findings of the 2019 Report. Reuters Institute for the Study of Journalism Digital News Report. Retrieved from http://www. digitalnewsreport.org/survey/2019/overview-key-findings-2019/

Nielsen, R. K. (2012). How newspapers began to blog: Recognizing the role of technologists in old media organizations' development of new media technologies. *Information, Communication, and Society, 15*(6), 959–978.

Nielsen, R. K. (2017). The one thing journalism just might do for democracy. *Journalism Studies*, 1251–1262.

Nielsen, R. K. (2018). *The changing economic contexts of journalism. RasmusKleisNielsen.net. Draft chapter for ICA Handbook of Journalism Studies,* edited by Karin Wahl-Jorgensen and Thomas Hanitzsch, 1–38. New York: Routledge. Retrieved from https://rasmuskleisnielsen.net/2018/05/02/draft-chapter-on-the-changing-economic-contexts-of-journalism/

Nixon, L. (2019, February 28). Writing indigenous truths: Trauma ethics. *QWF Writes.* Retrieved from https://qwfwrites.wordpress.com/2019/02/28/trauma-ethics-by-lindsay-nixon/

Noble, S. (2018). *Algorithms of oppression: How search engines reinforce racism.* New York: New York University Press.

Norris, A. (2016, March 21). Lessons on driving digital business. FIPP: The network for global media. Retrieved from https://www.fipp.com/news/features/lessons-on-driving-digital-businesses

Olivarius, A. (2018). AnnOlivarius.com. Retrieved from http://www.annolivarius.com/

Onwuachi-Willig, A. (2018). What about# UsToo: The invisibility of race in the# MeToo movement. *Yale LJF, 128*, 105.

Owen, T. (2017). Unpublished research on not-for-profit journalism in Canada. Personal communication.

Owen, T. (2018, May 25). Data governance in the digital age: How Facebook disrupted democracy. *Financial Post.* Retrieved from https://business.financialpost.com/opinion/data-governance-in-the-digital-age-how-facebook-disrupted-democracy

Palmater, P. (2018, February 25). Why Canada should stand trial for Tina Fontaine's murder. *Now Toronto.* Retrieved from https://nowtoronto.com/news/why-canada-should-stand-trial-for-tina-fontaine-murder/

Papacharissi, Z., & Oliveira, M. (2012). Affective news and networked publics: The rhythms of news storytelling on #Egypt. *Journal of Communication, 62*, 266–282. doi:10.1111/j.1460-2466.2012.01630.x

Papacharissi, Z. (2015). Toward New Journalism(s): Affective news, hybridity, and liminal spaces. *Journalism Studies, 16*(1), 27–40. doi: 10.1080/1461670X.2014.890328

Pao, E. (2017). *Reset: my fight for inclusion and lasting change.* New York: Spiegel and Grau.

Pember, M.A. (2018, March 2). Sherman Alexie and the longest running #MeToo movement in history. *Rewire.* Retrieved from https://rewire.news/article/2018/03/02/sherman-alexie-longest-running-metoo-movement-history/

Paradkar, S. (2016, November 4). Lack of racial diversity in media is a form of oppression. *Toronto Star*. Retrieved from https://www.thestar.com/news/gta/2016/11/04/lack-of-racial-diversity-in-media-is-a-form-of-oppression-paradkar.html

Paradkar, S. (2017, May 12). It was wrong to rein in Desmond Cole. *Toronto Star*. Retrieved from https://www.thestar.com/news/gta/2017/05/12/it-was-wrong-to-rein-in-desmond-cole-paradkar.html.

Parasie, S., & Dagiral, E. (2013). Data-driven journalism and the public good: 'Computer-assisted-reporters' and 'programmer-journalists' in Chicago. *New Media & Society*, *15*(6), 853–871.

Peryer, M. (2019, July 29). Native Hawaiians on coverage of Mauna Kea resistance. *Columbia Journalism Review*. Retrieved from https://www.cjr.org/opinion/mauna-kea-telescope-protest-hawaii.php

Peters, C., & Broersma, M. J. (Eds.). (2013). Rethinking journalism: Trust and participation in a transformed news landscape. London: Routledge.

Phillips, A. (2010). Old sources: New bottles. In N. Fenton (Ed.), *New media, old news: Journalism and democracy in the digital age* (pp. 87–101). London: SAGE.

Piapot, N. (2018, February 20). Colten—our relative, our warrior. *JSource*. Retrieved from http://j-source.ca/article/colten-relative-warrior/

Picard, R. (2013, March 29). [Re-]establishing the relevancy of legacy news organizations. *The Media Business Blog*, http://themediabusiness.blogspot.ca/2013/03/re-establishing-relevance-of-legacy.html

Picard, R. (2014). Twilight or new dawn of journalism? Evidence from the changing news ecosystem. *Digital Journalism*, *2*(3), 273–283.

Picard, R. (2016). Submission to the House of Commons Standing Committee on Canadian Heritage local media inquiry.

Plener, A. (2017, April 10). Trouble at 1 Yonge. *Ryerson Review of Journalism*. Retrieved from https://medium.com/ryerson-review-of-journalism/trouble-at-1-yonge-b304dfbef746

Pollock, A. (2012). *Medicating race: Heart disease and durable preoccupations with difference*. Durham, NC: Duke University Press.

Pollock, A., & Subramaniam, B. (2016). Resisting power, retooling justice: Promises of feminist postcolonial technosciences. *Science, Technology, & Human Values*, *41*(6), 951–966.

Popplewell, B. (2018). Inside the *Toronto Star*'s bold plan to save itself. *The Walrus*. Retrieved from https://thewalrus.ca/inside-the-toronto-stars-bold-plan-to-save-itself/.

Posetti, J. [JuliePosetti] (2018, April 18). Just published: Time to step away from the 'bright, shiny things?' Towards a sustainable model for journalism innovation in an era of perpetual change. My first report for @risj_Oxford Journalism Innovation Project **#NewsInnovate**. https://reutersinstitute.politics.ox.ac.uk/our-research/time-step-away-bright-shiny-things-towards-sustainable-model-journalism-innovation-era . . . [Tweet]. Retrieved from https://twitter.com/juliepposetti/status/1067955331173629952/photo/1

Reclaiming Power and Place: The Final Report of the National Inquiry into Missing and Murdered Indigenous Women and Girls. (2019). Retrieved from https://www.mmiwg-ffada.ca/final-report/

Powers, M., & Zambrano, S. V. (2016). Explaining the formation of online news startups in France and the United States: A field analysis. *Journal of Communication 66*(5), 857–877.

Prenger, M., & Deuze, M. (2017). A history of innovation and entrepreneurialism in journalism. In P. Boczkowski & C. Anderson (Eds.), *Remaking the news: Essays on the future of journalism scholarship in the digital age* (pp. 235–250). Cambridge, MA: MIT Press.

Pritchard, D., & Sauvageau, S. (1998). The journalists and journalisms of Canada. In D. H. Weaver (Ed.), *The global journalist: News people around the world* (pp. 373–393). Cresskill, NJ: Hampton Press.

Public Policy Forum. (2017, January 26). *The shattered mirror: News, democracy and trust in the digital age*. Report for Heritage Canada. Retrieved from https://shatteredmirror.ca

Public Policy Forum. (2018, February 27). PPF welcomes policy measures that support Canadian journalism. PPF website. Retrieved from https://ppforum.ca/news/ppf-welcomes-budget-measures-support-canadian-journalism/

Raboy, M., & Taras, D. (2005). The trial by fire of the Canadian Broadcasting Corporation: Lessons for public broadcasting. Nordicom. Retrieved from http://media.mcgill.ca

Rankin, J. (2019). Personal communication.

Rao, S. (2018, March 13). Critics say *National Geographic*'s attempt to 'rise above' its 'Racist' past falls short. *Colorlines*. Retrieved from https://www.colorlines.com/articles/critics-say-national-geographics-attempt-rise-above-its-racist-past-falls-short

Rao, S., & Wasserman, H. (2007). Global media ethics revisited: A postcolonial critique. *Global Media and Communication, 3*(1), 29–50.

Rankin, J. (2019). Personal Communication.

Rasmussen, L. (2015). The (de)evolution of a genre: Pain memoirs and sequential reading as an ethical practice. *Biography*, *38*(1), 118–134. doi: 10.1353/bio.2015.0000

Rave, J. (2018, December 6). *American Indian media today*. Indigenous Media Freedom Alliance and Democracy Fund. Retrieved from https://www.democracyfund.org/publications/american-indian-media-today

Reardon, J., & TallBear, K. (2012). 'Your DNA is our history': Genomics, anthropology, and the construction of whiteness as property. *Current Anthropology*, *53*(S5), S233–S245.

Reardon, J. (2009). *Race to the finish: Identity and governance in an age of genomics.* Princeton, NJ: Princeton University Press.

Rector, K., & Bogel-Burroughs, N. (2018, June 29). Five dead in 'targetted attack' at *Capital Gazette* newspaper in Annapolis, police say; Laurel man charged with murder. *Baltimore Sun*. Retrieved from www.baltimoresun.com/news/maryland/crime/bs-md-gazette-shooting-20180628-story.html

Red Press Initiative. (2019). Native American Journalists Association. Retrieved from https://najanewsroom.com/red-press-initiative/

Reese, S. D. (1990). The news paradigm and the ideology of objectivity: A socialist at the Wall Street Journal. *Critical Studies in Media Communication*, *7*(4), 390–409.

Reguly, E. (2017, October 26). Star power. *The Globe and Mail*. Retrieved from https://www.theglobeandmail.com/report-on-business/rob-magazine/star-power/article18419304/

Reiner, R., Livingstone, S., & Allen, J. (2000). No more happy endings? The media and popular concern about crime since the Second World War. In T. Hope & R. Sparks (Eds.), *Crime risk and insecurity: Law and order in everyday life and political discourse* (pp. 107–123). New York: Routledge.

Rendell, M. (2017, June 26). *Toronto Star* abandons Star Touch tablet app, lays off 30 staff members. *The Globe and Mail*. Retrieved from https://www.theglobeandmail.com/report-on-business/toronto-star-abandons-star-touch-tablet-app/article35473859/

Rhodes, J. (1993). The visibility of race and media history. *Critical Studies in Mass Communication, 10*(2), 184–190. https://doi.org/10.1080/15295039309366859

Rhodes, J. (1999). Fanning the flames of racial discord: The National Press and the Black Panther Party. *Harvard International Journal of Press/Politics, 4*(4), 95–118. https://doi.org/10.1177/1081180X9900400406

Robinson, G. (2005). *Gender, journalism and equity: Canadian, US, and European Perspectives*. Cresskill, NJ: Hampton Press.

Robinson, S. (2017). *Networked news, racial divides: How power and privilege shape public discourse in progressive communities*. Cambridge, UK: Cambridge University Press.

Roitman, J. (2013). *Anti-crisis*. Durham, NC: Duke University Press.

Rosen, J. (1999). *What are journalists for?* New Haven, CT, and London: Yale University Press.

Rosen, J. (2006). The people formerly known as the audience. *Pressthink* blog, June 27. http://archive.pressthink.org/2006/06/27/ppl_frmr.html

Ross, K., & Carter, C. (2011). Women and news: A long and winding road. *Media Culture Society, 33*(8), 1148–1165.

Roth, L. (2005). *Something new in the air: The story of First Peoples television broadcasting in Canada*. Montreal and Kingston: McGill-Queen's Press.

Roy, A. (2004, November 3). The 2004 Sydney Peace Prize lecture. University of Sydney. Retrieved from http://sydney.edu.au/news/84.html?newsstoryid=279

Royal, C. (2012). The journalist as programmer: A case study of the *New York Times* Interactive News Technology Department. *#ISOJ: The Official Research Journal of the International Symposium for Online Journalism, 2*(1), 5–24.

Ryan, M. (2001). Journalistic ethics, objectivity, existential journalism, standpoint epistemology, and public journalism. *Journal of Mass Media Ethics, 16*(1), 3–22.

Sacco, J. (2013). *Journalism*. New York: Metropolitan Books.

Said, E. W. (1979). *Orientalism*. New York: Vintage.

SembraMedia. (2017). Inflection point: Impact, threats and sustainability. Retrieved from http://data.sembramedia.org/download-the-study/

Schaffer, J. (2007). *Citizen media: Fad or the future of news?* J-Lab: The Institute for Interactive Journalism.

Schmidt, C. (2017, November 20). Three years in, Discourse Media looks to membership to power its national expansion. *Nieman Lab*. Retrieved from http://www.niemanlab.org/2017/11/three-years-in-discourse-media-looks-to-membership-to-power-its-national-expansion/

Schrode, E. (2018). Eringschrode.com. Retrieved from https://www.erinschrode.com/

Schudson, M. (1978). *Discovering the news: A social history of American newspapers*. New York: Basic Books.

Schudson, M. (1989). The sociology of news production. *Media, culture & society, 11*(3), 263–282.

Schudson, M. (1995). *The power of news*. Cambridge, MA: Harvard University Press.

Schudson, M. (2001). The objectivity norm in American journalism. *Journalism*, 2(2), 149–170.

Schudson, M., & Anderson, C. W. (2009). Objectivity, professionalism, and truth seeking. In T. Hanitzsch & K. Wahl-Jorgensen (Eds.), *The handbook of journalism studies* (pp. 88–101). Mahway, NJ: Lawrence Erlbaum,

Schultze, U. (2000). A confessional account of an ethnography about knowledge work. *MIS Quarterly*, 24(1), 3–41.

Shapin, S. (1995). Cordelia's love: Credibility and the social studies of science. *Perspectives on Science, 3*(3), 255–275.

Shapin, S., & Schaffer, S. (1985). *Leviathan and the air-pump: Hobbes, Boyle, and the experimental life*. Princeton, NJ: Princeton University Press.

APTN. (n.d.). Sharing the stories only we can tell. APTN website. Retrieved from https://corporate.aptn.ca/

Shirky, C. (2009). Newspapers and thinking the unthinkable. Clay Shirky blog. Retrieved from http://www.shirky.com/weblog/2009/03/newspapers-and-thinking-the-unthinkable/

Siles, I., & Boczkowski, P. J. (2012). Making sense of the newspaper crisis: A critical assessment of existing research and an agenda for future work. *New Media & Society*. Retrieved from http://nms.sagepub.com/content/early/2012/08/21/1461444812455148.abstract

Silva, N. K. (2004). I kū mau mau: How kānaka maoli tried to sustain national identity within the United States political system. *American Studies, 45*(3), 9–31.

Singer, J. B., Domingo, D., Heinonen, A., Hermida, A., Paulussen, S., Quandt, T., . . . Vujnovic, M. (2011). *Participatory journalism: Guarding open gates at online newspapers*. Malden, MA: John Wiley.

Singer, J. (2007). Contested autonomy: Professional and popular claims on journalistic norms. *Journalism Studies, 8*(1), 79–95.

Singer, J. (2008). The journalist in the network: A shifting rationale for the gatekeeping role and the objectivity norm. *Trípodos, 23*, 61–76.

Simpson, A. (2014). *Mohawk interruptus: Political life across the borders of settler states*. Durham, NC: Duke University Press.

Simpson, A. (2016). The state is a man: Theresa Spence, Loretta Saunders and the gender of settler sovereignty. *Theory & Event, 19*(4).

Skelton, C. (2018, February 21). There are fewer journalists in Canada than 15 years ago. But not as few as you might think. Retrieved from: http://www.chadskelton.com/2018/02/there-are-fewer-journalists-in-canada.html

Skinner, D., Compton, J. R., & Gasher, M. (Eds.). (2005). *Converging media, diverging politics: A political economy of news media in the United States and Canada*. New York: Lexington Books.

Smith, P. C., & Warrior, R. A. (1996). *Like a hurricane: The Indian movement from Alcatraz to Wounded Knee*. New York: The New Press.

Smith, S., & Watson, J. (2010). *Reading autobiography: A guide for interpreting life narratives*. 2nd ed. Minneapolis: University of Minnesota Press.

Smith, V. (2015). *Outsiders still: Why women journalists love-and leave-their newspaper careers*. Toronto: University of Toronto Press.

Spivak, G. (1988). Can the subaltern speak? In C. Nelson & L. Grossberg (Eds.), *Marxism and the interpretation of culture*. Urbana: University of Illinois Press.

Spivak, G. (2004). Terror: A speech after 9-11. *Boundary 2, 31*(2), 81–111.

Spurr, D. (1993). *The rhetoric of empire: Colonial Discourse in journalism, travel writing, and imperial administration.* Durham, NC: Duke University Press.

Squires, C. (2014). *The post-racial mystique: Media and race in the twenty-first century.* New York: New York University Press.

Squires, C. (2009). *African Americans and the media.* Cambridge, UK: Polity Press.

Stabile, C. (2006). *White victims, black villains: Gender, race and crime news in US culture.* New York: Routledge.

Stanley, A. (2014, June 29). Hot spots, anyone? Racy preferred. *New York Times.* Retrieved from http://www.nytimes.com/2014/06/30/arts/television/Vice-the-news-entity-grows-on-hbo-and-online.html?_r=2

Star, S. L. (1990). Power, technology and the phenomenology of conventions: on being allergic to onions. In J. Law (Ed.), *A Sociology of monsters: Power, technology and the modern world* (pp. 26–56). Oxford, UK: Basil Blackwell.

Steel, E. (2017). At Vice, cutting-edge media and allegations of old-school sexual harassment. *New York Times.* Retrieved from https://www.nytimes.com/2017/12/23/business/media/vice-sexual-harassment.html

Steiner, L. (2012). Failed theories: Explaining gender difference in journalism. *Review of Communication, 12*(3), 201–223.

Steiner, L. (2018). Solving journalism's post-truth crisis with feminist standpoint Epistemology, *Journalism Studies, 19*(13), 1854–1865. doi: 10.1080/1461670X.2018.1498749

Subramaniam, B., Foster, L., Harding, S., Roy, D., & TallBear, K. (2017). 14 Feminism, Postcolonialism, Technoscience. In U. Felt, R. Fouché, C. A. Miller, & L. Smith-Doerr (Eds.), *The handbook of science and technology studies* (pp. 407–433). Cambridge, MA: MIT Press.

Sullivan, M. (2018, July 16). After a stunning news conference, there's a newly crucial job for the American press. *Washington Post.* Retrieved from https://www.washingtonpost.com/lifestyle/style/after-a-stunning-news-conference-theres-a-newly-crucial-job-for-the-american-press/2018/07/16/720a7c64-891b-11e8-a345-a1bf7847b375_story.html?noredirect=on&utm_term=.3511d9a12a79

Swisher, K. (2015). Ellen Pao has some things to say (full video). *Recode.* Retrieved from https://www.recode.net/2015/6/22/11563772/here-comes-that-troublesome-ellen-pao-full-video

Taboada, M., & Torabi Asr, F. (2019). Tracking the gender gap in Canadian media. *The Conversation Canada.* Retrieved from http://theconversation.com/tracking-the-gender-gap-in-canadian-media-110082

Takenega, L. (2019, January 17). Why the *Times* published a disturbing photo of dead bodies after an attack in Nairobi. *New York Times.* Retrieved from https://www.nytimes.com/2019/01/17/reader-center/nairobi-kenya-photo.html

Talaga, T. (2017). *Seven fallen feathers: Racism, death and hard truths in a northern city.* Toronto: House of Anansi Press.

Talaga, T. (2018). *All our relations: Finding the path forward* (CBC Massey Lectures). Toronto: House of Anansi Press.

TallBear, K. (2013). *Native American DNA.* Minneapolis: University of Minnesota Press.

TallBear K. (2014). Indigenous bioscientists constitute knowledge across cultures of expertise and tradition: An indigenous standpoint research project. In J. Gärdebo, M.-B. Öhman, & H. Maruyama (Eds.), *RE: Mindings co-constituting indigenous / academic / artistic knowledges* (pp. 173–191). Uppsala Multiethnic Papers, 55. Uppsala, Sweden: The Hugo Valentin Centre, Uppsala University.

TallBear, K. (2014a). Standing with and speaking as faith: A feminist Indigenous approach to inquiry. *Journal of Research Practice, 10*(2). Retrieved from http://jrp. icaap.org/index.php/jrp/article/view/405/371

TallBear, K. (2018, March 30). 'Sorry for the Racism' segment of Episode 108. MEDIA INDIGENA. Retrieved from https://mediaindigena.libsyn.com/ep-108-reading-the-larger-lessons-of-the-sherman-alexie-story

The Economist. (2018, November 29). The rise of Native American politicians: Indians are unlike any other minority group. Retrieved from https://www.economist.com/united-states/2018/12/01/the-rise-of-native-american-politicians

The Islamic State. (2014). Vice Media. Retrieved from https://www.youtube.com/watch?v=AUjHb4C7b94&has_verified=1&bpctr=1552689051

Todd, Z. (2016). An indigenous feminist's take on the ontological turn: 'Ontology' is just another word for colonialism. *Journal of Historical Sociology, 29*(1), 4–22.

Tokbaeva, D. (2016, July). When media and management collide: An interview with Lucy Küng. *Westminster Papers in Communication and Culture, 11*(1), 26–30. doi: http://doi.org/10.16997/wpcc.233

Toronto Star. (n.d.). Strong, united and independent Canada. Toronto Star website. Retrieved from https://www.thestar.com/about/strong-canada.html

Trahant, M. (2019, April 10). Spring fundraising drive builds on lessons from election night; goal is a nationwide broadcast. *Indian Country Today.* Retrieved from https://newsmaven.io/indiancountrytoday/news/spring-fundraising-drive-builds-on-lessons-from-election-night-goal-is-a-nationwide-broadcast-jBEABSd-eo0eKvScg2QkIVw/

Traweek, S. (1988). Beamtimes and lifetimes: The world of high energy physicists. Cambridge, MA: Harvard University Press.

Tsing, A. L. (2015). *The mushroom at the end of the world: On the possibility of life in capitalist ruins.* Princeton, NJ: Princeton University Press.

Tuchman, G. (1972). Objectivity as strategic ritual: An examination of newsmen's notions of objectivity. *American Journal of sociology, 77*(4), 660–679.

Tuchman, G. (1978). *Making news.* New York: Free Press.

Tuck, E., & Yang, K. W. (2012). Decolonization is not a metaphor. *Decolonization: Indigeneity, Education & Society, 1*(1), 1–40.

Tufekci, Z. (2014). The medium and the movement: Digital tools, social movement politics, and the end of the free rider problem, *Policy & Internet, 6*(2), 202–208.

Turkle, S., & Papert, S. (1990). Epistemological pluralism: Styles and voices within the computer culture. *Signs, 16*(1), 128–157.

Turner, F. (2005). Actor-networking the news. *Social Epistemology, 19*(4), 321–324.

Turner, F. (2013). *The democratic surround: Multimedia and American liberalism from World War II to the psychedelic sixties.* Chicago: University of Chicago Press.

Tworek, H. (2018). Tweets are the new vox populi. *Columbia Journalism Review.* Retrieved from https://www.cjr.org/analysis/tweets-media.php

Tworek, H. (2019). *News from Germany: The competition to control world communications, 1900–1945*. Cambridge, MA: Harvard University Press.

Usher N. (2013). Marketplace public radio and news routines considered: Between structures and agents. *Journalism, 14*(6), 807–822.

Usher, N. (2014). *Making news at the* New York Times. Ann Arbor: University of Michigan Press.

Usher, N. (2015). Newsroom moves and the newspaper crisis evaluated: Space, place and cultural meaning. *Media, Culture & Society, 37*(7), 1005–1021.

Usher, N. (2016). *Interactive journalism: Hackers, data and code*. Urbana: University of Illinois Press.

Usher, N. (2018). Women and technology in the newsroom: Vision or reality from data Journalism to the News Startup Era. In L. Steiner & C. Carter (Eds.), *Gender and The News Media*. London: Routledge.

Vice Media. (2013a). I posed as a prostitute in a Turkish Brothel. In *Correspondent Confidential*. Retrieved from https://video.vice.com/es_latam/video/i-posed-as-a-prostitute-in-a-turkish-brothel/56a0f855a1b8d38d234ee2c9

Vice Media. (2013b). I was kidnapped by a Colombian Guerilla Army. In *Correspondent Confidential*. Retrieved from https://video.vice.com/es_latam/video/i-was-kidnapped-by-a-colombian-guerrilla-army/56a10ceca1b8d38d234ee2d3

Vice Media. (2014a). A bizarre night in Thailand. In *Correspondent Confidential*. https://video.vice.com/en_us/video/a-bizarre-night-in-thailand/56a298b8366ad919056c73c6

Vice Media. (2014b). Investigating KKK murders in the deep South. In *Correspondent Confidential*. Retrieved from https://video.vice.com/es_latam/video/investigating-kkk-murders-in-the-deep-south/56a297bc6eff7245021208cb

Vice Media. (2014c). Strange border kidnappings in Kosovo. In *Correspondent Confidential*. Retrieved from https://www.vice.com/en_ca/article/nnqdy7/strange-border-kidnappings-in-kosovo

Vice Media. (2014d). Uncovering a mysterious cholera outbreak in Haiti. In *Correspondent Confidential*. Retrieved from https://video.vice.com/es_latam/video/uncovering-a-mysterious-cholera-outbreak-in-haiti/56a29ab893d848fb7a1f904c

Vimalassery, M., Pegues, J. H., & Goldstein, A. (2016). Introduction: On colonial unknowing. *Theory & Event, 19*(4).

van Dijk, T. A. (1987). *Communicating racism: Ethnic prejudice in thought and talk*. Los Angeles: SAGE.

van Zoonen, L. (1998a). A professional, unreliable, heroic marionette (M/F: Structure, agency and subjectivity in contemporary journalisms. *European Journal of Cultural Studies, 1*(1), 123–143.

van Zoonen, L. (1998b). One of the girls? The changing gender of journalism. In C. Carter, G. Branston, & S. Allan (Eds.), *News, gender and power* (pp. 33–46). New York: Routledge.

van Zoonen, L. (2012). I-Pistemology: Changing truth claims in popular and political culture. *European Journal of Communication, 27*(1), 56–67. doi: 10.1177/0267323112438808

Vigh, H. (2008). Crisis and chronicity: Anthropological perspectives on continuous conflict and decline. *Ethnos, 73*(1), 5–24.

Wagemans, A., Witschge, T., & Deuze, M. (2016). Ideology as resource in entrepreneurial journalism: The French online news startup Mediapart. *Journalism Practice 10*(2), 160–177.

Wahl-Jorgensen, K. (2012). The strategic ritual of emotionality: A case study of Pulitzer Prize winning articles. *Journalism*, published online June 14. doi: 10.1177/1464884912448918

Wajcman, J. (2010). Feminist theories of technology. *Cambridge Journal of Economics, 34*(1), 142–152.

Waldman, K. (2018, July 23). A Sociologist examines the 'white fragility' that prevents white Americans from confronting racism. *New Yorker*. Retrieved from https://www.newyorker.com/books/page-turner/a-sociologist-examines-the-white-fragility-that-prevents-white-americans-from-confronting-racism

Ward, S. J. (2004). *Invention of journalism ethics: The path to objectivity and beyond.* Montreal: McGill-Queen's University Press.

Ward, S. J. (2011). *Ethics and the media: An introduction.* Cambridge University Press.

Ward, S. J. (2014). Radical media ethics: ethics for a global digital world. *Digital Journalism, 2*(4), 455–471.

Watts, V. (2013). Indigenous place-thought & agency amongst humans and non-humans (First Woman and Sky Woman go on a European world tour!). *Decolonization: Indigeneity, Education & Society, 2*(1), 20–34.

Wente, J. [JesseWente]. (2018, January 30). Just so I'm clear: After centuries of genocidal policies, violent oppression, slavery, residential schools, prejudicial police, denial of voting rights, and ongoing laws based on ethnicity . . . . It's us who make everything about race? Huh. Cool story. [Tweet] Retrieved from https://twitter.com/jessewente/status/958400979094986753

Wente, J. [JesseWente]. (2018, January 31). #TinaFontaine and #ColtenBoushie are not on trial. We see you Canadian media. #JusticeForColten #JusticeForTina. [Tweet]. Retrieved from https://twitter.com/jessewente/status/958791533389664261?lang=en

Wente, J. [JesseWente]. (2018, February 10). If you want to see Canada, look at my mentions and many other FNMI peoples mentions today. That is the mirror to find Canada's reflection. [Tweet]. Retrieved from https://twitter.com/jessewente/status/962380909990248448?lang=en

Wente, J. (2018, February 16). 'We need to break these cycles and tell different stories': Jesse Wente on coverage of Colten Boushie. *Unreserved*, CBC. Retrieved from http://www.cbc.ca/radio/unreserved/after-colten-boushie-where-do-we-go-from-here-1.4535052/we-need-to-break-these-cycles-and-tell-different-stories-jesse-wente-on-coverage-of-colten-boushie-1.4537466

White Eye, B. (1996). Journalism and First Nations. In V. Alia, B. Brennan, & B. Hoffmaster (Eds.), *Deadlines and diversity: Journalism ethics in a changing world* (pp. 92–97). Black Point, NS, & Winnipeg, MB: Fernwood Publishing.

Whyte, K. P. (2013). On the role of traditional ecological knowledge as a collaborative concept: a philosophical study. *Ecological Processes, 2*(1), 7.

Whyte, K. P. (2016). Indigenous experience, environmental justice and settler colonialism. In B. Bannon (Ed.), *Nature and experience: Phenomenology and the environment* (pp. 157–174). Lanham, MD: Rowman & Littlefield.

Whyte, K. [KenWhyte3]. (2017, January 26). but, in the end, if they're going to spend another 100 million, at least this time it goes to my friends #ppf #cdnpoli. [Tweet]. Retrieved from https://twitter.com/KenWhyte3/status/824647505430401026

Whyte, K. [KenWhyte3]. (2017, January 26). overall, reads like terrified response of high priests of Ptolemaic astronomy to the spread of the Copernican hypothesis #ppf #cdnpolo. [Tweet]. Retrieved from https://twitter.com/KenWhyte3/status/824646621271117824

Winseck, D. (2010). Financialization and the 'crisis of the media': The rise and fall of (some) media conglomerates in Canada. *Canadian Journal of Communication, 35*(3), 365–393.

Winseck, D. (2017). Media and Internet concentration in Canada, 1984–2017 (Updated). Retrieved from http://www.cmcrp.org/media-and-internet-concentration-in-canada-1984-2017-updated/

Wolf, M. J. P. (2000). *Abstracting reality: Art, communication, and cognition in the digital age.* Lanham, MD: University Press of America.

Wolfe, P. (2006). Settler colonialism and the elimination of the native. *Journal of Genocide Research, 8*(4), 387–409.

Young, M. L. (2005). Crime content and media economics [Unpublished doctoral dissertation]. University of Toronto.

Young, M. L. (2016). Scoop was king: Media Competition, Crime News, Markets and Masculinity. In R. Smith-Fullerton & C. Richardson (Eds.), *Covering Canadian crimes: What journalists should know and the public should question* (pp. 357–396). Toronto: University of Toronto Press.

Young, M. L., & Beale, A. (2013). Canada: A step forward? The paradox of women in news. In C. Byerly (Ed.), *The Palgrave international handbook on women and journalism* (pp. 109–121). Basingstoke, UK: Palgrave Macmillan.

Young, M. L., & Callison, C. (2017). When gender, colonialism and technology matter in a journalism startup. *Journalism*. Retrieved from http://journals.sagepub.com/doi/abs/10.1177/1464884917743390

Young, M. L., & Giltrow, J. (2015). A mobile responsive expertise: Thinking more productively and generatively about journalism education. In G. Allen, S. Craft, C. Waddell & M. L. Young (Eds.), *Toward 2020: New directions in journalism education* (pp. 46–63). Toronto: Ryerson Journalism Research Centre

Young, M. L., & Hermida, A. (2015). From Mr. and Mrs. outlier to central tendencies: Computational journalism and crime reporting at the *Los Angeles Times. Digital Journalism, 3*(3), 381–397.

Young, M. L., Hermida, A., & Fulda, J. (2017). What makes for great data journalism? A content analysis of data journalism awards finalists, 2012–2015. *Journalism Practice*, 1–21. doi.org/10.1080/17512786.2016.1270171

Young, M. L., & Hermida, A. (2018). WMEMC conference paper, Cape Town, South Africa.

Yu, S. (2016). Instrumentalization of ethnic media. *Canadian Journal of Communication, 41*(2), 343–351.

Zelizer, B. (1993). Journalists as interpretive communities. *Critical Studies in Mass Communications, 10*(3), 219–237.

Zelizer, B. (2000). What is journalism studies? *Journalism, 1*(1), 9–12.

Zelizer, B. (2015). Terms of choice: Uncertainty, journalism and crisis. *Journal of Communication, 65*(5), 888–908.

Zelizer, B. (2017). *What journalism could be*. Chichester, UK: John Wiley & Sons.

Zuckerman, E. (2008). Meet the bridgebloggers. *Public Choice, 134*(1–2), 47–65.

Zuckerman, E. (2014). New media, new civics? *Policy & Internet, 6*(2), 151–168.

INDEX

For the benefit of digital users, indexed terms that span two pages (e.g., 52–53) may, on occasion, appear on only one of those pages.

Figures are indicated by *f* following the page number

Chan, J.B., 61–62
Cherokee-Phoenix, 39
Ching, Carrie, 80, 88–90, 91–92, 96–98,
    102, 104–5
Choy, Tim, 44, 72–73, 221–22n132
civic engagement, press's role in, 63
civic epistemologies, 47, 76–77
civic imagination, 47
civic journalism, 73–74, 77–78
civic media projects, 40
class, making of, 36
climate change
    adaptation and, 12
    coverage of, 12, 110–11
codes of ethics, 31–32, 60–61, 93, 99,
    154–55, 169–70
Cole, Desmond, 117–19, 121–22, 132
Cole, Matthew, 125
collaboration, 157. *See also* communities
    challenge of, for journalists, 154
    professional resources for,
        141–42, 154–55
    technology and, 205–6
colonialism, 5, 6–7, 25–26, 36, 107
    authority and, 97
    Indigenous resilience and, 169
    journalism and, 39, 78
    in journalism startup studies, 140
    knowledge production and, 202
    media and, 158–59
    news coverage and, 90–91, 108
    power generation and, 193
    relationships with sources and, 93
    witness roles and, 52
#ColtenBoushie, 56, 57t, 79. *See also*
    Boushie, Colten
commercial media, failure of, 102
communication studies, 37
communities
    collaboration with, 135–36,
        150–51, 155
    expertise in, 196
competition, as masculinist proxy, 150–51
Compton, J., 113
confessional accounts, 96
Cormier, Raymond, 53, 54, 55, 56

Correspondent Confidential (Vice Media),
    21, 80, 81–82, 87–100, 87*f*, 92*f*, 97*f*,
    102, 104, 105, 106–7
Coulthard, G., 153–54
counterpublics
    Twitter and, 52–53
    witnessing by, 52
court reporting, 204
Coward, R., 85
Craig, Sean, 130
credibility, 72–73, 77–78, 224n66
    authority and, 207–8
    goal of, 33
    narrative field and, 104–5
    production of, 72–73
Crenshaw, K., 203–4
crime journalism, 177
crisis
    framing of, 114
    narratives of, 5
    understandings of, 111
    as unitary phenomenon, 2–3
crisis journalists, 95
critical race scholarship, 6–7, 37, 75–76
CRTC. *See* Canadian Radio-Television
    and Communications
Cruickshank, John, 109
Cukier, Wendy, 19
cultural relativism, 85–86
culture, fluidity of, 15–16
culture studies, 6–7
Current, The (CBC), 115
current affairs television, 31–32

Dahlgren, P., 78–79
Dale, Daniel, 121–22
Daley, P.J., 39
data
    integration of, into traditional news
        stories, 127–29
    interpretation of, 128–29
data journalism, 22, 122–32,
    145–46
    audience and, 125–26
    continuity view of, 126–27
    defined, 122–23

data journalism (*cont.*)
   integration of, into legacy
      newsrooms, 127–29
   methodological values explained for,
      127, 128
   nonprofit funding and, 141–42
data journalists
   identity of, 124–25, 149–50
   roles of, 125–26
de Certeau, M., 40, 202
decline, narratives of, 5
decolonization
   approach to, 155–56
   effects of, 171
   process of, 172
Deerchild, Roseanna, 160
de Fatima Oliveira, M., 56–58, 75
deficit model of reporting, 163, 165
defined journalism, 152–53
Demby, Gene, 27–28
democracy
   journalism and, 5, 31, 32,
      42–43, 61–62
   mainstream/legacy media and, 40
Democracy Now (Big Noise Films), 40
Deuze, M., 30–31, 32, 74, 124, 140–41
Dhillon, Sunny, 100, 212, 225n4
difference, as memoir theme, 91–92
digital journalism. *See* data journalism
digital media
   as corrective for mainstream
      media, 11, 51
   emphasizing interpretation, 31–32
   knowledge production and, 8
   rise of, 111–12
   users' centrality to, 75
digital platforms
   journalists' discussions on, 81–82
   providing voice to multiple publics, 50
digital technologies
   activating publics and
      relationships, 56–58
   as diagnostic, 20 (*See also* technology)
   platforms offered by, 23
   research focused on, 41
digitalization, 41–42, 209

discrimination, 20–21, 63–64, 109, 169
dissonance, 20
distance, as memoir theme, 91–92, 93
documentary filmmaking, computer
   imaging in, 104–5
Domingo, D., 74–75, 76–77
Dotan, Hamutal, 119
Duarte, M.E., 40
Dumit, J., 17
Dunbar-Ortiz, R., 189
Durham, M.G., 44–46, 49–50
Dyer-Witheford, N., 113

economy, decline in, 2–3, 5
Edwards, Breanna, 27–28
#EllenPao, 64, 67–68. *See also*
   Pao, Ellen
Ellis, R., 75–77
emotionality, journalism and, 62–63
epistemology
   civic, 47
   foundations of, for journalism, 2
erasure, 28, 148, 161, 163–64, 189
Ericson, R.V., 8, 30–31, 61–62
Estes, N., 189
ethical plateaus, 15–16
ethics
   codes of, 31–32, 60–61, 93, 99,
      154–55, 169–70
   difficulty of navigating, 99
   Indigenous journalists and, 195
   literature in, Western orientation
      of, 98–99
ethnic media, 140
ethnography, experimental, 210
Europe, journalism and objectivity
   in, 31–32
evidence, ranking of, 47
exclusion, 7
expertise, 12–13, 196, 217n5
   claiming of, 93
   credibility and, 72–73 (*See also*
     credibility)
   middle ground for, 77–78
   performance of, 98
   production of, 72–73

settler-colonialism, 7, 47–48, 49–50, 161
  acknowledgment of, 171
  brutality of, reconstructed, 61
  Canada's history and, 129–30
  impacts of, 166–67
  Indigenous women's issues
    and, 48
  intersectionality and, 203–4
  journalism and, 48–49, 79,
    154–55, 166–72
  legacy media and, 116
  media structure of, 161
  media's support of as policy of clearing
    the plains, 60
  representations and power relations
    in, 47–48
Seven Fallen Feathers (Talaga),
    11–12, 165–66
sexual abuse, 69–72
sexual assault. *See* Oxford, Kelly
sexual harassment, 69, 102
sexuality, making of, 36
sexual violence, Indigenous women and,
    media representations of, 60
shaming, social media and, 51
Shapin, S., 33, 34–35
"Shattered Mirror: Democracy and Trust
    in the Digital Age" (Public Policy
    Forum), 112–14, 115–16
Shepherd, D., 106
Silva, N.K., 39
Simpson, A., 49–50, 129, 169–70
simulations, computerized, 104–5
Sisk, Caleen, 190
situated knowledge, 9–10, 12–13, 45–46,
    65–66, 81, 100, 101, 106–7, 117–18,
    182, 198–99, 208, 212–13
Smith, S., 85, 86
social locatedness, 44–45
social media
  changes resulting from, 20–21
  crowdsourced critique on, 51
  identities emerging on, 78–79
  Indigenous communities and, 162,
    181, 188
  mapping gaps in media coverage, 55

quit lit and, 106–7
responding to news events, 20–21
witnessing function of, 52
social movements, 34, 204–5
social movement scholarship, 52–53
social order, 43
  emotionality and, 62–63
  facts and, 35
  fluctuations in, 34–35
  journalism and, 49–50, 98, 209–10
  transformation of, 161
Society of Professional Journalists, 31–
    32, 60–61, 154–55
Solomon, Linda, 115
somewhere, view from, 16–17, 46,
    101, 124, 184 (*See also* situated
    knowledge)
sources
  accessing of, 94
  behaviors of, moral issues
    with, 91–92
  bypassing gatekeepers, 63–66
  connectedness to, 90–91
  personal stories of, focus on, 64
  power relationships with, 92–93
  trustworthiness of, 72
spam accounts, 68
speculative memoir, 225n5. *See* memoir
  fragments
Spence, Theresa, 183
Spivak, G., 9, 46–47, 93, 104
SPJ. *See* Society of Professional
  Journalists
sponsored (branded) content model,
    103, 107
Spotted Bear, Jodi Rave, 181–82,
    187, 191–92
Spurr, D., 85, 97
Squires, C., 38
Standing Rock, 161–62, 184, 185–86,
    187–88, 189, 190–91
standpoint epistemology, 45–46
standpoint theory, 45, 49–50
Stanley, Gerald, 54, 55, 56
Star, Leigh, 7–8, 33–34, 45–46, 49–50,
    202, 208

startups, 6, 22–23, 102, 135–37, 139–40.
    See also Indigenous journalism
    audiences for, 143
    community involvement of, 145
    demographics for, 140
    digital, in Canada, 116–17
    editorial strategy of, 146–47
    funding of, 142–43, 146, 147,
        149, 235n25
    goals of, 139, 140–41, 145, 150, 158
    innovation in, 140
    journalism studies and, 151
    manifestos of, 145
    partnering with other media
        outlets, 150–51
    reinforcing traditional journalism
        practices, 139–40
    repair function of, 142, 143–46
    reporting by, 136–37
    studies of, 139–41
    successes of, 141–42
    women-founded, 146–47
Steiner, L., 7, 44–46, 47–48, 49–50
Stelter, Brian, 18–19
stereotypes, 30–31, 38–39, 153–54, 163,
    166, 168–69, 173–74, 206, 209–10
Sterritt, Angela, 174–75, 176–77, 193, 194
storytelling
    Alaska Natives and, 39
    audience included in, 105–6
    autobiographical journalism and, 85
    co-creation and, 75
    data-driven, 135–36
    Indigenous framework for, 165
    Indigenous journalists and, 174–76,
        182, 193–94
    newer forms of, 20, 25
strong objectivity, 6–7, 44–46, 47–49,
    101–2, 212
STS. *See* science and technology studies
subaltern, 9, 46, 93, 104
subjectivity, 82
    embrace of, 55–84
    navigation of, 86–87
    role of, 106
Subramaniam, B., 10–11, 49–50, 170

subsidies for journalism, 113, 114, 115–16,
    132–33, 137–38, 140–41
Sullivan, Margaret, 3, 8–9
Swisher, Kara, 64, 65, 66–67
systemic stories, 150–51
systems, 211–12
systems journalists, 13, 212, 213

Talaga, Tanya, 11–12, 132, 163, 165–66,
    196, 204–5, 240n17
TallBear, K., 7–8, 28, 30–31, 49–50, 101,
    161, 170–71, 206
technological determinism, 41
technology
    amplifying journalism's problems, 43, 200
    changes in, 2–3, 5, 108
    colonial assumptions about, 153
    crisis in, 108
    decentering of, 43
    as diagnostic tool for journalism, 43–44,
        81–82, 108–9, 111, 205–6 (*See also*
        data journalism)
    disrupting journalism and democracy, 5
    as force vs. presence, 110–11
    gender and, 151–52
    identity crises and, 149
    Indigenous journalists and, 162
    journalism studies of, 41–42
    production of, 151–52
    startups and, 151
    as tool for gauging power relations, 122
Teen Vogue, 59–60, 69–70
theTyee.ca, 115
Thompson, Hunter S., 226n16
#TinaFontaine, 56, 57t, 79. *See also*
    Fontaine, Tina
Topping, David, 119
Toronto
    demographics of, 108, 119
    diversity initiatives in, 109
    history of, 229n1
    media businesses in, 230n40
Torontoist, 119
Toronto Star, 22, 107, 113, 114
    activist journalism at, 117–19
    colonialism and, 108

columnists for, 121–22
data expertise at, 124–25
data journalism at, 126–27, 130, 131
gender and, 108, 109
history of, 123–24, 129
layoffs at, 110–11, 124–25
losses at, as news story, 109
market research categories at, 232n79
newsroom demographics of, 117–18,
119, 131–32
power regimes at, 132
race and, 108, 110
sense making at, 129
technological change at, 108
Toward Reconciliation, 154
traditional media, 141 (*See also*
legacy media)
Trahant, Mark, 178–80, 182, 187,
188, 191–92
Trahant Reports, 178–79
transparency, goal of, 33
Traweek, Sharon, 7–8, 33–34, 35, 202
Troian, Martha, 173–74, 175–77
Trump, Donald, 3, 52, 69, 207–8
truth
multiple perspectives on, 86
pursuit of, through life stories, 86
seeking of, as journalism's task, 30
truth claims
ideological bases for, 45
messiness of, 106
Truth and Reconciliation Commission
(TRC; Canada), 135, 161–62, 163
truth regimes, 8
Tuchman, G., 8, 29–30
Tuck, E., 47–48, 166–67, 171, 172
Turkle, S., 152
Twitter, 161–62
ambient journalism and, 75
counterpublics' use of, 52–53
network and textual analysis of, 52–53
as news source, 188
used as form of accountability, 56–58
Tworek, H., 52–53, 134
UBC. *See* University of British Columbia
Unicorn Riot, 187–88

United States
Indigenous journalists in, 163–64
Indigenous people erased in
media of, 28
media ignoring minority
perspectives, 168–69
reporting in, on Indigenous
issues, 164–65
University of British Columbia, 241n48
Usher, N., 139–40

Vega, Tanzina, 18–19
Vice Media, 21, 80, 102–4, 107,
228–29n115
victim blaming, 55, 56
victim trope, 78
video feeds, Standing Rock and, 187–88
view from nowhere, 3–4, 7–8, 20, 21, 22,
23, 24–25, 44–45, 46, 84, 101, 170
view from somewhere, 16–17, 46, 101,
118, 124, 170, 184 (*See also* situated
knowledge)
Vimalassery, M., 129–30

Wagemans, A., 139–40
Wahl-Jorgensen, K., 62–63
Walker, Connie, 176, 177
Walker, Sebastian, 89, 94–95, 96
Walking Eagle News, 183–84
Ward, Dennis, 188
Ward, S.J.A., 30–31, 33
Wasserman, H., 98–99, 152–53, 177–78
Waterton, C., 75–76
Watson, J., 85, 86
Watts, V., 172
Wawatay News, 194–95
Welles, B.F., 52–53
Wente, Jesse, 54–56, 60–61, 77–78, 79, 204
Westlund, O., 8
What Are Journalists For? (Rosen), 73–74
White Eye, Bud, 172–74
white masculinity
journalism and, 8–9, 43, 44, 46–47,
62–63, 65–66
power of, obscured, 48–49
of STS scholars, 41

Whitestone Hill massacre, 185
Whyte, Ken, 114
Wilson, Tiar, 176
Winseck, D., 116–17
witnessing, 34–35, 169
    by counter-publics, 52
    identity and, 72–73
    masculinity and, 35–36
    role of, 51–52
    social media and, 51
Wolf, M.J.P., 104–5
Wolfe, P., 169
women. *See also* feminist media
    studies; gender

broadcast ownership and, 148–49
    media's glass ceiling and, 148
    startups and, 146
work, organization of, 152
Wynne, B., 75–76

Yang, K.W., 166–67, 171, 172
Yesterday's News (Miller), 119–20

Zambrano, S.V., 140
Zelizer, B., 33, 36–37, 61–62,
    111–12, 115–16, 120, 126,
    128–29, 168–69
Zuckerberg, Mark, 181

CPSIA information can be obtained
at www.ICGtesting.com
Printed in the USA
BVHW072240180920
589013BV00004B/25

9 780190 067083